Upstream Living
in a
Downstream World

Reflections on Ministry

DANIEL A. HAUGEN

(BA, MDiv, STM)

 **FriesenPress**

Suite 300 - 990 Fort St
Victoria, BC, Canada, V8V 3K2
www.friesenpress.com

Copyright © 2015 by Daniel A. Haugen
First Edition — 2015

All rights reserved.

No part of this publication may be reproduced in any form, or by any means, electronic or mechanical, including photocopying, recording, or any information browsing, storage, or retrieval system, without permission in writing from the publisher.

All Scripture quotations, in this publication are from the HOLY BIBLE, NEW INTERNATIONAL VERSION ® NIV ® Copyright © 1973, 1978, 1984, 2011 by Biblica, Inc.®. Used by permission. All rights reserved worldwide.

ISBN
978-1-4602-6327-3 (Hardcover)
978-1-4602-6328-0 (Paperback)
978-1-4602-6329-7 (eBook)

1. Religion, Christian Life, Professional Growth

Distributed to the trade by The Ingram Book Company

TABLE OF CONTENTS

Dedication..i

Foreword..iii

Preface..1

I. Early Beginnings: Home... Foundations from
People of the Pew (1947-1965)..21

II. The Early Struggles: University Years, 1966-1971..................41

III. Upstream Again:
Internship and Last Year of Seminary (1971-73).........................53

IIII. First Call: Preeceville Lutheran Parish: (1973-77).................69

V. Wrestling with the Need for Change (Spring 1977)................119

VI. The Second Call: Nelson Evangelical Lutheran
Church (1977-83)...131

VII. Grad Studies: Time out for Evaluation and
Back to Work (1981-83). 161

VIII. Call number three: Lutheran Collegiate
Bible Institute (1983-1985). 175

IX. A New Chapter: President (1985-1991). 191

X. Fired: And The Aftermath (1991-2002). 213

XI. The Call to Messiah Lutheran: Joy Under a
Cloud (2002-2010). 265

XII Postlude: Time for Contemplation (2010-retired)
with Thanksgiving for the Letter of Call................................299

DEDICATION

To my dear wife Beverly who has been an amazing partner, best friend and support in life. To our three children Tim, David and Amanda who shared this journey and blessed our lives; who in their adult lives have been such wonderful friends and gifts to us and to those they live among. And to Patti and Shawn who have joined our family and now eight grandchildren... with deep gratitude to God for each one of you: May God bless us all (together with all God's people) with the joy and challenge of exploring and living upstream lives as followers of Jesus in this struggling world that God still deeply loves.

FOREWORD

Upstream Living In a Downstream World is the story of one pastor's journey in ministry, a journey that carried the Reverend Daniel Haugen through several parishes; to president of the Lutheran Collegiate Bible Institute in Outlook, Saskatchewan; and back into parish ministry.

The book is more than stories of one person's ministry, for each story or group of stories become the foundation for broader theological and pastoral reflection on ministry and the church in our contemporary world.

Rev. Daniel Haugen was ordained into ministry of the Evangelical Lutheran Church Canada (ELCC) in 1973. The ELCC in 1986 merged with the Canadian Synods of the Lutheran Church in America to become the Evangelical Lutheran Church in Canada.

The foundation for Pastor Haugen's ministry is the Lutheran doctrine of grace and the presence of Christ in the lives of the people he served. This grace of God is reflected in each story and in each broader theological and pastoral reflection on the joys, blessings, and frustrations of ministry.

As a pastor, Rev. Haugen always has been and continues to be deeply affirming of the people to whom he ministered. He saw and experienced grace and God's presence again and again and again in those whom he served. In this book he affirms over and over their grace and discipleship, as well the struggles so many of us face as we journey through life. He wrote in his resume: *Over the years I have had a wonderful experience in ministry. Each parish I have served has been very different, but the people have been a delight to work with and for.*

As the reader will discover, Pastor Haugen can be quite forthright in his critique of the church in today's world. Yet despite occasional frustrations with the church, Pastor Haugen has been and remains steadfast as a disciple of Christ and a bearer of God's grace, and he remains faithful to the church at the parish, synod and national levels. His critiques, when they are expressed, are not meant to disparage the church or ministry, but rather to raise issues confronting the church in Canada in today's world, a world significantly different than the world in 1973 when he was ordained. His deep hope is that productive discussion will arise from reading his observations about ministry and the church.

It was a privilege to both read an early copy of *Upstream Living in a Downstream World* and to be asked to write this foreword. God's blessing to all who, as children of God, know themselves to be disciples of Christ and bearers of God's grace.

Rev. Wilburn Nelson, Ph.D.
Retired Professor of Pastoral Care
Lutheran Theological Seminary
Saskatoon, Saskatchewan

Upstream Living *in a* Downstream World

PREFACE

Going "upstream" is sometimes just the stubborn exercise of an adventurous spirit in a person who simply likes challenge. I remember seeing how far I could canoe into the Stanley Rapids, near Stanley Mission in Northern Saskatchewan by paddling upstream. It was exciting though certainly not particularly productive. One time I got close to the centre of the rapids and stepped off onto a rock where I fished for pickerel. In half an hour I had caught my limit. It was a challenge well worth the exercise. Beyond that, it was just adventure.

The upstream adventures in a downstream world which one encounters in ministry are so much more than the simple exercise of an adventurous spirit. It is a calling. With that calling is a commission that begins with "go". This commission to go has a defined purpose: make disciples, baptize and teach. It comes with a promise, "I am with you always to the close of the age (Matthew 28:18-20)." This promise might suggest that we will be called to go into places and circumstances sometimes even against our will, and sometimes into circumstances where we will be in over our heads. We will need help. Without this "One" who promised to be with us, we would be lost and overcome with the task and the circumstances.

On the journey we are called to be faithful to the Lord of life who has given this commission. We are called to be faithful to the business of God's kingdom. We are called to be faithful in the business of the church, the body of Christ where all God's people find a place with their varying gifts and abilities.

The pastor is one among many who serve. The corporate gifts of the whole body of Christ (pastors and lay people) are the adequate resources providing both the equipment and the personnel for the task. The development of those gifts and equipping those servants is an essential part of the pastor's work. Pastors play an important role to prepare that great priesthood of all believers for their role in the kingdom of God.

When that great priesthood of all believers enter this journey, we are drawn into an adventure in the lives of all kinds of people in every kind of circumstance. And in every circumstance is the holy challenge to share in the redemptive work of Jesus in the world that God still loves. These experiences will stretch and bend us and continue to shape us into the servants God calls us to be.

Some might think "downstream" is a negative view of the world. It is not meant to be negative. It is meant to be descriptive of a reality that surrounds us. We are born and we all move toward death. This reality is not overcome by any human initiative. We reproduce life in and through our children. They enter the same process. Similarly, we buy a new vehicle, and with time it deteriorates. We replace it with another.

In the journey of life we can care for life. We can follow instructions to avoid abusing our bodies. We can support life with a good diet, exercise and rest. This works against some of that downstream pull. All the measures we take to care for the gifts we have received are measures to slow (at best) the downstream process and at the very least not to accelerate it. These are ways we seek to fight some currents in life. We do not escape the pull. We are mortals.

There are other realities in our world that take life on a downstream course. Inherent in every human creature is a twisted heart. This is identified in the teaching of our church in the phrase "by nature sinful". (See Augsburg Confession, Chief Articles of Faith, II Original Sin.) This phrase identifies the process of a reflex that comes from the core of our being and has an incredible power to take us in directions that can degrade and even destroy life and relationships on the face of this world.

A street friend of mine described a new direction for his life in this way, "I have lived my whole life by my stomach, now I have to start living from the heart." Appetite without some measures of restraint and discipline can undermine and finally degrade life in one's self, and in the lives we touch around us.

In Galatians we have this description:

> *The acts of the sinful nature are obvious: sexual immorality, impurity and debauchery; idolatry and witchcraft; hatred, discord, jealousy, fits of rage, selfish ambition, dissensions, factions and envy; drunkenness, orgies, and the like. I warn you, as I did before, that those who live like this will not inherit the kingdom of God.* (Galatians 5:19-21)

This destructive quality of the human spirit unfettered produces a downstream current that has a visible effect on every aspect of life. Paul speaks of this reality and the challenge of the gospel:

> *Those who live according to the sinful nature have their minds set on what that nature desires; but those who live in accordance with the Spirit have*

their minds set on what the Spirit desires. The mind of sinful man is death, but the mind controlled by the Spirit is life and peace; the sinful mind is hostile to God. It does not submit to God's law, nor can it do so. Those controlled by the sinful nature cannot please God. (Romans 8:5-8)

There is a trend in current thought to assume a far more optimistic view of human life. In my university years and the years that have followed there has been a tendency to believe that the human spirit unfettered would rise to its highest state of being.

I like optimism, but one should not have to close their eyes to be optimistic. Ideologically, one can hold such positive views, but when one walks into the reality of our world, and as history unfolds, it is much more difficult to be convinced of this particular optimism.

The human creature, especially when alienated from God, ends up as lords of their own lives and masters of their own fate, which almost always leads to the abuse and neglect (if not rejection) of God and the use and abuse of those over whom they gain power in order to provide for themselves. The victims in this process are many.

There is another reality at work causing life to be drawn downstream. The scriptures speak about the real power of evil that works on the human spirit to turn it against God. When Jesus prayed for his followers this was a part of His prayer

My prayer is not that you take them out of the world but that you protect them from the evil one. (John 17:15)

Paul later writes in Ephesians 6:12 *For our struggle is not against flesh and blood, but against the rulers, against the authorities, against the powers of this dark world and against the spiritual forces of evil in the heavenly realms.*

The power of the "evil-one" seems to work well with the twisted human heart. Evil loves to take the human mind and play with it in the shadows. Evil spawns the degradation of life. Evil frolics in downstream living.

Evil seems to always come masked. Jesus talked about evil coming as the "wolf in sheep's clothing" (Matthew 7:15)and the apostle Paul as the "angel of light"(2 Corinthians 11:14). From the temptation in the story of creation to Jesus' temptation in the wilderness one sees the attempt to twist even God's words in order to turn the tempted against God.

The call to be followers of Jesus has many challenges, not the least of which is to test the spirits. All of these, and many more are the realities at work in this world that God loves. The work of God's people will not escape these realities. We are called to work in the midst of them.

The call of the Church is defined in the commission that Jesus left with his followers:

> *Then Jesus came to them and said, "All authority in heaven and on earth has been given to me. Therefore go and make disciples of all nations, baptizing them in the name of the Father and of the Son and of the Holy Spirit, and teaching them to obey everything I have commanded you. And surely I am with you always, to the very end of the age."* (Matthew 28:18-20)

Daniel A. Haugen

This commission in the first centuries of the life of the Christian church sent Jesus' disciples throughout their homeland. It sent Jesus' disciples into the Roman world. They had no invitation to "come"; they went by commission and compassion for a struggling world. They challenged the direction of the flow of life in the Roman world, but they did not go as invaders. They did not go as oppressors. They went as people who had good news to share that would bring change to human life wherever that human life was found. The gospel focused on the change of the human heart, not the immediate change of human institutions. And those new hearts in community brought a testimony of life and practice in the daily business of living that reached quietly and brought renewal into the life of the communities in which they lived.

This good news was for the whole world. The call to go was not fulfilled within the confines of the Roman Empire; and the call to go was not fulfilled in the confines of one generation of disciples. The heart of that call was directed by Jesus' summary of the law and the prophets:

> *Jesus replied, Love the Lord your God with all your heart and with all your soul and with all your mind. This is the first and greatest commandment. And the second is like it, love your neighbour as yourself.* (Matthew 22:37-39)

Here is the affirmation of the "holy" which is the heart of the life of God's people. Love is focused on the holy shaped by God. Love uses the "common" stuff to serve the holy. "Holy" in the Hebrew language meant "to be set apart." Human life created in the image of God was "set apart" from all other life on the face of the world. Every human life was "holy" by definition. Holy lives are not to be abused, used or denigrated in any way. However, in this world, holy lives have been deeply profaned. Redemption of life was the work to restore that holy gift of life in relationship with God and with people.

The call to go is not always a trip into open arms of human compassion. Jesus had his own warning for his disciples for this journey:

> Remember the words I spoke to you, 'No servant is greater than his master'. If they persecuted me, they will persecute you also. If they obeyed my teaching, they will obey yours also. (Luke 15:30)

"Love" will challenge those human practices that abuse and degrade life. In the defence of life, love will oppose evil. The call of God will always be a call to repentance, to new directions for life. It will challenge people individually and in community. It is a radical call denying so much that the struggling human spirit, by reflex, adores and pursues. It calls people to live upstream.

Love is also the focus on how to deal with enemies and those who cause powerful currents against the way of Jesus. Followers of Jesus are instructed to love their enemies and to pray for those who persecute them on the journey (Matt. 5:44). This is grace in action, not just in thought. It gives direction in those deeply challenging currents against which God calls his people to move and serve in a most upstream way.

The upstream adventure is not only a challenge to the flow of society, but it may also be a challenge to the flow of our own will and ways. Are we ready to go upstream against our own will and desires when that is necessary to fulfill our calling?

Daniel A. Haugen

> Then Jesus said to his disciples, "If anyone would come after me, he must deny himself and take up his cross and follow me. For whoever wants to save his life will lose it, but whoever loses his life for me will find it." (Matthew 16:24-25)

What do we do when we face those times in which a higher calling challenges us to "forget about ourselves" and take up the burden of the day and follow Jesus?

This is another dimension of upstream living, for it calls us to move against those currents in our own lives which flow so freely into pools of self interest, self indulgence and the stagnant pools of personal comfort and security. Here our love for "self" can so gently replace our love for God that we no longer want to reach out to care for the lives of others.

Much of the stimulus to the life of faith comes through the corporate church. Even here there are times when there is a need to go against the flow.

The books of Kings and Chronicles in the Bible constantly remind us of the propensity even within God's people for "everyone to do what is right in their own eyes" and how, even among God's people, this repeatedly led kings, priests and people away from God and into many great sources of grief.

In the corporate expressions of our lives and as members of the Christian church, we are vulnerable to the lure to buy into our own thoughts and ways. Those in leadership positions are in some ways the most visibly vulnerable, though it also affects people in their everyday lives. Power is alluring. The call to be servants of God and people so easily drifts into becoming their masters. This current is accelerated by the flow of our society that views the life of servants as demeaning. To be "masters of one's fate and captains of one's soul" is much more the stream of the day.

For both pastors and people, contemporary wisdom often elevates us above history and sometimes above God. We reshape God to our own image and to our own ways of thinking (if we hold on to God at all). Then we attach God as a talisman to legitimize our course. Sometimes in the community of faith, we take the soiled robe of Jesus at the foot of the cross and hang it on the ideology of the day to call it Christian. It looks more relevant to the society in which we live, but no longer sounds like Jesus. The church then flows in harmony with the culture of the day. However, one wonders where it will take us, and quietly expects that we will find the evidence for an answer to this question washed up on the downstream shores.

Reality may not reshape itself to accommodate the "higher wisdom" of the contemporary mind. One will have to allow time and history to prove or disprove what is happening. In the Old Testament, the test of the prophets was to see if what they said indeed came to be. I think we can learn something from the pedagogy of Jesus. Jesus did not demand submission to what he taught. He asked his followers to walk it into life. He seemed to know that what he taught would be confirmed in the reality of the world in which we live.

Obedience is sometimes the discipline that gets us on the road. The journey will provide its own discoveries. So when obedience is not forthcoming, followers of Jesus have to walk their own road and pay the price of discovery. Sometimes people have to learn the hard way. It is the work of God's word and spirit to convince us and sometimes it takes the hard lessons of life to open hearts and eyes and ears to learn. Experience is a good teacher; although, the tuition can be very high.

Daniel A. Haugen

Upstream living is a humbling task. It claims no authority in itself. It also has its own snares. God's upstream people can turn from faithfulness to crusades that leave a trail of destruction. The cures can be as bad as the diseases they fight. Zeal can sometimes replace faithfulness. Righteousness can spawn its own ills. Physicians become judges. Grace succumbs to "rights". Demanding justice out of others or over against them replaces the call to "do justly" (Micah 6:8) and to fight oppression one becomes oppressor.

Sometimes we are ready to take the journey that may call us to challenge the currents of the day. The snares are there. We are not always enthused about the circumstances into which the journey might take us. We may wonder what to say, and what to do, when to speak, and when to be silent. These are always issues that challenge us to seek to discern the will of God. As human beings this is an approximating enterprise in which (not just sometimes) we always need help from God who calls us into this venture.

Jesus described his work in this image:

> On hearing this, Jesus said to them, "It is not the healthy who need a doctor, but the sick. I have not come to call the righteous, but sinners."
> (Mark 2:17)

There is a striking difference between the image and work of a judge and the image and work of a physician. When a judge identifies wrong, the judge demands justice as the solution to the wrongdoing, which is usually "correction through punishment". The physician identifies what is wrong, and seeks to find something redemptive.

Both the judge and the physician identify evil. Having discovered evil, by nature we seem to be most attracted to the work of the judge. However in Jesus' instruction for his followers, there was no doubt about this matter:

> *Do not judge, or you too will be judged. For in the same way you judge others, you will be judged, and with the measure you use, it will be measured to you.* (Matthew 7:1-2)

Upstream living is embodied in the image of a physician who lives in a world where there is sickness. The redemptive work seeks to bring healing where there is sickness. The downstream world, as tragic as it might be, is not an offence, but a motivation for compassion and care and more often tears than indignation. (Jesus agonized over Jerusalem in His time (Matthew 23:36-38) and indeed, as Jesus life reveals, compassion might speak with harsh words (Matthew 23:32-34) at times to seek to open eyes and ears.

It is good to remember that in this venture, the spirit helps protect others from us. For even with the best intentions, it is easy to do harm.

The call of God through Jesus challenges us with thoughts that are not our thoughts and ways that are not our ways (Isaiah 55:8). It challenges us to live in a different way and with different values and priorities.

This "new life" comes with a different spirit than the spirit of the world. This different spirit builds new characteristics that grow in God's people as they live upstream lives.

> *But the fruit of the Spirit is love, joy, peace, patience, kindness, goodness, faithfulness, gentleness and self-control. Against such things there is no law. Those who belong to Christ Jesus*

> have crucified the sinful nature with its passions and desires. Since we live by the Spirit, let us keep in step with the Spirit. Let us not become conceited, provoking and envying each other. (Galatians 5:22-26)

None of these are goals we can achieve. These are the fruit that God seeks to nurture in His people through His Word and through the spirit he has given us. This fruit nurtures life in a struggling world. Nurture always has a time line, and the growth experienced in life comes with a journey. Quite often we do not like the time life needs to grow for ourselves or for those we serve.

In 40 years of ministry, life has not always been turbulent. Upstream at times was just quiet plugging along in normal currents that are quite tolerable. I think that is most of what ministry is about. We live most of our life in what seems mundane . . . but in this normal business of life we still discover the surprises of God's power and faithfulness. God does some of his best work in the mundane realities of ministry.

Upstream can also take us to circumstances in which we exhaust our human energy and will. But, if the journey is important and it takes some times of heavy upstream living, then it is an important part of the journey even if not the most enjoyable.

A senior pastor (one of the many mentors in my ministry in the early years) once suggested to me that we do not have to go out looking for crosses to carry. Instead, he suggested when crosses come to your door; you should be prepared to carry them. "And God will never give you more than you can handle."

We share in that history where God has worked and through those whom He called to be His servants. It is a deeply humbling experience to seek to follow Him, and it is a richly rewarding experience to venture where He leads us.

Early in parish ministry I saw the delightful and quiet work of people who were light and salt in a community. Let me share a story. There were plans to build a new arena and the ever-present problem of raising the money for this venture came up at a community meeting. The suggestion was to have a community event but the main concern was the need for a bar because that was where they would raise the most money.

One of the men of the community, a local farmer, rose up to speak. In a very gracious way he affirmed the need to provide healthy recreation for the young people of the community, but he was also concerned that the plan was to raise money by playing on the weaknesses of so many people in the community and further nurturing more problems for people in the community.

He concluded, "I am only one person and I have only one vote, but I want you to know why I will vote against this proposal." He then affirmed his support and encouraged other ways to get together to achieve this task in their community. The community voted down the proposed fundraising event and produced a new project that did the job.

This one quiet voice brought some thought and seasoning into the life of the community. This man spoke from experience, for he recalled his own time of struggle with some of the abuses with which so many in this community were still struggling.

I remember a person who worked in providing community services to many of those people with deep needs in our city. He was highly respected in the community. His life and faith informed the work he did. It influenced how he worked with his employees. It shaped the nature of the care he sought to provide to all those who received the services provided.

Another person was the CEO for the largest employer in our community. He lived a quiet, but deep life of faith and fellowship with God and with the people he encountered. He was recognized and highly respected for the way he handled his work and the people with whom he worked. The media even recognized the way he could deal with labour conflict. Once, he shared his life and faith at a gathering of men and teenage guys at his church's Men's Breakfast Fellowship. That morning was a turning point for the men and teenagers of our church. He and his family made worship a central part of life. This man, who shared in that great priesthood of all believers, was a wonderful gift to so many.

It is our first calling to love the Lord our God with all our heart, with all our soul and with our entire mind. The great gift of weekly worship keeps our focus in life on love for God and for people. The message of forgiveness frees us. The "torah" (instruction) of God's word challenges our thoughts and ways, and the thoughts and ways of our communities. The instruction of God's Word both informs and equips us to evaluate the cultures in which we live and gives measures for evaluation in the decisions we have to make. It helps keep our orientation and direction. It gives us contrast so we can see. It keeps us salty and givers of light and life. We come also to hear and learn to trust in God's promises which secure the future.

Through this encounter with God's word and spirit, we learn and are equipped to live upstream lives in our downstream worlds and God shapes the human heart.

There is a sub-theme I would like to weave through this story of adventure: It is not about us. We will have a story, but the goal is not to build our story, but to live our calling. Though I want to share a personal journey of pastoral ministry, it is a journey that includes the call to forget about ourselves. All of those who make up the "priesthood of all believers" will also have a story. All of our stories will always be of a highly imperfect journey in which there is always much to learn and always more to do. But the great adventure is to forget about ourselves as we reach out to honour God and care for life and be surprised what God can do.

When we forget about ourselves, we are allowed to enter places and experiences that we would never otherwise have the freedom to enter. We could miss much of the adventure and we would miss the reward (that comes mostly by surprise), but most of all we would miss our calling, which can bring new life to people.

The Christian Church on Earth is called into this venture and adventure by Jesus. The call of the Gospel and the Great Commission are our common challenge.

The reformation, over the years since the sixteenth century has fragmented the Christian church much like a prism fragments light. The denominations like the red, orange, yellow, green, blue, indigo and violet identify our different wavelengths as the refracted light of Jesus. It is at once humbling, and beautiful.

It is humbling, because none of us can claim to be "the" light. So as denominations, we who confess Christ are each a part of the greater whole. Fragmented into denominations we appear weaker. We sometimes fight with this. We see human attempts in both "ecumenism" and "non-denominationalism" to try to gain greater mass and to have greater influence and power. If only we could "wag emperors" again and exercise more power and influence in the world.

Maybe the humbled church of denominations is God's wisdom to remind us that His power is made perfect in weakness. Maybe the humility of the church is still in some way our greatest strength. For in weakness it is not about us, but about the power of the One we serve.

There is also beauty. Where there is mutual respect and encouragement of one another, the presence of denominations brings colour and dynamic that serves a broader base of people in every community. It will also bring some human struggle as those called by Jesus to be children of God sort out life in God's grace as we encounter our differences: that struggle can also help us grow.

We share in that mission to bring light into this world that God deeply loves. We each have strengths, and equally have weaknesses.

This book is written by a Lutheran pastor who lives in Canada. Though the experiences are drawn from a particular Lutheran context, the exploration of the call of the Gospel and the Great Commission is something we all share. We will each see it from the unique perspectives of who we are as followers of Jesus and in our different ways we will struggle with that upstream calling in our struggling world.

When I was thinking about writing on the experiences of ministry I asked a number of people how they would approach it. Three people gave me advice that seemed to fit together.

I used to take private communion to Mary Phillips each month. Mary had run a newspaper with her husband. When I told her of my goal to write about ministry I asked her for her advice of how to go about it and she said, "Focus on something that is really important and mostly forgotten."

Later I was visiting with the president of our Lutheran seminary in Saskatoon. I told him of Mary's advice and asked him (in the light of Mary's suggestion) what he thought. He replied without hesitation, "The people in the pews."

I also discussed this with a former intern with whom I worked in Nelson, B.C. (1981-1982) and who was now a member of the congregation I recently served in Prince Albert, Saskatchewan. His reply, "Tell the stories."

So, I will share some stories from the personal journey into the adventure of the calling to pastoral ministry, which I shared with the whole priesthood of all believers. These are the people of the pew. These are the people who enriched life so deeply. These are the people who put flesh and blood into the theology we studied at seminary, and who embodied the teaching of Jesus that made life so rich and the faith we teach so much more than mindless ideology. Upstream living was a humbling and challenging experience we shared together.

It was easy to fail and fumble. It was encouraging to remember the story of Peter and the post-resurrection encounter with Jesus at the time he felt most disqualified:

> When they had finished eating, Jesus said to Simon Peter, "Simon son of John, do you truly love me more than these?" "Yes, Lord," he said, "you know that I love you." Jesus said, "Feed my lambs." Again Jesus said, "Simon son of John, do you truly love me?" He answered, "Yes, Lord, you know that I love you." Jesus said, "Take care of my sheep." The third time he said to him, "Simon son of John, do you love me?" Peter was hurt because Jesus asked him the third time, "Do you love me?" He said, "Lord, you know all things; you know that I love you." Jesus said, "Feed my sheep. (John 21:15-17)

Jesus called the struggling disciple to nurture and care for the flock. If you read on in this text, you will find that Jesus did not pretend it would always be an easy road for Peter and there is no promise it will be easy for us as well.

One day a student came into my office and talked about his life. He talked about some of the responsibilities he had as a student that he really did not like. "But that is not fun ..." was his recurring refrain.

When he was done I asked him, "Who said it had to be all fun?" Some of the greatest rewards in life do not come out of the "fun" stuff. Some of the greatest rewards come from daily faithfulness in the midst of all kinds of different experiences. At the dark end of that spectrum, some experiences are just plain hard.

Ministry is not all fun, nor is anything that is worth doing. Ministry sends us into the broadest spectrums of human experience. Ministry takes us from the most mundane basics of daily living to that which borders on mystery; from the depths of human struggle to its highest joys; from some of the most superficial appearances of life to the very depths of the human reality. The Lord of life walks with us and sends us and the people we serve into the middle of these vast experiences.

I hope this story of pastoral ministry is not some oppressive dirge. Indeed, an upstream adventure can be challenging, but it is also invigorating and because the business of God's kingdom is life giving, it is filled with celebrations of rich joy.

I hope this writing will encourage more people, young and old, to consider the call to ministry and for all of God's people, to consider the challenge of loving God and people whom we encounter in the daily routines of life.

For too long many have talked about ministry as a life sentence to a dentist's chair. If ministry is oppressive for the pastor, it is likely going to be a ministry of oppression imposed on the congregation and the people we serve. And in a spirit of oppression, there is no delight in the ventures that otherwise turn into adventure as one seeks to follow Jesus and enter into the mainstream of the lives of the people and communities we are called to serve.

In a world so skilled in technology, we may assume everything has changed. I think we will find that although technology has changed, humans can still read and understand ancient history because we still have so much in common with human life across the ages. In this same world I have never been more convinced that the teaching of Jesus transcends the greatest thoughts of our time and walked into life still proves to be equipped to deal with the heart of our lives in a life giving way.

The community of faith will never recover its confidence till it returns to the living God, who through Jesus brings new life to us humans that is eternal and life giving.

May the hymns of praise to God be mixed with great thanksgiving, while with longing hearts, God's people seek opportunities to share God's gifts with the people in this world that God still deeply loves.

I. EARLY BEGINNINGS:
Home... Foundations from People of the Pew (1947-1965).

My thoughts about pastoral ministry began at an early age. I was about four years old when I found an old wooden apple box. I set it on end, so it was about the right height to be a pulpit for a four-year-old preacher. I placed it in the middle of the floor of our bedroom. After singing a hymn with all the gusto a four-year-old could muster, I was ready to preach. I stood up to the apple box pulpit with great confidence and suddenly became aware of a harsh reality . . . I had no idea what to say. I put the box away and pursued other goals, likely with toys and adventures more suitable for a four-year-old.

That experience; however, was not the last time I would face the void. How often, throughout one's years of ministry, did one ask . . . what do you have to say? What do you have to offer the people who will gather in the pews on Sunday morning? What do you have to offer these young people at school? What do you have that might bring some gift of life to people you meet every day?

In those times of question, one returned to the scriptures. One returned to the testimony of that which had been seen and heard and recorded in the scriptures. One returned to the Confessions to enter the debate and one returned to work, taking this equipment into the lives of the people one served.

As the years went on, one experienced the power and reality of that Word in the mainstream experiences of daily living among people. Slowly one came to see with new clarity the pedagogy of Jesus at work:

> To the Jews who had believed him, Jesus said, "If you hold to my teaching, you are really my disciples. Then you will know the truth, and the truth will set you free." (John 8:31-32)

Learning was an adventure and that adventure never seems to end.

Over the years it became more and more clear, as empty as that four-year-old, we have nothing to offer that comes out of ourselves. Of course it is good to remember, it is not about us.

I had been raised in a home where both my father and mother had one thing in common: they both had worn out Bibles. Here they found thoughts that were not their thoughts, and ways that were not their ways. This was an upstream adventure. They wrestled with the scriptures and allowed the scriptures to wrestle with them. Even when Mom could no longer see well enough to read, her joy was a small CD player on which she could play the Bible in the background as she went about her day.

That upstream adventure is likely why they both loved teaching. Mom taught Sunday School for 50 years and Dad taught adult Bible studies well into retirement. It shaped and reshaped their day-to-day living as they sought to be faithful to God who had called them to be His people. The study of God's Word was a passion, which they never lost.

Upstream Living in a Downstream World

I am sure it was this daily experience of life in our growing up years that nurtured many of my perspectives to this day. The scriptures brought challenging thoughts that did not fit with the way I would deal with life by reflex. If reflexes were driven by the reality "by nature sinful" then one needed some measure that would give basis for something different. And to live something different required self-control and often required a change of direction. Of course, self-control was often on holidays or pushed somewhere into a different corner of life.

Even self-control was not something one could muster, but it seemed to grow with the journey. Self-control sometimes demanded one take a difficult course because there was a reason to do so. It sometimes meant going "up stream" when one would prefer an easier route.

According to my mother, I was the child who struggled the most and rebelled in my early years. Discipline sometimes had to come through external means. My parents wrestled with its use. It was not always obvious how it should be done, but their love for me pressed them to seek ways to affirm some things and caution against other things. And sometimes, in my mother's words, "It took a little heat to bend good metal."

My oldest brother named me Daniel. There was a record we had on which there was a song, *Dare to be a Daniel, dare to stand alone. Dare to have a purpose firm, dare to make it known.* How I came to hate that song. Whenever I was drifting in my early teenage years my mother would often remind me of that song. Here was the call to live upstream, not for the sake of simple rebelliousness, but with purpose.

As much as I came to hate this song in my early teens, over time I also came to realize that this was the call for all God's people. In a wonderful way, that song seemed to embody that which I struggled with during my teenage years and early adult

23

life. I admired my older brother for his courage to stand for values drawn from his faith that were not always popular among his peers. He dared to stand alone if necessary. It was sometimes hard on him, but I also saw the respect he gained. His model had a great influence as I was growing up.

I was raised on a farm at Birch Hills Saskatchewan where my father farmed two quarters of land (later a third) and had a poultry farm. He operated his own grading station and marketed eggs to the stores in our neighbouring city of Prince Albert. During hatching season, he sold eggs to the hatchery for broiler farms.

There was one girl and five boys in our family. My sister and I shared the middle (though she was younger by just over a year) with two siblings who were important because they were older, and two siblings who were special because they were young.

My father had been raised in the Spruce Home District, north of Prince Albert, Saskatchewan. He was one of eleven surviving children (one sister Hanna died of whooping cough at the age of seven). My father's family lived off the land, hunting and trapping and cultivating a small acreage of cleared land on their small homestead. It was a humble life. My father's favourite line was they were never affected by the Great Depression of the 1930s because, "We lived in constant depression."

My father loved to take photographs in his early life. He had several albums of pictures. Though poverty was real and in some ways living was hard, there was never any doubt when our father showed us the albums of pictures he had taken - though they were poor in material things, life was "rich" and they shared much joy in its living.

In my father's early years my grandfather often led worship in their home and was involved in the development of the congregation in Spruce Home. They often provided shelter for the itinerant pastors who came to serve them in those early years.

The Lutheran congregation eventually formed in this community and became a significant part of the roots that were to later form Messiah Lutheran Church in Prince Albert.

My mother was raised on a farm near Birch Hills, Saskatchewan. Her father had emigrated from Norway to North Dakota in 1902 in his late teens. In 1905 he came to Canada and homesteaded northeast of Birch Hills. My mother also had some pictures of growing up, which gave us a glimpse of her early life. These photos were a wonderful gift to help us know and understand something of our roots.

After becoming established on his homestead, my grandfather went back to Norway in 1909 to find a wife. On October 23, 1909 he was married and brought his wife back to Canada. The bachelor cabin required some immediate renovations and a major order of furnishings. In 1917 he built her a beautiful new home on the farm and later added running water, sewer and full electrical service provided by their private power plant. My mother was one of eight surviving children. One sister Kerna, died as a child from typhoid and my mother was named after her. By standards of the day, they were very well off. My mother's father had provided land on the corner of their homestead on which the community of Lutherans built a church.

My mother and father were in many ways opposites. My father loved the outdoors. My mother didn't. My father loved sports. My mother didn't. My mother loved refinement. My father saw little point in it. My mother wished she could have some of the finer things in life like the rest of her family. My father wished he could give it to her, but could not afford it.

My mother had a grade 12 education. She attended Bible school for a short time in 1940; studied Latin; went to a business college; worked at the mental hospital in North Battleford;

worked as a secretary at the provincial legislature in Regina; and later worked at a business in Prince Albert.

My father had a grade eight education, and was a sharp mathematician and later attended Bible school. These two very different people got married and moved to a little house my father had built for this occasion. This small house, situated on the Little Red River (about 20 km north of Prince Albert) right next to my grandfather's homestead, was my father's pride and joy, but it was a hard life.

Some years after my father died my mother told me how hard that first year of marriage was. She often cried herself to sleep. She had never experienced such poverty. She described it like this, "Dad was so proud of this little house. But it had no water, no sewer and no electricity, and dad skinned skunks in the basement."

My mother's father, it seems, could not stand seeing his daughter in such poverty and just a few years after they were married, encouraged them to move into a big brick house near Birch Hills (about 40 km south of Prince Albert). This is the house we grew up in.

There was one thing my mother and father had in common that surpassed all the differences. They both shared a deep faith. That faith was deeply nurtured in God's Word. The source of their daily nourishment was visibly identified in their worn Bibles. In our growing up years they encouraged us to read a chapter from the Bible every night before turning out the lights. This became a common practice well into our teens.

Both Mom and Dad attended a Bible Camp at Christopher Lake. It was here where they first met. Later, they both attended Bible School when Outlook College reopened as the Saskatchewan Lutheran Bible Institute in 1940, though mom was there for only a very short time. Dad completed a term there. I found Dad's academic records when I served as president of that school. He had "A's" in every subject.

I remember seeing Dad's pictures from his time in Outlook. The picture that seemed to best represent his time and the heart of his life, was a picture taken while he sat studying in his desk.

He had wanted to become a pastor, but his brother also wanted to be a pastor. In the end, my dad offered to stay home and take care of the farm so his brother could go to seminary.

The common faith of our parents was the centre of our life on the farm. Every morning Dad would lead the family in devotions following a hardy breakfast. He would read a scripture and a devotional article before he prayed for whatever was on his heart and mind that day, and then together we would recite the Psalm, "... this is the day that the Lord has made, let us rejoice and be glad in it ..." and conclude with the Lord's Prayer.

Every night my mother and father had devotions together which my mother led before ending the day after everyone was tucked away for the night. And it was an exceptional Sunday if the whole family was not at worship together Sunday morning.

The one luxury we had over the years was a week at Christopher Lake Bible Camp (about 50 km north of Prince Albert). Dad had been involved in the camp from its inception, and was one of eight men who had picked out the 120 acres of forest on a half-mile shoreline of Christopher Lake where the first Camp was held in 1940. The land was purchased by the young people's organization called the Luther League. The purchase price: five hundred dollars. A man from Birch Hills, Saskatchewan lent the money interest free to the Luther League.

Every year our family attended a week of Bible Camp and when we were old enough, we attended Youth Camp while the younger family and Mom and Dad attended family camps. Here life and fellowship were enriched and as children and young people we got to know many pastors and friends. For our family, the Camp was an extension of our home.

In our growing up years it was not uncommon to attend special services held in neighbouring Lutheran churches. There was a broad fellowship of Lutherans who came together for these special events.

These formative years shaped our early understandings of life and faith and introduced us to many different models for ministry seen in the pastors we came to know. Of course it was not uncommon for Mom and Dad to sit at the table the next day and evaluate what they had seen and heard. It was always tested against their knowledge and understanding of the scriptures and often inspired some time to study particular issues that might have arisen.

Dad spent many hours in the evenings grading eggs and putting them in cartons ready for sale. While doing this work he always listened to the radio. In those years there were many religious broadcasts.

I am sure from the time we were five or six years old, we all had various duties helping pack eggs. As we worked together, Dad would often run commentary on the radio preacher as he worked. Some were excellent . . . and I remember on occasion when he would be fed up and change station. This was all part of life on the farm.

The broader fellowship of the church was a rich fellowship that we treasured even as children; from potlucks to hearing special preachers, we mixed with people. Sometimes we were bored, but most of all, this was normal life for us. It was a source of rich friendships that we enjoyed for years to come.

My father was always delighted to attend conventions of the church. He would come home and share stories of the conventions in conversation around the table at meals. We came to know the pastors of the church and a lot about the life of the church through these conversations even as children.

On the farm we worked together as a family from the time we were very young. Everyone had chores to do: feeding chickens, pumping water, picking or grading eggs and packing them. During the summer when I passed into grade four, I would get up at six o'clock in the morning to drive the tractor and cultivate the fields in order to avoid twenty minutes of chores. I did not enjoy the daily tedious routine of chores that never ended.

Dad knew how to take the edge off the worst jobs. One of those annual jobs was butchering over two thousand chickens, plucking and cleaning and putting them in plastic bags ready for the buyers. And when that was done, we had to clean the three-story barn in the hottest weather of summer to get ready for the young flock that was moving in.

Dad could make a one-day fishing trip with his boys into a two-week occasion. He would go to a calendar, put a finger on the day when the ugly jobs would be completed and declare, "This is the day we are going fishing." Dad seemed to realize that the length of anticipation proportionately extended the significance of the event itself. Looking back, we were always going fishing. In reality we went on two one-day trips every summer.

As we grew older there was a great bond of friendship and fellowship in our home. As we worked together we talked a lot. It was advice I received from my father while we worked together on the farm that was for me the most influential.

I don't recall the year, but we were cleaning the three-story poultry barn. Something led us into conversation about occupation and vocation. In that conversation I remember a number of things my father shared. "I really do not care what you children choose to do. You have to sort out what gifts God has given you. Then develop those gifts and find a place where you can use those gifts in a way that honours God." "In whatever you choose to do, put your best into it. If you have given your best, even if you fail at what you are doing, you never have to be ashamed. No one can do better than their best." He continued, "Others can maybe do things better than you, but that is their business. Your job is to do the best that you can. If you decide to be a ditch digger, then do it to the best of your ability and honour God as you do it."

In those conversations his own dream of being a pastor came up. Maybe his own journey in agriculture instead of ministry shaped his thinking but he also said, "Some people are called to be pastors, but whether a pastor or a farmer we are called to serve God and take care of people." There was never any pressure from my parents for any particular vocation.

As we grew older Mom and Dad made it clear to us children that if we wanted to take the last two years of our high school studies at the Lutheran Collegiate Bible Institute in Outlook, Saskatchewan, they would find a way to make it possible and if we wanted to take another year for Bible School, they would also support that. Christian education was a high priority, which they held for their children. It was no small sacrifice in a family of six children to make this kind of commitment.

Once, I remember being in town with my father on some farm business when we met a local member of our congregation. Two of my brothers were away from home and at school. In the conversation my father was severely reprimanded by this man for sending his children away to school especially when we had a perfectly good school in town. And then he concluded, "Besides, you really can't afford it."

My father's response left an indelible impression on my heart and mind, which I have often thought about. "Some people invest their money in things, we decided to invest it in our children." I believe that is also where the conversation came to an end.

There was a little indignation in his voice, but there was also a deep conviction.

It was true that our parents struggled to pay the bills for these years of schooling. I remember Dad commenting one day that he did not know where the money would come from, but he also assured us that it always seemed God provided all we needed for the things that were important. He found peace in this certainty and it always seemed to work out.

When it came to further university education we were encouraged to find ways to earn the finances necessary on our own. As much as they would like to help, they just could not find a way to do this. Of course they assured us that if we were running out near the end of the year, they would try to find something to help us through.

Our oldest brother set the pattern and the rest of us just seemed to follow. He worked and saved each summer and put himself through four years of education. As a result, the rest of us couldn't say it couldn't be done since he had already done it. Everyone in our family went on for post-secondary study, totalling 27 years plus four degrees earned later. It would seem our parents gave us more than can be measured that equipped us for life's journey.

There was always a lot of mischief in our home. As we sat at the family table where we shared all our meals there was serious talk, and light-hearted banter. On one occasion, when Mom and Dad were involved in playful banter, my mom took off her shoe and threw it across the table at Dad. It was playful, but when Dad ducked it hit and broke the rather large window behind him. There was a sudden pause, a little discomfort, and then much laughter: windows could be fixed.

One time someone suggested that our mother was going gray. She immediately jumped onto the kitchen table and did a jig to prove she was young. Just as quickly, she was suddenly embarrassed. My mother was normally a very dignified person, but underneath there was a lot of mischief. Six children kept her busy in the home. She still found delight in those times we gathered around the table.

Of course the human reality of good days and bad days existed in our home too. There could be sibling conflict and in those transition years to adult life my parents encountered the challenge of budding adult minds that tested their roots and sometimes lived out that rebellion of the human heart. I remember thinking we were a pretty average home (and sometimes a bit below average). I was several years into the parish before I realized that our home was likely one in a million.

Through my high school years I concluded that I wanted to be a farmer. In the fall of 1966 my father bought a new tractor and we talked about the possibility that I might rent some land the next spring and farm with him. The previous spring, after I had completed a year of Bible school and had spent the summer working on my uncle's farm for five months, I had saved enough for my first year of university in Saskatoon. Getting an education and farming seemed a compatible mix.

That winter, we received a phone call from the train station in Saskatoon. Mom and Dad were heading for Kelowna (British Columbia) to look at a poultry farm in the Rutland area. An aunt saw an advertisement in the **Western Producer** for a poultry farm and they decided to check it out.

This was a shock to us as a family. We had never heard our parents hint of moving. On returning from Kelowna they called to inform us that they had bought the poultry farm and planned to move the next summer. That ended my plans to farm.

There had been some conflict in our local congregation. Dad had challenged some of the teaching happening in our church.

Dad and the pastor still had a good relationship even though they had disagreements. Dad called it "modernism". We would hear a lot of discussion on this topic at the kitchen table.

On one of the few occasions Dad was ever in the hospital, as it happened the pastor was also there. Dad and the pastor had daily devotions together. While in the hospital a delegation from the church council of the congregation came to visit Dad to inform him that he had caused the pastor to have a nervous breakdown. Other issues seemed to accelerate this situation beyond its normal bounds.

The whole environment was becoming very difficult for my parents. This was the first serious conflict I witnessed over the years of living at home. The conflict continued. I was living away from home attending school, and on one occasion being home for the weekend I was shocked to see how Dad had aged.

When they were sorting out the business of moving they finally concluded that their work was done in the community where they lived. The congregation they treasured had some problems and they decided that for the sake of the congregation it was likely time to move. They felt that the congregation might be better able to work out the circumstances without them being there. It was a difficult decision.

Dad had always said, "My occupation is where I make my living, but my work is in the church." For Mom and Dad, the move seemed to be a part of God's leading though they had never considered it before these circumstances.

This was a major change in life. They were leaving family behind. They were severing roots with a community in which they had lived and shared for almost 30 years. It was a difficult decision, but it was also an adventure. It seemed to be time for a change. They had peace with the decision. The sale of their farm and many of their possessions went smoothly. They would move into a much smaller house and would live on one acre of land.

During the summer of 1967 I helped Mom and Dad move to British Columbia. I remember the day we loaded and headed down the highway. I never looked back. Something in me thought I should, but I found no need. In Dad's words, the house and land were just "stuff". We were not leaving our home; we were moving our home to a new place.

It was a great summer. The weather was hotter than normal. We rose every morning at five o'clock to work before it got too hot. We did a lot of renovations to the poultry barns and the acreage. By eleven o'clock it was often so hot, we shut down and headed for a swim in Okanagan Lake, or played horseshoes in the back yard under the huge weeping willow trees that shaded us and spit a pure refreshing mist of fresh water, which served as a natural cooling system.

There were a lot of water fights and enjoyment of the lighter workload. On one occasion that summer we tied our sister in the soaker hose and cooled her down! Another time we had a good water fight going which included our mother, when a neighbour came over to introduce herself to the new family in the community. My mother immediately became her dignified self, but when she saw her teenage kids coming around the corner of the house with buckets of water just for her - she panicked.

She got out a few gestures to redirect our frivolous behaviour just before she got hit full on. There she stood drenched, trying to recover some dignity as she attempted to explain the behaviour of her family and assure this new neighbour we were not crazy. She laughed after, but not in that moment.

She was always equal to the task. A young family friend passing through the Okanagan stopped in unexpectedly. My mother saw him coming, ran to the sink and filled her water pistol. When she opened the door to greet him he was blessed with a stream of water in the face! It was all part of the joy that overflowed from a rich life.

Mom and Dad joined Christ Lutheran Church in Kelowna. The congregation was served by an elderly German pastor. He came to visit us shortly after we moved. He spoke of his congregation with deep love and also deep sorrow. I remember him saying in tears that it seemed most people just wanted to be, "… hatched, matched and dispatched." There was little spirit of joy or commitment in the life of that congregation in those days.

When our pastor found that Dad loved teaching adult Bible study classes he was delighted. He asked if Dad would start a study at the church. He said that he had tried many times and could not get one started.

Dad was hesitant to try what the pastor had not been able to do, but the pastor suggested sometimes lay people could do what pastors cannot do. (He understood something about the "priesthood of all believers".) He convinced dad to try and it turned out to be a wonderful experience. The study even ran through the summer months because people wanted it to continue.

Over the years this wonderful pastor became a great source of wisdom and a friend. Our paths crossed often and I learned a lot from this great man of faith.

In the years that followed, I received many letters from home. Both Mom and Dad marvelled that the move could be so good. The workload was so much better for both of them. The poultry business went well and they revelled in the beauty of the Okanagan. They marvelled at how God worked through all the circumstances that brought them to this new place of grace and the new fellowship and opportunities to serve at Christ Lutheran Church.

Daniel A. Haugen

Christ Lutheran had its times of struggles over the years. My mother had a cousin always pushing them to go to her church, which was so alive and dynamic. My parent's response was, "But this is our church." They hung in through all the struggles; walking through the hard days and celebrating the good days. Meanwhile, my mother's cousin had, over the same years, run to almost every church of her persuasion in the city of Kelowna. When she was on a visit with our mother years later she said, "I would give anything to have the fellowship you have."

I have often thought of my parent's journey. They left Birch Hills because they thought the congregation might be able to work out their struggles better without them.

In Kelowna they hung in with the on-going commitment to the fellowship they shared. In many ways each decision (though on the surface so different) was moved by the same concern for others.

In the fall of 1967, now uncertain about my farming career and equally uncertain about my alternatives, I returned to Saskatoon to continue my arts program at the University of Saskatchewan. I still felt the call to ministry, but was not attracted to the possibility.

I had given the "response to the toast" to the graduates at my grade 12 graduation at the Lutheran Collegiate Bible Institute in 1965 and I have no idea if what I said was even coherent. All I remember was the panic and fear, the difficulty to get my breath, and the sweat running down my back. Public speaking was not my forte. God had a rare sense of humour to think this person should be a pastor.

So many things shape us, and we receive more than we sometimes recognize from God and from others. I am sure these formative years had already shaped many things in my life. I am also sure that I was totally unaware this was happening

I remember sitting in the coffee shop years later with men from the community. Some were quick to affirm they had worked hard for everything they had and often shared scorn for those who had less. I remember challenging these men to pray that God would take away every gift He had given them, and leave them with everything they had acquired for themselves. I often wondered what they chose to do.

The great challenge in life is to use what we have received. Do we use if for our self-interests? Is life only about us? Is it all about gaining some significance, or position and power? Do we develop our gifts simply for our own purposes? Do we add knowledge to these gifts simply for the achievement of our personal goals?

I became convinced early that . . . if what we have received is only for self-acquisition we have already lost our direction in life. This thought is certainly counter culture, but Jesus' instruction to his disciples was this:

> *"If anyone would come after me, he must deny himself and take up his cross and follow me. For whoever wants to save his life will lose it, but whoever loses his life for me and for the gospel will save it. What good is it for a man to gain the whole world, yet forfeit his soul?"* (Mark 8:34-36)

Following Jesus was a radical calling. I was not sure I really wanted to consider this calling. Whatever else this calling was, in some way it included "forgetting oneself". Whatever gifts we have received are merely equipment for that journey in loving God and people. And Jesus had a sobering addition for this perspective:

> *From everyone who has been given much, much will be demanded; and from the one who has been*

Daniel A. Haugen

entrusted with much, much more will be asked.
(Luke 12:48)

In all, it seemed like a dusty trail. Does one really want to face this responsibility to God and to others?

It was easy to challenge others with these "thoughts that were not our thoughts, and ways that we not our ways". The more challenging issue was focused in the questions: "Are you prepared to live it as well?" "Do you really believe what you are saying?" "Are you ready to live what you are called to preach and teach?" "Are you really ready to live your life in love to God and to people?"

There were other complications. How do you come to understand the scriptures and one's faith enough to put it into words? This is the heart of preaching. (And of course one needed the courage to stand in front of people.)

I felt ill equipped. It was one thing to have faith that one lived in one's own life. How does one relate that to others? It was all a blur to me. I was just a simple country boy who had been graced with a rich life and wonderful relationships.

In high school I met a girl who had a similar background to my own. Her father and mother farmed and also had six children. Her father had devotions every morning with the family; faith and life had been woven through every fabric of their lives.

Quite by coincidence her parents attended the same Bible School at the same time as my parents in 1940. I soon found out that my father used to skate with her mother. They didn't meet again till we started dating.

This family gave me a new place of acceptance and deep fellowship. They worshiped in a small rural parish near Hawarden, Saskatchewan. They had come from the Lutheran Free Church background. The Lutheran Free Church had joined the

Evangelical Lutheran Church of Canada when it became an autonomous church in Canada in 1967.

This family introduced me to another community that proved to be a rich "life support" community where there was deep joy and a fellowship seen in work, in play, in worship, and in service to others.

I remember driving an elderly retired pastor through this rural parish during those dating years. He made this comment about that man who would later become my father-in-law. "I have never met a man like Harry. He is the best friend of the finest saint and worst sinner."

When I was a high school student at LCBI my mother would write and almost always place a scripture passage at the bottom of the letter. At first, just like most teenagers who did not like to be lectured, it offended me. Over time I realized there was something she wanted me to think about. I knew she cared very deeply for all of us children. After that, I memorized every scripture she shared. It was a way to absorb what came from my mother's way of caring.

One of those scriptures was a text from the Apostle Paul's instruction to early Christians in Rome. This passage from Romans was part of the picture:

> *Therefore, I urge you, brothers, in view of God's mercy, to offer your bodies as living sacrifices, holy and pleasing to God—this is your spiritual act of worship. Do not conform any longer to the pattern of this world, but be transformed by the renewing of your mind. Then you will be able to test and approve what God's will is—his good, pleasing and perfect will.* (Romans 12:1-2)

Conforming to the world was something I had already learned as a teenager. What does it mean to be transformed? What does it mean to have our minds "renewed"?

I think I began to recognize this in my parents, and in my future in-laws. These "people of the pews" lived their life and faith each day. I saw it in many pastors and people in the communities of faith we had shared. As I considered the future, I also considered how important this would be for pastoral ministry. Over the years I began to see how important this is for everyone in order to live in this world and then that last line stimulated the question that would prevail throughout all those years of wrestling with ministry: What is God's will?

II. THE EARLY STRUGGLES:
University Years, 1966-1971.

I thought it an irony that God might call a person into ministry who was so shy and uncertain in front of crowds. I could barely state my name in public. I seemed more suited for agriculture.

My girl friend at the time made it clear that she did not want to marry a pastor. The equation got even more complicated when we got engaged at her graduation from nurses training and at the end of my second year of university.

I took Greek and Hebrew in case the road led on to seminary. A major in Western European History from the third to the nineteenth century seemed to be good background as well. Much of that history focused on the early influence of the church and the end of that era which brought about the beginning of (what I call) the "great secular experiment".

Political philosophy was my minor. I was surprised at the influence of early Christianity in the political developments of the Western World as it fit into that same history. I was also intrigued by the shift of the enlightenment when a new paradigm sought to understand political life apart from God. These years of education were challenging. If this dusty trail should continue toward pastoral ministry, I hoped I would have the academic background and some awareness of the world in which I lived that might support that next chapter.

In my last year of university the girl who did not want to marry a pastor decided to enter the uncertainty and on the fourteenth day of December in 1968 we were married.

I was a student, not by passion but by determination. It was a grind, especially in the first years. The courses I chose required a lot of reading. It was not till the third year that I discovered a new thrill through reading. Most of the time I read 25 to 30 pages an hour, and had trouble remembering the details since my mind wandered to other things while I read.

Bev worked at the University Hospital in Saskatoon. After taking her to work one evening, I returned home to read *Renaissance to Romanticism, Art Literature and Culture of Western Europe*. There was a tutorial the next day on this book of over three hundred pages. At my normal reading speed I would read all night and end with little knowledge, great fatigue and likely a migraine.

I decided to take a new approach to reading. I would run my eyes systematically across every line. The human mind should be able to follow the words. I decided whether I got anything or not, I would simply see if I could muster the discipline to look at the words on each line as fast as I could run my eyes over them: something happened. On page 42 I remember being surprised that I was getting everything, and not only that, I even noticed page numbers. I finished the book in an hour. The next day I could remember paragraphs and page numbers when the discussion began. Education became a new adventure; but if education became a new adventure the issue of calling was still a struggle.

Zion Lutheran Church in Saskatoon was a wonderful church and home for us through our student years. I worked with the Boy Scout Troup at Zion for five years. With the normal program of training in outdoor skills we went on many camp-outs including winter camping in pine bow lean-to's in minus 30 degree weather. Today I wonder how parents allowed us to take their children into these conditions. We also had a great fellowship at Zion with a broad fellowship of other university students.

One Sunday after worship I remember asking . . . how can I become a pastor when I have difficulty getting excited about worship? It was the era of the 1960s, which, in retrospect was likely a quite dysfunctional era. Everything was questioned. Nobody seemed sure what to do with worship at seminary. Zion was still quite traditional, though sometimes dull.

However, every Sunday after worship I was glad I had taken the time. Why was this? It always seemed to make life richer and more complete even though I sometimes found it distasteful. J.B. Phillips book *The Ring of Truth* was popular reading at this time. I seemed to hear that ring in worship, though I was only beginning to understand it.

Through these university years I had an aunt and uncle who moved (for the winter months)to Saskatoon from their farm near Watrous, Saskatchewan. Uncle Don and Aunt Clara had been a wonderful support through all our schooling years. We spent many Sunday afternoons playing games, staying for dinner and visiting in their home.

My Aunt Clara had extensive experience working with youth through the Lutheran Church in America (before she was married) and was sought after as a speaker throughout the church. My Uncle Don was an avid reader and a stimulus to thought, which made our discussions a renewing time. This relationship likely kindled my academic interest more than any other.

If the truth were known, I would have never got through my first year of university without their support. They invited me to their farm during "cram week" (the last week before finals). I had no car, so I hitchhiked to their farm. They provided me with a room; regular meal times and left the rest to me. I set up a study schedule that was rigorously followed. I am sure that was all that got me through that first year. During that "cram week" we also had to discuss politics, not the least being the election of Pierre Elliott Trudeau as leader of the Liberal party in Canada, which we watched on television during this time.

Graduation from Arts and Science with a B.A. in the spring of 1969 was uneventful. I had planned to skip the grad exercises but Bev insisted that I attend. Following graduation it seemed the dusty trail continued in the direction of seminary, so I registered at the Lutheran Theological Seminary in Saskatoon, Saskatchewan.

The connection with agriculture continued through my university and seminary years since I found summer work at the Beef Cattle Research Station on the university's campus. This was a reasonably good paying job and the manager held the position for me every year for as long as I needed it.

I felt quite at home working with an incredible variety of men. We cleaned corrals, fed cattle, put up 500 acres of hay each year, and made feed rations to specifications set out by professors doing research. The agriculture department of the university (among other things) did studies on health related issues and feed conversions for the beef cattle industry. The work proved interesting.

Of course the men who worked with the Beef Cattle Research Station knew I was going into seminary. It was interesting to see their initial uncertainty about a "preacher" working with them.

There were a couple reflexes that seemed very natural in these circumstances. Since then I have watched this reflex show up in other pastor's lives. (One recognizes these things quickly when you have seen them in yourself.) There is a reflex toward "impiety" to prove oneself a normal human being. To associate with things viewed as the opposite of piety was to affirm humanity.

Upstream Living in a Downstream World

The humour and maybe the sad reality is that we think we have to prove we are human. On our best behaviour I am certain that reality is never concealed, but the reflex was still interesting.

A second reflex was to be a bit aloof and hide in one's own insecurity. This narrowed one's involvement with people and tended to affirm that preachers must indeed be strange.

Working at the Beef Cattle Research Station was a good workshop to seek out a healthy response (instead of following the reflexes) to the discomfort of those who felt uneasiness in the presence of someone planning to be a pastor.

Of course I understood them because I was also uneasy with the image. In the end I decided to just be honest and be who I was; a farm boy who treasured the life I had received as a follower of Jesus and with time those I worked with started to talk about their faith backgrounds and everyone seemed to find a freedom to be themselves.

The head of the feed mill was one of the most vocal and dynamic characters. Dick had a church home for which he mostly blamed his wife. He was passionate about his politics. One of his lines was, "You can take away my church, but don't you dare touch my politics." If you wanted a dynamic conversation over lunch you could easily stir his passions.

I developed many close friendships with these men and with time I found out that most of these men in some form were "people of the pew". After five summers at the feedlot, I often went back to have coffee with these men to sustain the gift of friendship we shared.

The manager happened to be a member of Redeemer Lutheran in Saskatoon. He was quite open with the men about the importance of his faith. He was highly respected by everyone and credited with rebuilding the feedlot into a first class operation. For me, he was a mentor from the pew from whom I learned a lot.

Daniel A. Haugen

We became close friends and our friendship continued until his death many years later. I last visited him in the Lutheran Sunset Home in Saskatoon thirty years later when he was suffering with ALS from which he later died. We attended his funeral and shared in the family's great sense of loss and celebrated with them the gift of hope in the gospel.

I continued to trudge on into seminary with much uncertainty, some things learned, and so much more to learn. I wrote about the on-going inner struggles in a book of "random thoughts". In seminary the struggle became more intense and more focused as we delved into theology from a very academic perspective.

In one random thought I likened academic theology to the act of a mad professor. This mad professor had a little pet mouse, with which he was deeply fascinated. One day he decided to fully understand the little pet mouse. He dissected the little pet mouse. He carefully stretched out his little hide, and then identified and organized all its little organs in a row. He studied every little muscle and its skeletal structure and labelled every part. After he analysed everything: he ended in deep despair. For after such deep study, he had lost what he most treasured about his little pet mouse: its life.

I often felt that our theological endeavours had taken the pulse out of our faith. We would "do" prayers. We would "say" the Apostle's Creed. We would seek to be thorough practitioners of the sacred arts in the sanctuary, but with little passion or what seemed to me to be real. However, whatever we did had to be done well.

It was also the great age of relevance. There were attempts to shake people out of complacency. For example, one student jumped off the altar rail as a part of the service. I guess we did some pretty silly things.

We talked about God more as a theological proposition than from the perspective of the first article of the Apostle's Creed that speaks of God as "father, almighty, creator of heaven and earth". We talked of God as if He was the product of our mind. We seemed to miss the creedal reality that we were the product of His mind. (One remembered the great philosophers of the Enlightenment from university classes.)

Prayer seemed to become an expression of philosophical propositions. Prayer sometimes expressed a longing for peace in the world, or for some fulfillment of personal needs, and the future desire for the fulfillment of our aspirations, seemingly expressed to the gathered community more than to the living God.

Was God the talisman under which we expressed our human desires and aspirations and needs to each other? This is not a very gracious description, but it was how things appeared to this struggling student.

I began to believe that since the reformation there had been a gentle shift in academic Christianity to blend with enlightenment thought. The world without God was simply a place of cosmic accident. The human creature was the highest creature developed on the evolutionary ladder. As the creature evolved so did the creature's knowledge and the thought of contemporary humanity in some way transcended everything that preceded it.

Political philosophy was totally reworked in this new thought world. Political philosophers like Hobbes, Locke and Rousseau worked to explain the development of human society and political science through the human response to the fundamental needs of food, clothing and shelter. Natural law became the new template for the measure of life and relationships in human community. Though some still clutched to faith in God, it was relegated to a spiritual world connected with death, but had little to bring to the real world of this life. Where theology was once the queen of the sciences, in this new world "economics" became the queen.

This seemed to crescendo in nineteenth century German scholasticism and mainline academic theology from which we seemed to never escape. The influence on our seminary experience was striking.

This, in my perception, had moved us from the first article of the Apostle's Creed to the belief that God was the evolutionary product of our minds. God was an ever-changing concept shaped and reshaped over history to meet human need. It was no longer about God's compassionate heart that continued to struggle with the ever-drifting world of God's people and God's world. God seemed a concept but not an effective and functional power in the real world.

Ours were the active and living minds. Thoughts of the divine changed with our thoughts. The rest of the natural world was the product of mindless evolution through spontaneous adaptation and change, though we liked to extend a possibility that maybe somewhere God still might exist though with a lesser influence at least in the natural world.

In the study of scripture we seemed to have decided that all the writers and collectors of the sacred text thought just like a nineteenth century German scholastic. We had to discern how each author shaped events and stories to meet their own needs or fit some ideological preferences. There was a basic assumption that miracles were not possible, a striking enigma after confessing the Apostle's Creed proclaiming God as "almighty" and "creator of heaven and earth".

There seemed to be a background proposition that God was not a functioning reality. God could not reveal, or do, or call gather and enlighten the whole Christian Church on Earth as we read in Luther's small catechism. *But the Holy Spirit has called me through the Gospel, enlightened me with his gifts, and sanctified and preserved me in true faith, just as he calls, gathers, enlightens, and sanctifies the whole Christian church on earth and preserves it in union with Jesus Christ in the one true faith. (Luther's Small Catechism, Meaning of the Third Article of the Apostle's Creed.)*

Our confessions were no longer viewed with much interest. They had become "old thoughts". The study of scripture was mostly a process of theological deprogramming leaving one in an ambiguous world.

The statements in our Lutheran confessions, that the scriptures were the authority for life and faith, were interpreted into a mystical presence of the "word" only discerned by those who had the proper critical tools and intellectual abilities: that left congregations in a different world from pastors and church leaders.

While I was at seminary there were still some professors who had not made this transition in thought as much as others. In the classroom one was churned back and forth. Some still had a high regard for the scriptures as authority for life and faith and a real God who indeed was the mind behind all that this world was intended to be and the source of the coming of Jesus his son through whom we have life. Some seemed caught in a schizophrenic tension between academic theology and faith.

I had entered seminary with the struggle over my sense of calling. The agonizing struggle with a theology that seemingly had no pulse and the struggle between faith and our theologizing compounded the struggle.

In my second year of seminary I had a new crisis. One of my wife's uncles was retiring and offered to sell me all his land, his equipment, house and granaries for a very reasonable price. "I know how much you love farming Dan, so I want to offer this to you before anyone else. Take as long as you need to decide."

Daniel A. Haugen

There it was: the open door of escape from my hesitance to be a pastor and the confusion I found in theological study. My father-in-law heard about this offer and assured me that I could borrow all the money because he would sign for it.

I wrestled with this all fall. I remember a double ethics class in early November. At the end of the first class I went to my professor and informed him I would be missing the next class because I decided to go hunting with my uncle Emil at Pike Lake. This professor seemed to understand my struggle. He immediately assured me that he thought it was a wonderful idea. "Just go and relax and forget about everything for a time."

This uncle had provided great sanctuary to many of us nephews and we loved to hunt together. He also was a quiet faith-filled and wise man who always brought a healthy perspective to almost anything in life. He and his wife were faithful "people of the pews". Here was life and faith that reached into every aspect of life in such real and living ways. We talked a lot and hunting was quite secondary to our afternoon together.

By Christmas, in total frustration, I went to my father-in-law and suggested that he should buy the farm so I did not have to think about it anymore. I did not know why, but I could not escape the sense of calling, which I fought against daily.

In the second half of that year there was a new alternative. I thought seriously about going into law. This had great attractions and it seemed worth exploring. The background in political philosophy had certainly laid some foundations to support this venture. Paved road . . . or dusty road? As much as I struggled I could not escape.

These struggles throughout my education years had influenced conversation with my peers. As we sat having coffee together there were often conversations that explored many issues. I have often wondered how my personal frustrations influenced the conversation. None of us are at our best when frustrated. In spite of this, there was a grace in the fellowship we shared that resulted in deep friendships that continue to this day.

Internship was coming. The president of the seminary called me in to his office to see what I wanted to do. I had shared with him my struggle with the pastoral call, but the dusty road continued, so I told him I felt I should pursue internship. He seemed to think this was a good idea and I appreciated his support.

III. UPSTREAM AGAIN:
Internship and Last Year of Seminary (1971-73).

I interned in Burnaby, B.C., beginning in the fall of 1971. Tim, our first child was born the previous spring. I interned under Pastor Russel Melsness at Atonement Lutheran Church, a Mission Church just a few years old. Internships normally last for one year and afterwards there was one more year of study before completing the program and receiving a degree in theology.

"Green" is hardly an adequate description of that young student who appeared in Burnaby that fall of 1971. I have often wondered what my supervisor thought. I had no idea what I was going to do or how I would do it. Fortunately, the pastor was a gracious man and provided wonderful nurture and guidance.

We settled into an apartment in Burnaby just a short block off Kingsway Highway. The traffic noise twenty-four hours a day demanded the need to adjust to a significant environmental change. We scrounged furniture and found our new place quite comfortable: this was a new adventure.

There were a lot of people we had to get to know. My supervisor gave me the church records and directory with pictures. Getting familiar with names and faces before meeting those people helped to make the unfamiliar more familiar as names can be difficult to retain in those first days.

Daniel A. Haugen

My supervisor was a very organized person. We were soon set up with a schedule and we worked as a team. Every Tuesday we met over coffee to talk about what we were doing and how things were going. He taught me a lot and shared experiences that helped to give context to ministry.

Each month there was a congregational newsletter to share what was happening in the life of the congregation and a feature called *Seen and Heard*. It carried stories of members of the congregation and tended to be a mix of humour and information. The human-interest section was the first thing people read. The supervisor reminded me that if people do not read what we print, it is pointless to produce it. And people like to see their names in print. In my visits I found it was working well.

I set out to visit every family in the congregation in the first month. Did my supervisor smile when I told him? He told me to go ahead. The schedule provided 45-minute visits in the afternoon and some evenings set out for the whole month, five days a week with 15-minute gaps between visits.

After two weeks I experienced migraines like I had never experienced before. These migraines were so bad I could hardly stand. With the advice of my supervisor, we stretched the balance of the visits over a much longer period of time. The migraines left and life was good, if still very insecure.

Preaching was another challenge. I was assigned to preach every second Sunday. Sermon preparation was difficult and took a lot of time. What does one say? That challenge of the four-year-old came back to me. I tried to focus preaching by going back to the apostle's task. They were to proclaim (I John 1:1) what they had seen and heard and touched with their own hands.

The New Testament scriptures embodied what the apostles saw and heard and became the source of proclamation. I remember early in my internship when my supervisor (at our regular

Tuesday meeting) asked me why I kept using the phrase, "I think . . ." He suggested preaching is not about what we "think," it is about God's word.

I felt a little misunderstood at the time. The phrase was used as an attempt to be less dogmatic about what I was saying. It was my hesitance, not my self-asserting thoughts.

After this conversation, I tried to avoid that phrase. The observation was another circumstance that helped affirm for me that this business at its centre "is not about us". We are merely the servants in a greater enterprise. Indeed, what I think is quite secondary at best, but thinking was still necessary. Paul had called on the Romans:

> *Do not conform to the pattern of this world, but be transformed by the renewing of your mind. Then you will be able to test and approve what God's will is—his good, pleasing and perfect will.*
> (Romans 12:1)

How does the mind use the scriptures as the instruction for life and faith? How do we bring that word into the lives, homes, workplaces and every aspect of life? How does that change life from the inside?

My mid-year report to the president of the seminary forced some further assessment. I wrote that as long as life in the parish went well, there was no problem, but if there was any criticism, I was certain I would crumble. I was very fragile. So much of life was still about me. I had yet to find that freedom of self-forgetfulness.

I remember struggling with the question . . . what does it mean to be a pastor? Preach, teach, visit the sick, administer the sacraments (of course as a student presiding at the sacraments was not allowed), marry, bury and work with and care for the congregation.

People still had difficulty with pastors, but what is that mystery of being a pastor? People on the street treated you as normal until they found that you were planning to be a pastor. Pastors apparently were strange people. They were not normal. People acted differently when they heard you were going to be a pastor.

After a while, I found an opportunity to play hockey in Burnaby. I had a friend who attended British Columbia Institute of Technology (BCIT). They had a team that invited me to come and play. Ice time was at twelve o'clock midnight. What a wonderful opportunity. Sometimes we got the ice on Saturday night and I would get home by three o'clock (Sunday morning) and was in the office by nine o'clock. I guess that's a time it was good to be young.

This time provided me with some therapy to get some exercise and fellowship with a bunch of guys who in a short time seemed to have no problem having a pastor on the ice with them. I remember asking myself . . . how do we relate the story of Jesus to these people? This question would rise many times in the years that followed.

Whatever a pastor was, if anything I felt like a misplaced farmer. So began an identity crisis of not being, or feeling like a pastor. Though the issue reared its head many times, the solution I found (which seemed to be adequate for the time) was to just be one's self and get back to work. That turned out to be a long-term comfort and solution.

I feared funerals. I had a great distaste for visiting in hospitals. Although I loved meeting new people, I still found it stressful even under normal circumstances.

A friend worked with Vancouver First Call. They picked up bodies and delivered them to the morgue. One evening, while visiting over a cup of coffee, he got a call. He asked if I wanted to come along. I did not want to go, but in the pressure of the moment I went. A man died from a heart attack in his home. We had to take him out of the home on a stretcher and deliver him to the morgue. I was not really ready for this. I had never been in close contact with death. This was the beginning.

My first house call to a person in distress came at eleven o'clock one evening. A man wanted to see a Lutheran priest. He gave me his address and I said I would be right over. He did not live very far from our apartment. I arrived and rang the doorbell.

When I rang his doorbell there was no immediate answer. The lights were on and I could hear someone inside. I rang again and finally a man came and stared through the window. It took a while before he opened the door. I introduced myself and asked if he was the man who called and he finally invited me in.

I sat in the living room while he went to the kitchen and picked up a hunting knife on the kitchen table. He stood looking at the knife for some time. It seemed forever. I was beginning to wonder if I should have entered this house and I tried to strike up a conversation with him. He was slow to reply.

I was not sure if this knife was meant for him or me. I looked for some means of defence should it become necessary. As I continued to try to strike up a conversation, he finally put the knife back on the table and came out into the living room. That was a relief.

So began my encounter in ministry with a man and his family that had struggled with the bondage of alcoholism and despair. I visited with this man many times after this and shared his journey to sobriety and his struggle with faith that God in Jesus had called him to be one of His own. Forgiveness and new beginnings were not only important for this man but for his wife as well. They came to worship and I continued to visit with them. This being my first call from outside the community of faith, I wondered what the future would hold.

One striking experience for me was with a large family of faithful members of this congregation. The father was a very successful businessman. Often, when away on business trips, he would come back Sunday to worship with his family and have the day with all his children. Here was a faithful family of the pews. Then, late Sunday night or early Monday morning he would fly back to where he had to be.

They had a huge dining room table where the family would gather almost every Sunday night. The adult children would often be home and for the rest of the evening they would eat together and then play games. There was something about their life and faith that had a powerful impact on me.

Over the years that followed, I stayed in touch with this family. Years later, I went to see the parents. The father was in his 80s and his health was failing. He was in bed when I arrived and his wife insisted I go up to his room to see him.

He was a rather large and stately man propped up in his bed for my visit. I remember the gracious hospitality of his presence and the deep faith out of which he shared stories of his life. This life had also gone through many struggles, which he humbly acknowledged. Then in a most wonderful way, he gave me a "father Jacob" account of all his children. (At the end of the book of Genesis Jacob did this with his children.)

From the oldest to the youngest he described his children in life and faith with deep insight and affection. He recognized their strengths and weaknesses in a most gracious way. Here was a living faith that reached into the depths of this man's life. This faith was the foundation of all he did. It was the lens through which he saw and understood his children. From this man I learned a lot about the impact of the gospel. This follower of

Jesus took that faith into his home and his business world. He taught me a lot.

Then came another new experience for which I felt unprepared. My supervisor gave me the chance to be involved in a marriage preparation with one of the young couples of the congregation and to participate in the marriage service. He was Lutheran and she was raised Jehovah Witness.

I met the couple in a suite overlooking the calving area in a barn. Out of the picture window we looked down on the cows and calves and talked about life and relationships and how our life in fellowship with God finds a centre from which we gain the equipment and perspective to deal with life as sinful human beings. This was a new venture but a wonderful experience.

It turned out to be the beginning of a very special friendship that has continued throughout my ministry as I have stayed in touch with this couple. They have five children and it has been wonderful to see the family grow, and to share the life and faith of this family. On one visit I was asked to help one of their sons with his confirmation course work. It was a formidable task. Their pastor certainly took confirmation instruction seriously. It was fun to be a part of it.

I have also followed the lives of many other members of that congregation. Some have thrived and some have found their road difficult, sometimes because of their own choices, and sometimes because of the imposition of others. They are still people who hold great value and enrich our lives and for whom we pray and with whom we visit whenever we find occasion in their busy lives.

While on internship I had my first encounter with issues outside of the institutional church. This was the first of many encounters with community and political issues. My father had a poultry farm and in the fall of 1971 encountered problems with the egg marketing board, which governed the marketing of eggs throughout the province. This board had arbitrarily reduced my father's quota for marketing to half of what he had been assured of when he moved in 1967. The board offices were in Abbotsford and since I was living in Burnaby my father asked me to do some work on his behalf.

So began an interesting new venture that used up many of my days off. In a month I had a thick file of information suggesting there were deep problems in this organization.

They were threatening to take my father to court for not paying a penalty on over production that basically amounted to all his profit. My father retained a lawyer. The lawyer revealed to my father that the BNA Act (still in effect at that time) allowed farmers to sell all their produce on their own land. Thus, he was well within the law since his total production was marketed on the farm. The board then hired people to sit in a car on the side of the road in front of our house to watch the farm daily.

The details are too many to share. In the end I called the Minister of Agriculture's office in Victoria and requested a government inquiry into the activities of the board, suggesting that the board was in contravention of the Natural Products Marketing Act under which they operated and there were further indications of larger problems that we felt needed investigation.

The government set up a formal inquiry board as we requested. In the end they affirmed the breach of law related to the Natural Products Marketing Act, and acknowledged there were many issues they did not have the time to explore but generally swept everything aside with an affirmation that the board was doing a good job. It was a disappointing experience. In the end my father could not accept the pressure of the daily scrutiny on the road in front of our farm, and he finally sold out.

Some would call this a justice issue. I suppose one could make it an issue of justice and rights. In my mind, it was just another circumstance in life where the realities of a sinful world are a part of the environment in which we live. How do you love your enemies and pray for those who persecute you? One could work to crush opponents; one could seek some remedial action for the short term; one could seek remedial action for the long term, for the abuses would affect others as well. We did everything we saw possible. For all practical purposes we failed and life went on.

Luther talked about the needed role of civil government in society as a God given function. In this experience I became more aware of the challenging stewardship of civil office. I also became convinced of the need for God's people to be involved in areas of civil government. Over time, I have also become aware that many people in the pews have a deeper understanding of the issues than we as clergy will ever have and it may be more important for us to encourage them to discover their calling as God's people to bring their life and faith into these arenas of service.

One member of our congregation was a director for a major food wholesaler in the greater Vancouver area. In conversation I shared some of my involvement in this matter with the egg marketing board and I found out that he also had dealings with them. It did not take long to realize that here was a person who had a much deeper and far more profound understanding of the problems than I had. He had more to bring to this table than I ever would and was a great help on the journey. It caused me to think more about the work of "the priesthood of all believers".

It reminded me again that lay people can often do much more in a healthy way on these issues than we as pastors will ever be able to do. Maybe our job is to nurture the life and faith of our laity and as that great working force of the priesthood of all believers moves to their various places of work, they will have both opportunity and ability to do more than pastors can ever do in their respective fields of work and life as God's people of "salt and light". There was certainly more to learn.

A neighbour to my father-in-law had a heart attack during the winter and could not farm in the spring of 1972; therefore, he was looking for someone who could farm his land. He called to see if I was interested. This would shorten the internship experience, but it met other needs and was acceptable to everyone involved.

I returned from internship at the end of May 1972 to raise some additional financial resources for our last year of seminary as we had one more year of schooling. Our internship salary of $250 per month plus accommodation did not allow for much of a savings account at the end of internship. We had to find additional resources.

We moved back to Saskatchewan and into the small house on that land my father-in-law had bought near the town of Hawarden. This was very close to the land I was to farm. With creative determination, we furnished the house with $100 and had a wonderful summer enjoying this taste of our first "career love". Life was good. After the crop was seeded there was summer fallow to work. Then there was grain to haul from the previous season's crop.

On one farm a barn loft had been filled with ten thousand bushels of barley. During the winter the structure did not prove equal to the task. The floor had collapsed with the barley flowing into the main floor of the barn, filling the stalls and central ally. Cleaning up was a terrible job because the auger would only reach so far into the barn, and every nook and cranny required shovelling and a final clean up. There was also a machine shed with twelve thousand bushels of grain that had to be moved into nearby bins (that had been extended that summer) to hold more grain.

Much of the summer was just good healthy hard work. It was also a taste of being stewards of the land. I worked hard and enjoyed every day and had time for family outings, and Sundays we had time for worship and family and friends.

After harvest I went over every piece of equipment, fixing every mechanical problem I could find. I changed the oil on every motor, greased every bearing and then put the equipment into the machine shed.

I remember the sense of satisfaction the day I snapped the padlock and the farm work came to an end. It was as if I could hear my father's words, "I really do not care what you children choose to do. You have to sort out what gifts God has given you. Then develop those gifts and find a place where you can use those gifts in a way that honours God and cares for people. And in whatever you do, put your best into it."

There was a great sense of satisfaction and completion to this task. I think the farmer was satisfied as well that it had been a good summer. This was normal life. We were normal people among normal people. It felt great.

Then it was back to seminary in the fall of 1972. We were moving again. Just before we moved off the farm, we found a house to rent in Saskatoon. We had $800 in the bank to get through the coming year. The house allowed us to rent out a room to one of my brothers attending university. A little rent money would help and to our surprise, he paid more than we asked.

Shortly after we moved into our new home, an older brother and his wife came for a visit. This brother and I had roomed together for several years earlier till he completed his university. Before leaving, he handed us a check that covered the cost of our groceries for the month and informed us that there would be a check every month till we were finished school.

I remember sharing my concern that it would be some time before we could pay him back. And then he taught us something about pride and humility: he informed us that we would not be paying him back because this was a gift.

I told him that we could not accept it. I will always remember his reply, "We have saved for two years so that we could do this for you and you cannot deny us that privilege. If you need to pay us back just do the same for someone else who needs help."

Ever since I have called this "premeditated pride slaughter". They had been saving for two years. Every month the checks were more difficult to accept. But each month we learned something about humility, and I believe we also discovered through the life of this brother a theology that had a pulse.

I will always be grateful for this generous act of kindness. It defined grace. It was a gift that was undeserved, not even asked for, and non-repayable. And then there was the call to pass grace along to others:

> *The King will reply, 'Truly I tell you, whatever you did for one of the least of these brothers and sisters of mine, you did for me.'* (Matthew 25:40)

The last year of seminary had its own challenges. A new course in Pastoral Care and Counselling came into the seminary program during my internship. This new course was a graduation requirement. I found the course interesting and valuable until it came time to pick up a number of index cards with names and addresses of real people in the community with whom we were to make contact in a counselling role. We were required to write verbatim reports on these visits and discuss them in class. I didn't have a problem with the practice until I headed across the city to my first address.

Upstream Living in a Downstream World

As I drove across the city, I became more thoughtful about this whole process. I was taking real people and using them as guinea pigs for my academic purposes. Was this how one dealt with real people? I was doing this for my own benefit, not for theirs. And on top of this seeming abuse, I was to ignore a primary principal of counselling which was confidentiality. I had to prepare a full verbatim account of my visit and share it with others.

I drove halfway across the city before I locked up. I could not do this. This was all about me and not about the people who had real needs. I could not do it. I headed back to the seminary and asked for a meeting with my professor and shared my difficulty with him.

He did not believe I made a serious enough attempt to carry out the program's requirement and would fail me unless I showed that I made some attempt to do this part of the course. I would get an "F" in this class. I left in despair.

If I did not pass I would not graduate. Of course it also crossed my mind that this was my way out from pastoral ministry; however, something in me resisted. I continued to participate in all other aspects of this class, but could not find a resolve.

I finally appealed to the faculty to waive this course as a requirement for the degree on the basis that it had come onto the syllabus while I was on internship. This was the suggestion of the president of the seminary when I went to him for advice. I hope I still showed respect for the professor. I affirmed that a professor had the right to grade as that professor saw fit, and I was quite prepared to submit to any grade given. Though, I still had trouble accepting that it would not allow me to graduate.

I was called before the whole faculty to defend my request and that was one of the worst experiences of my life . . . and maybe that is enough said on this matter. In the end they waived the course as a requirement for my degree, and in the end I graduated. That is the first and only "F" I ever had on my academic record.

When I reflect back, it was a difficult place for a professor. It is difficult to discern what is happening in different circumstances with different students. The course standards were indeed his to set. It would be difficult to understand why some could freely participate and someone else could not.

How often would I be in the same position as this professor in the years ahead? I had much to learn.

Every time I see the "F" on my academic record I am reminded of this experience and I smile. The good news is that this professor is a good friend to this day. Grace and forgiveness are a wonderful and undeserved kindness we can experience and reconciliation one of the great gifts of life for all God's people.

But the struggles with issues of pastoral ministry were not over. Bev had bought a beautiful black cassock and had made a white surplus to go with it. She had also made stoles with symbols I had designed. There was one problem. I could not bring myself to put on the cassock, surplus, or stoles to see if anything fit.

Something in the clerical garb represented my struggle. I was repulsed by it. Finally, one day with a firmness that Bev used only when necessary, she informed me I would put it on. I did. She walked me in front of a full-length mirror so I could see myself.

This was a most difficult experience. The pastor looked back from the mirror. This was "the pastor" on the outside. This was the pastor so many shied from. This was the image that seemed unnatural. It did not look like the person I felt on the inside. I took it off as soon as I could without being offensive.

Ordination day was to be in May of 1973. I asked the president of the seminary to preach at my ordination. We were members of Zion Lutheran Church in Saskatoon and the senior pastor would led the service and be assisted by the assistant pastor at Zion. The

President of the Evangelical Lutheran Church Canada Dr. Ted Jacobson would preside at the ordination. (This was particularly meaningful to me since he was one of the first students my father taught in Sunday School.)

That Sunday arrived. My whole family came and we had a barbecue in our back yard. Chairs were limited, so I sat on a kitchen stool. One of my brothers saw me seated, pointed and said, "There is the pastor in his lofty position."

He never knew in that moment, that he could not have said anything worse. It was one of those lonely moments when one wished to simply dissolve and disappear.

From the barbecue we headed to Zion Lutheran Church. In the bag draped over my arm was the burden of a clerical garb once worn and ever so foreign. I left my family and met with the pastors in the sacristy. They were getting garbed and ready. I began buttoning up my cassock. It seemed like I had a hundred buttons and each one was more confining. I pulled the surplus over my head. When everyone was ready, we prayed together in the sacristy.

The procession began. We walked down the long aisle of Zion Lutheran Church. Four ordained officials proceeded in pairs and behind came the ordinand; like a lost sheep alone. I got to the front pew where I was to sit, but there wasn't any space. My Uncle Selmer had to move over to make room for me.

There I sat. The sweat ran down and pooled where the pew met my back. This was not a good moment.

I remember looking at the side door of the sanctuary. The service began, we sang, we stood, we sat . . . I had all the actions. I have no recollection of the service to this point. Then it was time for the President of the Seminary, Dr. Bill Hordern to bring the sermon for this day. It would be twenty minutes. It always was.

I remember informing God that he had twenty minutes to work a miracle. If he did not work a miracle I would be walking out that side door and my family would be embarrassed. How unfair for my wife Bev. She had endured these years of study and though she did not want to marry a pastor, she had even sacrificed that to be my wife... "Twenty minutes God... that is all the time left for a miracle."

I have gone back to this sermon many times since. I talked to the seminary president about that sermon years later and asked him if he knew what a gift it had been. That sermon systematically dealt with everything that bothered me. His sermon allowed me to be the person I was on the inside. It was not about me. It was about proclaiming what God in Christ has done and spoken. It was about taking care of the people.

When the sermon was over with the "amen," I felt freedom and walked forward for ordination. This was a holy moment. God calls normal human beings to be His servants. And with time, I would find that the work to which he calls us is real and designed to serve real people who live in this real world. I was not ready... so much more to learn, but I was ready to get started. I hadn't prepared anything to say when the time came for me to speak at the close of the ordination service.

A senior pastor and professor years later told me that he had been disappointed with what I had to say, but when I told him this story he graciously understood. And of course, since it is not about me anyway, to have blown it was really not the worst thing that could happen. It was a little hard on one's pride; but God had called this misplaced farmer into ministry.

I had some time to fill before moving to our first parish and a friend offered me a job. He was a partner in a large gravel crushing and hauling business. Sitting in a tractor/trailer unit was comfort again. I enjoyed this brief interim before beginning in the parish.

IIII. FIRST CALL:
Preeceville Lutheran Parish: (1973-77).

My first call was to the Preeceville Parish in east central Saskatchewan. Bev was seven months pregnant, and not in good shape for moving. We had a two-year-old son full of energy. We had intentionally tried to own as little furniture as possible through our schooling years since we moved quite often. So, before moving to the parish we had to buy furniture.

We took out a bank loan for $1000 and bought a new living room, dining room and bedroom suites (we still use some of that furniture today) and moved into a three-bedroom parsonage in Preeceville. Our second son was born that first summer, the day after we returned home from Bible Camp at Nelson Lake about six miles northwest of Preeceville (our daughter was born in 1976 about a year before we would move again).

We served a parish made up of three congregations: St. John's Lutheran, Preeceville; North Prairie (a country church north west of Preeceville); and Faith Lutheran Church, twenty-two miles south in Buchanan.

This was a federated parish made up of two congregations of the Evangelical Lutheran Church of Canada, and Buchanan, which was a congregation of the Lutheran Church of America, Canada Section. The Letter of Call stated that I was responsible to attend conventions for both church bodies and support both church bodies through the respective congregations within the parish.

The conventions revealed two church bodies that differed greatly in character and emphasis. These differences were not as identifiable in the congregations as in the formal gatherings of the larger church. I would reflect on those differences many times in the years ahead, not the least during the processes that led to the merger of these two church bodies in 1986 and in the years that have followed.

This misplaced farmer, now twenty-six years old, began a journey in ministry. This was a venture into the unknown feeling totally inadequate for the task (not much more confident than the four-year-old at the apple box), but challenged to be faithful, and to do the best one could with the abilities God had provided. I understood the challenge was to proclaim and to live that which we have seen and heard, holding to that gift of the Holy Scriptures, which we believe to be the sole authority for life and faith. Fortunately, in those first years, the parish was filled with some wonderful friends who were the embodiment of grace and wisdom.

Norm and his wife Lorna took us under their wings. They were much older than us. Norm was a blacksmith and Lorna was a grace filled and gifted member of the congregation who mastered in hospitality.

I went golfing with Norm quite often that first summer and when I made my first ventures to the coffee shop, he was there to make me feel welcome. This "family of the pew," full of faith and quiet grace were a source of wisdom and inspiration that carried us in those first uncertain years of ministry. Preeceville Parish was a great place to begin for this young pastor.

It did not take long to learn that much of what we studied at seminary was wonderful in many ways, but did little to equip us for many of the functional aspects of parish ministry. At the same time the parish gave one time to learn, and what is even more important it put a pulse back into what we studied and the gospel took on new life.

I never had an office before. How would one function? As a student the schedule we had was determined by class times and the rest was open and adaptable for anything one's heart desired... unless one found the discipline to study. There was a lot to learn.

The pastor was there to serve the people. The people showed up on Sundays. Some served on church council and others attended Bible studies and taught Sunday School. Some were involved in other ways in the life of the congregation. The rest of the time they were about their business and the pastor was alone.

In the beginning I didn't have an office schedule. Maybe a council meeting went late the previous night. Should one be obliged to be in the office first thing the next day? How adaptable should one make the work schedule? At first I made it quite adaptable, so much so that one did not know if one was working or not.

This also produced stress and there were enough sources for stress. With three congregations, work events were compounded. There were multiple services on Sunday, three Council meetings each month, Bible studies, confirmation classes and two hospitals (which served the different communities) and there was a need to get to know the people and the communities we served.

I remembered from seminary the relationship between the Hebrew understanding of "shalom" and "order". My life had no order. It was chaos. It was not long till I realized that I had to commit myself to some schedule to create some order for life. Too many things would drift and often remain undone. It was important for my well-being to arrange what I had to do with some predictability. It was also important for those I was to serve. So, I set regular office hours.

There was no one to know if I kept those hours. Self-discipline needed support (at least it did for me). So I announced to the congregation my schedule and had it printed in the Sunday bulletins. This provided an accountability that supported self-discipline. I would be in the office 9:00-5:00pm Tuesday to Saturday - unless I was elsewhere on parish business in the afternoons. People soon found they could actually call the pastor at the office and he might be there.

The areas of discipline grew. Hospital visits in Preeceville would be at one o'clock on Tuesdays. Wednesday was my day for Buchanan. I would be at the hospital in Canora at 1:30pm on Wednesdays before spending the rest of the afternoon visiting in the Buchanan congregation where each Wednesday evening we had mid-week church school and confirmation classes. Mondays were my day off.

Something in me fought the idea of having a regular schedule. I struggled to make this commitment, but once it was made, I found there was much less pressure. Life had some order, and other matters that came up would fit in before or after the scheduled events, and even those unscheduled events became a part of the ordered day. There was something pretty real in that Hebrew understanding of *shalom* as order.

I became convinced that much of the pressure and stress of ministry is not the work we do, but the chaos in which many choose to work. With this degree of order I found a new sense of well-being in my workdays.

Preaching was hard work in the early years. I planned to work 12 hours on every sermon. I put a lot of time into study, including research of the Greek or Hebrew texts; therefore, time was set aside every day for reading. I set up a file system for all my sermons. This seemed a good idea since the periscopes repeated every three years and I might find these sermons helpful.

With time I found I could never reuse an old sermon. It always seemed to lack freshness. If it was not fresh for me, how could it be good for the congregation? I did explore previous sermons from time to time but never found them useable except to help explore the texts when they came up in the three-year cycle.

Preaching was a rich experience - except for one thing. When I got deeply engrossed in anything I lost all sense of time. If I got deep into study I could think I had worked an hour and it might be four hours. When deeply engrossed in a sermon I could lose all sense of time as well. I worked off a full manuscript but would come up with added thoughts that sometimes escalated a sermon into an ordeal for the listener.

It was a most embarrassing struggle and became a great source of discouragement. I finally got a watch with a built in alarm and would set it for twenty minutes. In twenty minutes an alarm would go and I would quickly wrap up. It brought many smiles to the congregation and spared them much misery. Preaching should not drive people out of the sanctuary.

It seemed like a good idea to get some feedback from the congregation in those early years. I remember sitting in my office one day evaluating what was happening in the congregation and I decided to prepare a survey. The survey turned out to be a test of one's security.

Sometimes you ask people what they think and they tell you things you did not want to hear. I remember wrestling with that as I collated the responses. Most of the survey was quite reaffirming, but a few comments challenged me. Those few comments had 90 percent of the impact though they were not 10 percent of the response.

Daniel A. Haugen

There were some struggles, but finally I was smiling as that inner voice informed me that I was still my own harshest critic and the congregation had not begun to recognize all the weaknesses I had seen in myself.

One day I wrote a list of the areas of work in which I felt I should do a better job (my personal complaints). In a parallel column I accumulated every criticism I had heard directly or indirectly from the congregation. My list was much longer. Why be critical of your parishioners for recognizing what you know is real? One had to chuckle quite often and get back to work.

I began to recognize that generally there were more women in church than men and more children than teenagers. If we were going to serve the people of our parish, there were a lot of people who did not show up for the formal program of preaching the Word, administering the Sacraments and conducting public worship in harmony with the faith and practices of the church.

It would be so nice if more men and teenagers would come to church. This thought dominated my mind one day as I sat reflecting in my office. Then that inner voice spoke, "Preacher you can sit here till hell freezes over, they still won't come. Maybe it is time you go to them." My response was, "How?"

Questions are important, but one must be willing to seek answers. Questions can produce turning points because sometimes the elusive answers to our questions push us to adventure into new avenues.

One day I heard that the men met for coffee at the Century House (a restaurant in town) on a daily basis. I walked downtown to pick up the mail each day and decided to target mail pick up just before ten o'clock and then went to the Century House for a cup of coffee. I found a table where a parishioner was sitting and joined the group.

Introductions were made and some of the men got quiet. I guess preachers were perceived to be people who wore strange robes, had a very critical spirit and did strange things unrelated to life, as most knew it. Conversations were interrupted by the often remarked, "Oh pardon me pastor... for the language."

The first visits to the coffee shop were strained and that old reflex to do things to be accepted crept in but one tried to suppress it and just be oneself (for better or worse). It took some time till the day came when I walked in and someone called out, "Hey everyone, clean up your language the pastor is here..." and I knew I was accepted.

For the first period of time the coffee shop was a place to meet people and talk about politics, farming and the weather. In those early days I would have quit going if someone had complained. Sometimes, the conversation carried on far too long to be helpful for the work that was waiting in the office. One wondered if it was always a good use of time, but it took time to build relationships. I discovered it took more time before people found the understanding and language to sit and talk about life and faith as freely as they talked politics, weather and agriculture. But with time, life and faith became a normal part of their conversation in the coffee shop.

One disconcerting experience came early in the coffee shop ministry. I was sitting with a man who was just a little more righteous than most humans are able to attain. He was introducing me to people as they walked in the door or as they walked by the large window looking onto the sidewalk.

"See that man coming in... he is (so-and-so) and here's the kind of guy he is..." and sometimes with almost a delight he would conclude "...and he's a member of your congregation" especially when his comment was negative.

One day a man walked by the large window in front of the cafe. The righteous coffee companion commented, "There goes a man you will never get to church even when he dies."

By this time I had a great desire to meet the man who walked by the window. (And I must confess I was almost thankful the man I sat with was a member of a different congregation... I tried not to be.) I found the man I was with most difficult to appreciate.

Over time, I got to know the man who walked by the window quite well. He owned a business in town and had developed quite a reputation. We had coffee together many times in those years. One day while I was in his business to buy something he asked me to come back into his warehouse. There he poured out his life story with a great deal of regret as he expressed his sense of failure in so many things. One tried to share with this man that which we have seen and heard and touched with our own hands as followers of Jesus.

We grew to be good friends. Many years later I was back to this community and I met him on the street and with delight he told me how much life had changed since those days. It was wonderful to see his gratitude for the change. I was deeply saddened to lose a good friend when he died a few years later.

I met so many people I came to treasure in the coffee shop. There was a hermit that lived north of town. He always showed up with a two-week growth of beard. He was rather roughly dressed and always carried a little black satchel under his arm. It took me two years to get a natural meeting with this man. I had waited for some opportunity to meet him that would not be intrusive. I never liked imposing myself on anyone.

One day I came into the coffee shop and he was having coffee with someone I knew well. Here was an open door. I sat with them, got introduced and we visited. After that I met with him a number of times.

He had earned a degree in horticulture in his '60s. He lived in a small one-room shack on a little lake north of town. He had struggled for years with alcohol problems but still had a mind that was sharp and well read. We talked about everything including life and faith.

One day he came to the booth where I was sitting, sat down, and poured out his story. He informed me, with tears in his eyes, that he finally realized he had to quit drinking. So began his pursuit of sobriety. It was both penitence and celebration.

The coffee shop ministry often held me at the restaurant to the jeopardy of my office time, and I must confess on a number of occasions I got called to the bar where the only telephone was located. Bev would have to call to suggest it was maybe time to come home for lunch because by then it was often one o'clock.

The first criticism I received from a parishioner for the time I spent at the coffee shop came in my third year in this parish. A dear friend, for whom I had great respect, said, "You can no more have a ministry in the coffee shop than you can farm there."

It was a concerned reprimand. On the inside, though surprised, I confess I smiled a little. I was pretty certain that it would be a short time before this man realized that ministry happens where people are. I am sure he later wished he had not said what he did. He was a most faithful and astute man of faith, but from the outside looking in it had to look like the pastor was wasting a lot of time. It was very understandable, but by this time I had few doubts about the importance of this outreach into the community. (I am quite certain if it happened in the first year, I would have not continued this venture.)

Something happened through this venue for ministry. We had several men's breakfasts that attracted a broad spectrum of men from the community, many with little or no faith background. We also ended up with times in which there were more men in church than women, and there were four pews of teenage guys at the back of the church. It all came quietly and almost unperceived. When faith grows there is a growing reason to worship. It seldom goes any other way and real life takes time to grow and mature. There is no shortcut.

I became convinced there is a direct correlation between ministry to men and the impact of faith on the teenagers of our communities. It may be cultural conditioning, but it still remains a reality. I am sure one will find that wherever there is an active and effective ministry to men, there will also be teenagers in the church. Why, I am not sure. You can get women into the church, and children into the church, but if you do not get the men into the church it seems you do not get the church into the home or on a broad basis into the community. For now I will leave that for others to think about as I am sure this could produce some fruitful discussion.

In parish ministry I found it hard to see signs of results on a day-to-day basis as one worked and prayed and sought to care for people. It was easier when one could look back over a greater period of time. I liked carpentry because you can take wood, shape it and assemble it and there is tangible evidence of what one is doing. When a job is complete, one can look at it and say, yes, this was done well . . . or not.

In parish ministry you worked long days and hours without seeing much of anything. It took time for me to realize that when you work with living things, there is always a time frame for growth. The only things that happen with some instantaneous results are things that are destructive (or also things artificial). You can destroy a plant almost instantaneously. You cannot grow one without allowing for time. You can make an artificial plant quickly, but it is not real.

Indeed, one can create the artificial signs of life in a short period of time, but in real life there are no short cuts. Life begins imperceptibly. The first signs of life seem so inadequate. It takes time for living things to grow and mature.

When a farmer plants wheat, it will always be 90 days or more before one sees a harvest. Over the years I came to the conclusion that if the maturing time for wheat is normally 90 days; from the planting of God's word and the nurture of spiritual life it is three years before you see significant change. It seemed a fair expectation to work for three years with people before more tangible change could be seen in life and faith. I have no idea if Jesus' ministry of three years had any significance, but I could not help but think about that.

It also became evident that the first yellow sprouts of new life come long before the harvest. Those yellow sprouts of life are 100 percent new life, less than adequate, but if nurtured there could be great anticipation of what could come. I think I began to understand the farmer parables Jesus told. Indeed, some seed failed, but one plants, another waters . . . and then comes the harvest. One began to celebrate every new yellow sprout of growth with some anticipation for the future.

Often I visited with a certain man at the restaurant. He was a large man. He had come from Czechoslovakia as a young man after the Second World War. In the course of time he told me about life as a child in Czechoslovakia. He told me how they were forced out of their home during the war, and how his family was shot in the street in front of him as a child.

He told me about being an altar boy in the church and how one day he came into the priest's quarters and, in his words, "There were four feet in the bed." That had been the end of church for this man.

We talked about a lot of things over the years. He was not happy about being cut off from the faith that had been planted in him as a child. One day I suggested it was maybe time to go back to his church. The emotion was in his eyes as he affirmed that it was likely time and he returned to his spiritual roots.

I remember sharing my celebration of how this man changed with a member of the congregation. The response was immediate, "That man has always been the way he is. He will never change." Inside me a voice pleaded, "But he has changed ..." but I did not say it out loud.

Yellow sprouts of new life are often overlooked. I was buying parts for our snow machines when I met this man in the Chrysler garage by chance. He often picked up vehicles for the dealer. Word got out that I was taking a call to British Columbia and he asked me if it was true that I was leaving. I told him I was. This three hundred pound hulk of humanity stood and wept. Something had happened in this man's life; and through his life, something was also happening to me.

Some years later I came back to the same community. I phoned him and told him I would meet him for coffee . . . and he was buying. He finally asked whom he was talking to. I told him and immediately he invited me to his home. When I walked up to his house he greeted me with the biggest bear hug I have ever known, and the tears poured out of his eyes. Indeed over the years, life was changing. I remembered this scripture:

> "He who listens to you listens to me; he who rejects you rejects me; but he who rejects me rejects him who sent me." (Luke 10:16)

I wondered what this text meant in our relationships with people of the community. I still ponder this often.

Nelson Lake Bible Camp was another wonderful place for life and ministry. It was located on a small spring-fed lake six miles northwest of Preeceville. When we arrived at this parish we were informed that the little green cabin on the beach was the pastor's to use whenever we wanted to spend time at the lake. We were surprised at this generosity and enjoyed this cabin throughout those years.

This was a gracious place of retreat on days off and a place of many special memories. Not the least of those memories were two little boys who would stretch themselves out on the dock and fish for perch, or ride their Tonka trucks down the hill to the beach, often losing control halfway down and rolling the rest, truck and boys dirty and bruised but undaunted for another run.

We loved fishing, water skiing and canoeing on this lake. This was a place of many wonderful family times and memories - some included real foolishness as well.

Bev was nine months pregnant that first summer. In those days she water skied, drove the boat and took me skiing. On one occasion, during Bible Camp, I didn't change clothes to go skiing and was in my summer hat and short pants. I started from shore and was going to come in dry and run back up onto the shore. As I prepared for that final swing, there was this gracious wifely smile as Bev looked back and slowly reduced throttle till all that was floating was her husband's hat. She came back to pick me up. Back in the boat, I picked her up held her over the side and dropped her. The ladies on the beach were mortified. She floated well and we laughed, but it was likely foolish. A few days later our second son was born. (I wonder if pre-birth trauma affects a child?)

Shortly after coming to Preeceville I met a young man who had been in our Scout troop in Saskatoon back in university days. We met on the beach by chance and had a lot of scouting memories to share. One could see in his eyes that life had been difficult. As we visited the answers started to come. He opened his story with, "A lot of water has gone under the bridge since those days." He told me a story of conflict and drugs and the struggles in which he lived. How life had changed since I knew him last.

A short time later (I believe it was the following week) we had gone to the cabin Sunday afternoon to stay over till Monday, our day off. At eleven o'clock Sunday night there was a knock at the door and there stood this young man with family members. There had been a severe crisis with some violence. He wanted to stay with us that night in our one-room cabin. He had flash backs and was very unstable.

We gave him a bed on our couch. I lay awake all night. We had no way of knowing what he might do. At four o'clock in the morning he got out of bed and picked up the axe by the stove. I panicked and asked him what he was doing. He was cold and was going out to get some firewood. I was so relieved.

I spent a lot of time with this young man over that summer. He had a difficult journey, but we walked together through it looking for new directions and signs of hope. There was much uncertainty and at one point his greatest fear was that life had lost all value. He feared he had lost all feelings, and could do anything to himself or others. The concern alone was evidence that he still had feelings or he would not have shared this concern, but it was the low point of that journey before things started to turn around. I have followed his life since at a distance and it seems life has come together. One prays that God will continue to bring healing, hope and life to this man and that he will find people who will provide that added fellowship we all need in our journey with God and with each other.

The camp was in rather rough shape when we arrived. I loved carpentry so it was quite natural to spend spare evenings and days off with others, working at upgrading the camp. There was a group of men and women who treasured this place and dug in to make it a great place for families and youth. We renovated buildings and trimmed up the grounds.

The camp also had the best local party beach in the community. In some ways this was a problem, in other ways it became a great place to meet another side of the community.

We had two weeks of camp every summer. One week was for youth, and another week for families. Youth week was a magnet for young people from town. Of course some of those young people came and had their own reasons for being there and the property was not foreign turf for them. When the camp was not occupied, they made it their second home. It was their "party place".

Bev and I got to know a lot of the guys from town. Because we had a boat on the lake we would invite them over to water ski. They liked skiing so much it became difficult to get work done at the camp.

Problems need solutions. We took a calculated risk and I showed the guys where I hid the key for the boat and we made an agreement. They could use our boat any time whether we were there or not. There was one condition: they were to treat the boat like it was ours, because if they treated it like it was theirs they would likely wreck it. I also assured them that if they ever did anything that endangered anyone, they would never use it again. They agreed.

My friends in the coffee shop thought this rather foolish of me, and maybe it was. One had to accept that there could be a price and if there was, I could not complain because it was my decision. Thankfully it worked out well. I had a rather large fuel bill but it was a good investment.

Daniel A. Haugen

One of the first years at camp I had some senior pastors express concern that these guys were hanging around and would only cause trouble. "They were just coming to check out the girls." I remember commenting, "God uses good bait!" I immediately felt apologetic on the inside for having said it.

It took some time to negotiate an alternative. Finally, as a concession, it was agreed that the guys were welcome as long as they participated in whatever the campers were doing. If they wanted to come down and swim during swimming time they were welcome. If the campers were playing ball they participated or watched. They were welcome to everything, but if they wanted to opt out then they would leave the property for that time.

I wondered how I would get this message to everyone until I remembered we had a chain gate we locked each night. I decided to lock it early. They couldn't leave without finding me.

They found me. All their vehicles were waiting at the gate because they could not get out. I explained to them that I needed their help and that some people were not sure if they should be at camp, but I wanted them to be able to come. I asked for their cooperation so that they could be there (I think the young preacher also wanted to prove a point).

Their answer was direct, "No problem Pastor Dan." I opened the gate and we began a new chapter of exploration. Will this work? Will there be problems? We would have to see.

The guys came regularly and I do not recall any significant problems. I remember one time during youth camp some of these guys were asked to pull booze for some campers. I got wind of this and took one of the guys aside to inform him it was not a good idea, because if he did pull booze for these kids, they were minors and I would have to see that they were charged with providing alcohol to minors. I informed them that I wanted to tell them ahead of time so they wouldn't cry foul after if they carried through. I also informed them they were still welcome to come as long as they respected the terms and I assured them that if they did pulled booze I would know.

They seemed to understand and actually appreciated the frankness. After that I figured out who had asked them and let them know that there would likely be no booze that night. The campers were not sure how I knew, but a little mystery can be good. The week finished without any incidents.

They came every year after that. At first they just came for the sports and maybe to check out the girls. Soon they were joining in campfires and came for concerts. I ended up with several pews of teenage guys in the back of our church almost every Sunday. They were from all over the community. Some had huge problems and some less. They were our boys.

One year I worked late at the Bible Camp on a Friday night to finish up some odds and ends before the campers arrived. Saturday morning I was back at the lake only to find that the night before there had been a party on the beach. Bottles were scattered everywhere and there was broken glass in the sand and in the shallows of the swimming area. Camp was scheduled to open the next day.

I was angry as I worked to pick up all the glass. In the middle of my frustration a number of cars drove up. It was my boys. They greeted me as they came down the hill. "How are you Pastor Dan?"

My response was without hesitance. I was frustrated and angry. I showed the guys what had happened and how frustrated I was trying to make this place nice for everyone, "And then some jerks came down and did this." They were quiet. I don't think they had ever seen me angry. I asked of them a favour.

"No problem Pastor Dan. What do you want?"

I asked the guys if they would keep an eye on the camp property for me, and if they ever found anyone abusing it to take care of the matter and not tell me how they did it. The guys became the protectors of our camp. We never had a case of vandalism the rest of the years I was there.

Many different opportunities seemed to come by surprise. One year the principal of the high school had been using the movie *Jesus Christ Superstar* as a resource in his English program. He had portrayed Jesus as the sixties radical who overthrew all social convention. The principal gave me all the material he had been using along with the sound track to *Jesus Christ Superstar* and asked if I would take the Grade 11 and 12 students for two periods and critique what he had done for the class from a Christian perspective.

It was a fascinating assignment and I accepted it with some trepidation. To that day I had never been particularly impressed with Norman Jewison's production, but as I prepared and the more I studied the lyrics, the more profound they became. The principal had given me a full text manuscript, which I studied as I played the sound track in the background. The movie became the most powerful challenge to my ministry. It seemed like the voice of the community. It was in many ways the voice of the coffee shop. Their knowledge of Jesus was often sketchy and distorted, but there was something that moved them about this Jesus . . . and they wondered who He was and why He died. How would the church respond? How would I respond as pastor to these people?

I went to the school with some uncertainty as to how things would go. It was a large group of Grade 11 and Grade 12 students. I was amazed at the attentiveness of these students.

At the end of two hours some of the students wanted to continue the discussion so I offered to do a study on "Jesus and the crowds" from the Gospel of Mark. I believe they also were mystified by Jesus, and could resonate with those recurring questions in Jesus Christ Superstar... "Who was he and why did he die?" and the Mary Magdalene song *I don't know why he moves me.*

Eighteen young men and women from the community came to our home for a two-hour study of the Gospel of Mark looking at the response of the crowds to Jesus. This was followed by pizza and coke with the background music being the sound track to *Jesus Christ Superstar* played at a volume that only the hard of hearing and teenagers could appreciate.

We had a wonderful time and those questions reminded me that Jewison had captured the common question of many people who often do not find their way into the church. Even these young people had heard and seen glimpses of the story and they wondered and did not understand why there was something about this Jesus that moved them. It gave me a new perspective on ministry.

I got attached to the young people. I spent a lot of time with these guys. They told me everything, but knew I would keep confidence. I knew virtually every person who did drugs in town. I knew the traffickers. They even told me what drugs sold for, and when the traffickers were sold out. Trust is that fragile gift of relationship. One often wondered at what point one might push it too far.

The officer in charge of the RCMP was a member of the congregation and a good friend. If I breached the confidence with my guys I would lose the opportunity to do what I could to help them find help in sorting out things and to hear the good news of the gospel which was for them as well. There was always a bit of tension wondering just how to handle things responsibly.

One of our girls from town stopped by my office one day. She was concerned about her friends who did drugs. She told me she had also experimented with drugs and it scared her. She felt a need to do something for her friends, because she felt it was not caring to do nothing. She was not sure what to do. She asked if the kids would get into trouble if she reported them to the RCMP. I assured her that the RCMP would be more interested in the traffickers. I admired the seriousness of this young person and the grace and respect she had for those struggling with this problem.

After much wrestling with her questions, she finally asked to remain anonymous and wondered if I would take the list she had made to the local detachment. I told her that I would do that if she wanted me to, but I could only pass on the information and maintain her anonymity. She finally decided that was what she wanted to do.

I took the list to the detachment office the next day.

The officer in charge looked at me and said, "Dan, there are no drugs in this town. We shake down the primary kids on prime weekends. They are not smart enough to keep it from us."

I remember my reply, "What you do with this list is your business. I was asked to deliver it. Here it is. All I can tell you is that I know it is true." I left the list on the counter and walked out.

The RCMP did not inform me, but they decided to bring in the drug squad. In a short time there were four people held on twelve charges related to trafficking. Things got ugly in the community. A number of young people were taken into the country and beaten up to keep them quiet. Later, one young person was run off the highway when coming back from a dance at Endeavour and beaten. I have never seen a young man so black and blue. But the charges stuck. After we moved to British Columbia some of the young people continued to write me to inform me that there were no more drugs in town.

It was seventeen years later when I again met the girl whose courageous act of caring had brought about the circumstances that changed the community environment. I met her by chance in the lobby of the Bay Shore Inn in Vancouver while attending a conference in 1994. I asked her if she remembered this incident and then shared how her difficult decision had been such a gift to the community. I thought it important for her to know. Sometimes one person's action can be such a great gift to so many.

Thirty plus years later I still have connections with these young people. We have met in many different places from surprise encounters on opposing teams at Saskatchewan teachers' hockey tournaments, to chance encounters in restaurants.

I have joined them for a number of weddings and I was called to perform two funerals. One young man was killed in a plane crash in Dryden, Ontario the day he was coming back to get married and take over the family farm. He had been one of our boys. He had struggled with many things, but was also a wonderful gift.

Another one of these young men died in 2003 and I was asked by his wife to hold a memorial service on the deck of their home north of Calgary, Alberta. He died in his early 40s. All the guys came. They all were involved in reading scripture and prayers as they assisted with the memorial service. I will always remember that day.

That same day I remember apologizing to the guys. I sometimes felt I had failed them as a pastor. In response to my apology one of the young men assured me, "Pastor Dan, if it was not for you we would have no faith at all."

He went on to share his own story and that of some of the others, and the major changes they had experienced in recent years. What a reminder that God is at work even in our failures and long after we are out of the picture.

One prays for these young people. One prays for them because the cross reminds us that they are valued in God's eyes.

The Gospel is about God's gift and call to people that they might find life.

One prays that they will continue to hear the Gospel. One prays that they will grow to treasure the fellowship with God and with people that makes life rich. One longs for them to hear God's Word that instructs them in new directions that inform them on how we can live our love for God and for people. One prays that the Holy Spirit will work in their hearts and minds. The places where "upstream" can take life sure beats the places where "downstream" can end. This new life makes such a difference in how we live. It often directs us in new paths and away from some of the "destructive living" that has such high consequences for us and for others and in its place these lives can become a rich blessing to so many.

I began to wonder if we often forget the heart of ministry and have the risk of simply becoming social workers. We need social workers; but ministry is so much more. Ministry is about proclaiming God's Word through which he works to bring new life that is eternal. Oh yes, there is often a need to change direction. If one is living in directions that ignore God and in directions that undermine life, there is always a high price to pay. If we care, there is need to share our concern and maybe reveal options and new directions. One thought a lot about the Apostle Paul's instruction to young Timothy:

> *"All Scripture is God-breathed and is useful for teaching, rebuking, correcting and training in righteousness."* (II Timothy 3:16)

This raised questions. What was the role of "torah," that instruction of God for life? How do you bring this into the lives of these young people? This stirred my early thoughts about the difference between "instruction" and "law". (I still think a lot about this.) How important is Christian education along with other education? It also stirred the question about Jesus ... who was He and why did He die? How does the Gospel bring new life to the centre of these young lives? We deal with the externals of life . . . how does one reach the human heart with something new? One prayed that these young people would see the love of God in the relationships with which we were so richly blessed.

Confirmation ministry was a special challenge. Some years it was wonderfully easy and some it was not. I remember one member of the confirmation class. He was a gifted young man who could totally destroy a class. He could hold the whole class in the palm of his hand while the pastor was trying to teach.

One day I decided I had to try something new. This young man loved to play pool and he spent most of his spare time at the pool hall. Most parents did not want their children around the local pool hall because it was rumoured that the person who ran it marketed home brew and drugs to the youth who came.

Now, I had not been raised in a pool hall. I had been encouraged in my growing up years to steer clear of pool halls; though, one summer working for a farmer near Wiseton, Saskatchewan I had been introduced to the game. At seminary I had developed some limited ability since we had a wonderful full-size snooker table in the seminary lounge.

One evening, after having become totally frustrated with this young man, I informed him that after class I was going to take him down to the pool hall and whip him in a game. He never hesitated and accepted the challenge. We finished class and off we went to the pool hall with the whole class right behind us.

The game started slowly. I played my normal poor game and he was quickly ahead. Then it happened. I got hot and cleared the table.

Now that was a miracle. He lost. He immediately demanded we rack the balls for another game. Again I started slowly (not by choice) and then again I got hot. I dropped the last ball to tie him when the electricity went out throughout the whole community. It was dark and we had to feel our way through the darkness to get out of the pool hall.

I never played pool again in that pool hall, and apparently he quit too. I guess the kids at school heard about how the preacher had "waxed" him, but best of all he was no longer a problem in confirmation after that. We were friends.

Many years later I was sitting across from him, now a grown man at a wedding reception, and we talked about those years. I asked him if he realized that God had blessed him with an incredible array of gifts and abilities.

He was quick to affirm that he realized this, but he also expressed concern that he still did not know what to do with all his gifts. I suggested that he might have to get in touch with the giver of those gifts before he would know. He assured me he understood and kind of agreed. There was still more road ahead in his journey.

There were many experiences that included working with the RCMP in that first parish. The Department of Natural Resources Officer called me one day to ask if I would come with him. There was a dispute over a sawmill in a neighbouring community. As we were driving out of town, he informed me that the RCMP would be there because the two people involved were ready to start shooting at each other. When we arrived, there were two police vehicles already on sight. The RCMP wanted me to take one of the individuals aside while they dealt with the other person who happened to be an ex-con that they had dealt with before.

We took a good part of the afternoon before the issue resolved. I had not been prepared for this kind of negotiation; however, in so many ways what we learn from the scriptures gives us so much to share with others in all kinds of circumstances.

The situation ended and I heard of no further confrontations. I did not know it at the time, but I would meet up with one of these men again in another circumstance.

I had another situation where there was severe family abuse. I found this person in the hospital. It took some time to find out what had happened and I advised this person it would be helpful for everyone involved if she would report what had happened to the RCMP. If nothing was done to bring the problems to the surface, nothing would change. It was a difficult decision.

The RCMP was called and received her story. After visiting with the offender, the RCMP returned to let me know that the story could not be true. I had difficulty in accepting this. I pride myself in few things, but one thing I felt I did well was to know people.

There was one member of the family who could verify what had happened. I went to the school and asked this person about the circumstances. Although there was great fear; finally, there was a willingness to share this information with the RCMP. The RCMP carried on with their investigation, and eventually received a full confession. The days that followed had many uncertainties, but in the years that followed this sad story had a healthy resolve that did not end in alienation and more harm.

In those years I got to know all the officers in the RCMP. I played hockey with some and on several occasions they called on me to share their work struggles and some of the life issues that happened as a result. I came to realize that the life of police officers could be very difficult through their dealings with the public, but also with the internal politics of law enforcement. It was another form of education to share those friendships and professional struggles.

Daniel A. Haugen

I was very thankful for those police relationships after a couple guys travelling from Yorkton to Thompson (Manitoba) stopped by our house. They drove an old Buick Wildcat and asked for money to buy gasoline so they could get to their new jobs in Thompson.

I wondered how they found our house since it was not near the church; they must have asked around the community. They claimed to be out of gas and had a long journey to make it to Thompson. I was pressed for time (since I was getting ready to leave for a three day meeting in Saskatoon) and became quite short with them. I gave them a bit of a lecture. Leaving on a trip without the resources to do so seemed to come short of good judgment. I was not very gracious.

I apologized after doing this and told them that though they really likely did not deserve it, all of us are provided for many times beyond what we deserve. I directed them to a service station where I would arrange for them to get a full tank of gas and I would pay the bill on my way out of town.

I left shortly after and stopped to pay my bill. Steve at the garage chuckled about these guys. He told me their tank was almost full. He could hardly squeeze in any more gas. On my way to pay this bill I remembered seeing this Buick Wildcat in front of the local bar. I drove back to the bar, walked in and joined the two guys at their table. There was a ten-dollar bill in the middle of the table.

I don't feel I handled this properly but I was upset. I simply chewed these two guys out for their sob story and their fraudulent scam on the sympathies of the preacher. As I chewed them out, I saw they were getting angry. When I was done, I informed them that if I ever saw them again it would be too soon. However, if I did see them, and they were straight with me, they would have my respect. Then, I walked out.

As I drove away I looked in my mirror just in time to see them run out of the bar looking to see where I had gone. I left town and suddenly realized how absolutely foolish I had been. Bev and the children were home alone for three days (I was going to be gone) and these guys I had just ticked off knew where I lived.

A few miles west of town an RCMP friend of mine was parked where a number of people were fishing in a stream that crossed under the highway. I stopped and told him what I had done and asked him if he would keep an eye out for my family and if he ever saw that Buick Wildcat to shake them down good and make sure they were out of town. (I don't think anything I did that day had very good judgment.) At least I felt better knowing he would keep an eye on things: more lessons to be learned.

There were wonderful opportunities for recreation in the parish. Winters were a busy time. Every fall, on my days off, I hunted in bow-hunting season and later in gun season. I curled in the early years, and played hockey with the Preeceville recreational team. I played some with the Buchanan team as well, but when they played each other one had to choose sides. I played with Preeceville.

This provided a wonderful connection with many people in the community. It was not long till I decided I would have to choose between curling and hockey; I chose hockey.

In Buchanan, one of the spouses of a member of the congregation refereed. He was my favourite Ukrainian. There was nothing he loved better than to give the preacher a penalty! And he loved it if I would challenge a call. He would always threaten to throw me out. He had a wonderful sense of humour.

The congregation in Buchanan seemed to enjoy this involvement. During the winter months we held afternoon worship, and many of the games in that community were mid-afternoon. The congregation joked that the sermon would be short those Sundays.

At the end of the service, the congregation would often send me to the rink without shaking hands. They seemed to like that the pastor was involved in hockey and were regular spectators.

Bev and I had acquired matching snow machines. Our greatest recreational enjoyment was to get on our machines and head into the country. On our days off during the winter we often loaded our two sons (one four and one two years old) onto our skidoos and headed out to Annie Laurie Lake on the north side of town. From there we would go up a tributary that ran off the Assiniboine River to the Myhr farm.

From there, Gary and Patti and his brother Brian and wife Debbie would get on their machines and it was a short trip further northwest to the Thorson farm. There, three more machines were fired up and headed to the Sandagers where Rob and Therese would join us for the last leg to Laverne Olson's.

There were lakes and rivers and forests to explore as far as one wanted to go. We sometimes had wiener roasts out in the bush or by a frozen lake. We usually gathered for a chilli supper at the Olson farm, followed by a night run for the men after supper. An intense game of Rook, more coffee, and then back the same route heading home at ten o'clock in the evening. These were wonderful times of fellowship and enjoyment.

We were sometimes rather foolish as well. One night Bev and I decided we should go for a run into the country at ten o'clock in the evening. We called our faithful baby sitter and then we called friends of ours on a farm near town. They came on their snow machines and we headed south to another member's farm. His wife was not back from work; she was a nurse at the hospital. She would not be home until eleven o'clock so we waited for her.

There was a new family of Ukrainian background who had just started coming to church. They lived several more miles south, so we decided to go there for coffee. We roared into their yard near midnight and the lights were still on in their house. As we came into the yard we saw the lights go out. Do we crash them at this time of the night? We hardly knew them. Their two German shepherd dogs encouraged us to reconsider, but we were there for the adventure and fellowship, so we rang the doorbell.

The man of the house came to the door pulling on his pants. In helmets and winter gear he had no idea who we were. We announced that we had come for coffee. When he finally realized it was us; he was delighted. He got his wife out of bed and we had a great time together.

Shortly after one o'clock in the morning we headed back home. The neighbours might not have appreciated us roaring up to our house at that time of the night, so we parked at a service station on the edge of town and walked home. I wonder why we did not think more about our baby sitter. She deserved a medal.

This family we rousted out of bed so unceremoniously came to worship on a regular basis after that. Sometimes foolishness is not a liability. It provided the beginning of a great friendship and a deep fellowship within the community of faith. They became wonderful gifts to our congregation.

One wintery Monday, Bev told me to get on my skidoo and get out of town before the telephone rang or I would miss another day off. I put on my skidoo suit, went out and pulled off the tarp, pulled the rope and was just ready to leave when the phone rang. There was a lady on the phone and she was not happy. She wanted to see me in her office. Plans changed and I went to her office. I sat and did not say a word for at least forty-five minutes. I was severely reprimanded for having got involved in some family related issues.

When she was done, I remember sincerely thanking her for her honesty with me. She never had been very happy with the young preacher. We then talked about the family circumstances and I assured her that I had been asked by a family member to get involved - and that whether I was involved or not, there was still a need to face the issues.

We talked for a couple hours and something happened that day. I never did get out of town and I missed my afternoon off. We became very good friends and the family situation did find some resolve. It was well worth the interruption.

We do not always know how to deal with relationships either in the family or in the community of faith. Honesty is helpful. And if there are issues that need some adjustment it does not help to hide them in our fortresses. Grace, forgiveness, and the need to explore new directions (repentance) in order to care for life are wonderful gifts that come through the scriptures. It is our challenge to walk this into those real flesh and blood issues of life.

Just a few years ago I was asked to come back for her funeral. This was the deceased's request before she died. The Gospel breaks down the wall that divides us from fellowship with God and has the power to do the same in our human relationships.

Life in that first parish was rich and we had a lot of fun too. Bev decided to work enough hours to keep her registration as a nurse. Her work was part time. We decided she should open a separate bank account so we did not get used to living on her salary. She was to spend it or save it for whatever she wanted, but we would not use this money for normal living expenses. One's lifestyle can expand to consume everything. If we got used to living on the extra income, it would be difficult for Bev to quit if she decided to quit.

When Bev got her first paycheck we went to the bank together. I also had my check to deposit. Bev walked up to her teller and plunked her check on the counter and declared with some attitude, "I want my own account."

Upstream Living in a Downstream World

I had just given my check to another teller . . . I reached over the counter, snatched my check from her hand, walked over to Bev's teller, slammed the check on the counter and declared, "I want my own account too!"

Bev turned immediately and said, "You can't have one."

I hung my head, took my check back to the counter. The tellers looked shocked. I handed my check to the teller and said, "Don't mind her, she is one of those liberated women, put this in "our" account."

We laughed about it all the way home. The preacher and his wife having a fight at the bank . . . in the end I'm sure they laughed too. That night Bev wrote on two of our bank books, "Ours" and then on hers in capital letters "MINE". (There has been a "MINE" account ever since . . . but I must mention, about twenty years later Bev brought home a signature card for me to sign. I asked what it was for and she said, "I decided to give you your own account." Given time, sometimes us men catch up).

The congregation allowed the young pastor to learn. So many encouraged, supported and offered their friendship. I also came to know the gift of those old saints who had walked the journey of faith and shared it with so many.

Annie was a treasure. She had been raised in the rural community that surrounded North Prairie Lutheran Church. She had married a military chaplain, Rev. H.O. Gronlid who served as the first President of Outlook College, which opened in 1916 in Outlook, Saskatchewan. Earlier, he had been a pastor north of Melfort, Saskatchewan.

After they were married Annie's husband took a call to a major east coast city in the United States. She told me it was a wonderful experience for a young bride who moved into a beautiful home with wood panelling and a great staircase that rose to the upper floor. In Annie's words, it was every girl's dream.

They were there only a short time before her husband decided he could not avoid the call to serve the people who lived north of Melfort, Saskatchewan. They moved back to Canada, to the cold winters and a rustic life style. A short time after arriving, they moved into a small house, which Pastor Gronlid had built.

She told me stories of Gronlid's ministry. He loved the people he served. She told of their encounter with First Nation leaders and people whom they loved dearly who returned that love and respect. She told of the time they were invited to a special aboriginal ceremony, never before viewed by non-natives. They were guests of the chief as a sign of respect and allowed to sit in their buggy and from a distance view the whole event.

One Christmas the neighbouring community of Birch Hills didn't have a pastor and asked if Gronlid would hold a Christmas Day worship for them. It was a very cold day and he took the buggy to Melfort and caught the train to Birch Hills. After the service, he returned to Melfort by train. On the way home from Melfort, Gronlid found someone stuck in the snow, so he stopped to help the person out of the ditch.

Perspiring and weary, he continued his journey home. Shortly after Gronlid contracted pneumonia and was hospitalized. Annie told me he knew he was going to die. He asked her to get on her knees to promise before him and God that she would never ask why.

While telling the story Annie got a smile on her face and a twinkle in her eye as she acknowledged, "Of course that was a promise I couldn't quite keep."

Over a thousand people attended his funeral and later there was a town named after Pastor Gronlid in that area north of Melfort, Saskatchewan. He was highly respected for his ministry in the community and the little house he built still stands today north of Melfort.

For two years Annie looked after the parish. She commented, "If you think that was easy, it wasn't." She later had a dress shop and then moved to Saskatoon where she gave room and board to seminary students.

Annie had polio as a child and was partially crippled. One day, in Saskatoon, she fell and broke her bad hip when she was shovelling snow and could not walk anymore. She asked one of her seminary student boarders to put castors on her chair so she could pull herself around with her good foot. She continued to give room and board to seminarians for many years.

I met Annie in her late 80s. I remember going to give her private communion every month. It seemed strange that I presumed to be her pastor when she was ten times the person of faith that I would ever be. She was wise, faith-filled and most gracious with other's faults. She knew people well. It was as if they were transparent. She could see right through the young preacher also, but as you got to know her, you really did not care. She was "living grace" the embodiment of a Christ-like life.

Annie got Christmas cards from around the world. She catalogued her cards alphabetically by country and throughout the year answered every card with a full letter. She was quick to inform me that she had a lot of time to write. It was her delight. She stayed up every night for the eleven o'clock news because in her words, "I have to keep up with what is happening in the world."

As I heard Annie's story I came to realize that Annie's faith was the product of many years on life's journey. She had walked a road that was often difficult, but she had seen over and over the reality of the faithfulness of God. God's care was no longer theory to Annie: it was a reality in which she found deep rest and peace.

The memory of Annie reminded me so many times to be more patient as a young pastor. I had a lot to learn and there were no shortcuts in life's journey to learn it. One grows confident in God's faithfulness by experiencing it over and over again.

It also reminded me to be patient with those beginning that journey of faith. A yellow sprout of new life is 100 percent life. It may be inadequate in its frailty, but it is the way life always begins. New life needs nurture. How easy it is to crush it for being inadequate. Over the years one saw so many ways the bruised reeds or dimly smouldering wicks were quenched. How different the ways of Jesus:

> *"A bruised reed he will not break, and a smouldering wick he will not snuff out"* (Matthew 12:20)

The time came when Annie was hospitalized and she knew she was going to die. I asked Annie if she had many questions.

She replied, "You can't imagine how many questions, but God can handle it." There was peace.

Annie's elderly sister came to stay with her at the hospital. She told me that just before Annie died, they had prayed together, *"Now I lay me down to sleep, I pray the Lord my soul to keep. If I should die before I wake, I pray the Lord my soul to take."* With the Amen she was gone.

The funeral was at North Prairie Church. We had been instructed by Annie not to be sad, but to sing hymns of praise to God. After the interment, I walked back from the cemetery in the country churchyard with three widows who had been her friends. Each mopped the tears from their eyes and one commented, "Annie wanted us not to be sad, I hope we didn't disappoint her too bad." One had to smile.

I found that ministry was a constant education in the gracious working of God. One day at the hospital I met a man I did not know. He was miserable to the core and I heard stories about this man from people in the community. I visited him every Tuesday. We talked about whatever came up; I would wish him God's blessing; shake his hand and leave. I was really not sure what I should do when I visited people in the hospital. Some people wanted you to pray with them, while with some it seemed an imposition that was unnatural and artificial.

In my uncertainty, I visited him for several weeks. Then one day when I came in he looked at me and declared, "You're not a preacher, you're a fraud."

Now, this is not something I was prepared for since I was not confident in what I was doing. The statement seemed to demand some clarification so I asked him why he thought I was a fraud.

He replied, "You don't preach at me when you come to see me. Any preacher who ever came to see me always preached at me. How come you don't preach at me?" He was firm in his demand.

I replied, "I didn't think you wanted me to." He calmed down and we continued our visit. It was like the barriers came down. We were friends and when the visit was over, I wished him God's blessing and left.

This man's health deteriorated. One Sunday night, before I left for Sunday evening worship, the family called and asked if I would stop at the hospital to see him. This was the only time he had seen me in a clerical collar. The family was with him. I met with the family and we prayed together by his bed before I left.

The next Tuesday I stopped at the hospital and he started to tell me a wild story about how he and I had taken off in a space ship from North Prairie Church. He knew it was me because I had that strange collar on. He went on with his story and suddenly threw up his arms and hollered, "Horrors, horrors ..." And he did not quit.

The nurses heard the commotion and came, but they could not calm him down. I was shocked and wondered what I had done to this man. I am sure the nurses wondered as well. They strapped him into his bed and gave him a sedative. I tried to find a quiet and gracious way to leave.

The next week I was not certain that I wanted to see this man, but I did. He was fine for a while but as he told his story again, the same thing happened and the uproar brought the nurses. His condition did not change.

A couple weeks later the family came to see me. I was at Nelson Lake since camp was on. The family had been asked to sign papers to have this man committed for psychiatric care and wondered what they should do.

I remember my immediate response, "Don't sign those papers. He's going to come out of it." And then I had this deep sense of doubt, and that inner voice said, "You don't know what you are saying. You are out of your league. How pretentious can you be." And then I said it again, "Don't sign those papers." I was really convinced he would come out of it, yet so uncertain about the advice I had given them.

I kept visiting this man. Finally, he decided that he had died and we were all ghosts. He seemingly had lost all contact with reality. He even refused to eat because dead people don't eat.

Finally, one day I thought I would try something different. How could I help him reconnect with reality? I walked into his room and there was a bowl of fruit by his bed, so without any hesitation I picked up an apple and a banana and an orange and commented on each as I did. He was shocked.

"You mean you can see that?" he asked. I assured him I could. Then the surprise came that reminds one again that we are not in this business alone.

He called me over to his bed, and on his bed lay an open book, "What do you see there?" he asked.

"A book," I replied.

"No," he said, "what is the picture?"

I looked and saw a white traditional style church so I told him so.

"No," he said, "read what is under the picture."

It was about a small church in Denmark.

"That is the church where I was baptized," he replied. And then he said, "But God wouldn't have a person like me, because I am a murderer."

Here at last was the mystery of this man's soul that had haunted him since a young man. We see the externals of people's lives, but so often we have no idea what lies in the human heart that can have such power to shape the way we live.

Before leaving that day, I shared the first thing closest to a sermon with this man. I told him to remember a picture. The picture was of three crosses on a hill. In the centre was Jesus and there was a thief on each side who could have also been murders. One man said, "Jesus remember me when you come in your kingly power." And Jesus said, "Today you will be with me in paradise."

I looked at him and said, "If Jesus could accept that thief on the cross, may be he can handle you as well. Think about the picture." And I wished him God's blessing and left.

The next week I walked in and greeted him. He looked up at me and his first comment was, "I've been thinking about the picture."

But he continued to doubt whether God could accept him. Over the weeks that followed he told me the stories that haunted his soul. He fought in the First World War, and was one of the living wounded that survived the battle of Vimy Ridge. He told me graphic accounts of that brutal battle and the wounded friends who had pleaded with him to put them out of their misery. It was a harsh story that had haunted this man for years. He had built a wall around himself that people saw as uncaring. He seemed to push people away. Most saw him as a miserable man and had no idea what burdens tore at his soul.

He kept getting weaker, but could not believe that God could accept him. One day he was so weak he could hardly raise his hand to mine. I gave him my hand and held his. I sat on a chair by his bed. I did not know what to do or say.

As I sat in silence, I finally thought he had died. I even checked his pulse. This had been months now. I was frustrated. I did not expect him to hear me, but I said it out loud, mostly for my own sake, "You are such a miserable old beggar, I really don't know why God would want you but he does." And then came the after-shock.

He turned his head, looked at me and said, "I guess you are right."

He was home a short time after. He lived with his son and family. I went to visit him as often as I could. He loved to play cribbage. We played several games, and when I was about to leave I asked him if he would like me to bring him Communion.

He paused, "It has been a long time since I had communion." I explained to him that here was that gift of God's forgiveness in the body and blood of Christ. Forgiveness was the only freedom from the past.

He said he would think about it and immediately suggested we needed to have another game and dealt the cards. We played another game.

As I was leaving he shook hands and said, "I would like you to bring me Communion."

The next visit I brought Communion. We had Communion together as both he and I shared in that great gift of God's forgiveness. I remember the tears in his eyes, and the gentle spirit that pervaded his whole being from that day on.

I asked some people in the congregation to visit this man. Most were afraid, but one courageous "saint from the pew" went to visit him and marvelled at the gracious man she met. He died some weeks later in the arms of his son.

During this time I met his grandson at the hospital. He had been orphaned when his parents left him at six weeks of age and lived a difficult life. His story; however, is too holy and personal and special to share. He moved in and lived with us in January 1974.

He has been a part of our family and our lives ever since and taught us much and blessed us in a thousand ways. He and his wife have now been married for over 25 years and we still see them often and seldom miss a Christmas together. God indeed blesses us in this journey.

One learned a lot about God's grace in that journey of faith and the adventures of ministry. Theology took on a pulse and I began to realize that we serve the living God who works in the middle of our human frailty.

Since I met this elderly man in the hospital, I have been attracted to the rough and crusty lives of the community. Almost always under that tough exterior there was a gentle heart that was deeply wounded. You never broke through the crust. The miracle was being allowed in and I remember often praying that God would protect them from me. For being allowed in, one could so easily bring harm again without intent when one only wanted to see healing and new life happen for these people.

Buchanan congregation was another life experience that taught me much. The population was likely not more than 200 people plus the surrounding rural population. In the first year our worship attendance was quite often twelve people. We did not have an organist so our music was less than inspiring and I doubt the preacher was much better. The church roof leaked in the summer, and in the winter the building was cold.

A number of times (from the congregation) I heard the voice of despair and the gracious concern for their pastor. They wondered if they should continue since they were such a burden and so few. I assured the congregation I was happy to come and lead them in worship as long as they wanted to worship.

There was a Doukhobor lady in town. Someone heard she could play the organ. The congregation invited her to come and play. Sometimes she played only the melody, but in time her confidence and skill grew and she became a wonderful organist.

I tried to visit as many homes as I could on Buchanan days (every Wednesday after my visit to the Canora Hospital.) I found here were some wonderful people in this community. One couple, Ralph and Pat, taught me more about evangelism than I had learned before.

I would often stop at their home and sometimes I was tired and did not want to visit. Sometimes Pat met me at the door to inform me I looked terrible. She would send me to their couch where I was instructed to have a sleep till supper.

Ralph and Pat had connections through the whole community. They just seemed to love people. They invited many to worship, but they also reminded me that some people are not ready to worship yet, so they just kept in touch with them. They told me people knew their faith was important to them so they never had to initiate conversations about their faith. People whom they knew would do that as a matter of course and they would respond.

The little congregation had a few new faces every once in a while. I remember seeing a new family one particular Sunday. I met them at the door and asked their names. The names rang a bell, but I could not figure out why. On the way home that day it finally dawned on me that they were one of the families Ralph and Pat had told me about. They came one Sunday and did not come for several weeks. They came again and then it was a time before they returned. It seems as their faith grew, they became more regular. Over time I kept meeting more families whose names preceded them and I tried to visit everyone.

I saw at least a dozen new families show up to worship and they were all connected to Ralph and Pat. I doubt Ralph and Pat even knew the affect they had on people. They lived their faith in love for God and people. When people from all over the community needed help they seemed drawn to this couple. The power of the priesthood of all believers was reflected in this home.

During the summer months I tried to get in some golf (when I was able) on my day off. I had a dear friend from Buchanan who met me at the Crystal Lake Golf Course. He was a farmer who raised Hereford cattle. I used to smile because he was built like an Angus! We had a great time together.

One day while waiting for some golfers to finish the fourth hole, he asked me a question, "How can you be a Christian and have doubts?" He told me he became very discouraged in earlier years, because he had often been told that you couldn't have doubts and be a Christian.

I affirmed that it was pretty easy to have doubts; but God could handle that too. Jesus did not seem to shy from Thomas who had trouble to believe till he could have some visual confirmation of the resurrection.

On the other hand, in our times of doubt there is often something even stronger than our doubts. Sometimes we forget that which we have seen and heard has been so powerful, and sometimes we have to wait again for that confirming assurance. It was the beginning of a conversation that took the rest of the game.

Years later we attended a church convention in Ottawa. The first people we met in Ottawa were this man and his wife, delegates to the convention. One hot and humid evening we went walking with them. It was a night I will always remember. This peace-filled evening affirmed again that great gift God's people receive in the rich fellowship and friendship we share. Indeed we have been blessed with a rich life.

On this journey of faith, once in a while one forgets about oneself. There was a couple that had difficult marriage struggles. I visited the wife who had moved out on her own. They were not young and many things complicated the relationship. On one visit I must have said some things that were not appreciated; she got up from the couch and informed me I could show myself to the door and left the room.

Driving home that night I felt bad that I had offended her, though I felt it important to say what I had said. I often talked with God while driving and I finally told God that if she had to hate me that was all right. If God could not work through this preacher to help this family, then I asked that God would find someone who could. What was important was that they find what they needed to bring healing to their life and relationship even if the pastor was disqualified. It was okay.

It was freeing to be disposable, but the concern for this family was still what really counted. I thought back on my internship mid-year report to the president of the seminary. Something had happened. I could survive even rejection because it is not about me. It was all about the God we serve and the people we serve. I continued to pray for this family.

The alienation with me remained unresolved but the family stayed together. It was not till the farewell service in that parish that the wife came to me, took my hand in both her hands and looking me in the eye said, "You will never know how much your ministry has meant to us." How quietly surprises come.

By the third year the congregation was talking about building a new church. They had a hundred and fifty people coming on special occasions and over eighty people at regular worship. The fascinating thing was no one could put a finger on when they grew.

That seems to be one of the qualities of real life. It grows imperceptibly and one recognizes it only after it has happened and one looks back. It was difficult for the congregation to think they could build a new church when they seemed to have difficulty to meet their annual budget.

So, I encouraged the congregation to work to raise half the money they needed to build before looking at specific plans.

In our stewardship of God's gifts, people often live on the gifts of tomorrow instead of practicing a stewardship that celebrates the gifts of today. Debt can become such a burden for a congregation. The burden can press so heavily that they lose sight of their mission and it can strangle the joy and focus of a congregation and turn it inward seeking only survival. Instead of serving people it is easy to get the flow shifted into using people.

One man looked at debt another way and commented that if he wanted a new car he would quite freely borrow money to do it and would have no problem with the payments. He then (as if thinking out loud) made the observation that if they needed a new church he thought maybe he could do the same.

The congregation, at the end of the discussion, decided to start a building fund with the goal to raise half of the projected cost based on standard building costs and the square footage of space they felt they would need. This was a new adventure in faith that tested the hearts of the people. They were committed to provide an adequate facility to house their fellowship so they could gather for worship and Christian education, and to carry out their mission.

Daniel A. Haugen

Most of life is lived in the mundane business of seeking to be faithful to those routine tasks of caring for and nurturing life and faith in the parish. New adventures always came by surprise and I remember one visit to the Canora Hospital.

I met Helmar, a man in his seventies who lived as a hermit. He was in pretty bad condition when he came to the hospital. They soaked him for a long time to try and clean him up. I visited him several times at the hospital and when he was ready to be sent home I told him I would stop by for a cup of coffee. He gave me instructions to his home ... turn at the well; follow the tracks into the bush ... take the path to his house.

I mentioned to someone in the congregation that I was going to visit Helmar. The first response was deep concern and I was informed he hated preachers and that he would very likely run me off with his shotgun. They were serious and tried to discourage me from going.

I found it a little disconcerting, but I had told Helmar I would come so I went anyway. I had trouble finding the right road. The trail led into the bush and opened into a small clearing where the road looped in a circle to come back out. There were some old tractors grown into the trees. They had been there a long time without being moved.

I finally found a trail. I walked the winding trail into the bush, came around a corner and there it stood, a little one-room house. I walked around the corner of the house and as I rounded the corner there sat Helmar on a wooden chair, which stood on a small square of boards that formed the step to his home. With his elbows perched on his knees, he was reading the **Western Producer**. I said hello and Helmar was startled as my voice broke his solitude. Regaining his composure he looked up and said, "Hello" and still leaning on his knees, went back to reading his paper.

I thought he must not recognize me so I reintroduced myself, "I'm Pastor Haugen, the one who visited you in the Canora Hospital."

Helmar replied with some sarcasm, "I remember you." But he immediately returned to his reading.

I was not prepared to be brushed off this easily. There was a little retainer wall built on the corner of the house preventing further erosion from the water, which at times must have run down this path. I sat on the retainer and continued to make conversation. Helmar responded and finally, as if disgusted, put his paper aside and turned sideways on his chair to face me in conversation. We visited for over an hour. I finally suggested I had to go and he offered to walk me to my car.

When he saw my car he was surprised. I drove a brand new blue American Motors Gremlin with a hockey stick stripe on the side and blue Levi denim interior. He thought it a strange car for a "sky pilot" (his name for a pastor).

Meanwhile he had to show me his new truck. I had to sit in it and feel the comfort and turn on the radio to hear the sound. He was proud of his truck. I got in my car to leave and Helmar leaned in the window to visit for another twenty minutes. I finally informed him I had to leave.

His face clouded over and he told me, "I always fight with preachers."

I responded, "I always like a good fight, but I don't have time today. I'll have to come back."

To this Helmar stepped back, did a little jig with his hands made into fists and replied, "I'll have to get in shape so I can handle you!"

I wished him God's blessing and assured him I would come back.

Daniel A. Haugen

I visited Helmar many times. His one-room shack was stacked with barrels and boxes with a cot in the middle of the floor and a narrow aisle around it. He was dirty and the air was not fresh in the house. Yet, Helmar was a well-read man. He had stacks of magazines and books and had been a blacksmith at one time.

On every visit he would show me some of his treasures. The first was a man's ring. It was perfectly formed. He told me to polish it with the cloth in which it had been wrapped; you could see yourself in it.

"Bet you can't guess what I made that out of," he confidently challenged me. I couldn't guess. He had made this ring by melting old American quarters, which were pure silver. The ring was perfect.

Another time he showed me a three-hundred-year old pocket watch contained in a silver case. The watch had a chain drive, which was broken. He had gotten this watch from a friend.

"Bet you can't guess what I made the new chain out of" . . .again his confident challenge to the young preacher. I couldn't guess but he had to show it to me. He had replaced it with the E-string from a violin.

Another time he brought out a hunting knife. It was beautifully made, with a bone handle with brass end. And then of course the confident challenge, "Bet you can't guess what I made it out of." You could see your reflection in the blade.

Helmar had made this knife from the inside race of a bearing. He cut the bearing race, and in the forge, heated and opened in up to a flat piece of steal and forged this knife blade. He used some deer horn for the handle and a shaped brass end all fitted perfectly. He told me to wet my arm and see how sharp it was. Gillette could not have shaved it better.

This was an amazingly gifted man. What had made him retreat from people? I never did find out. One day I invited him to come and worship with us and he responded that he was not much for worship.

As I left that day I took his hand in mine as I said good-bye, I looked him in the eye and said, "Helmar, you just remember that when Jesus died on that cross he died there just as much for your sins as for anyone in that church, and he wants you as one of his people just as much as anyone in that church. You better never forget that." He thanked me and I left.

Helmar was suffering from congestive heart failure. One fall when I stopped by I found he could not put up his winter supply of wood, so I cut him enough wood for a few days before I left. Then, I went to talk him into moving into town, but that was futile. Every time I had broached the idea, he would either change the subject or bring up other concerns.

"Maybe if I moved into town I would start drinking."

I had no idea if Helmar had trouble with alcohol in his earlier life, so I took his concern seriously.

He laughed and said, "I've never drank before, why would I start now?" and he would laugh some more and change the subject.

Later on in the visit I brought the conversation back to the idea of moving.

"Maybe I will find a widow in town." The twinkle in his eye let you know that you had met your match.

Finally, I asked Helmar if I could bring out some men from the church to cut up some wood for him. Since, he was going to stay where he was, he would need wood.

He would not accept my proposal, so I told Helmar if he was going to be that stubborn and stay in the country then I would be equally stubborn and bring some men out to help put up his wood. I waited a short time to see if he would change his mind. He didn't.

Daniel A. Haugen

A week or so later after worship one Sunday, I asked if there were some men who would come and help cut some wood for Helmar. Twenty people showed up the following Saturday. There was a tractor with a saw on front, chain saws, wagons, men and teenagers. Helmar was surprised, but also seemed grateful and quite excited about the venture. He was quick to get his brand new chainsaw out of its case for someone to use.

In half-a-day there was a pile of wood almost as large as Helmar's house. As the day ended Helmar came down into a meadow where the men had been working. He stood there with his hands behind his back. Standing before these men and with quiet grace and formal presence he said, "Gentleman, I am not much for making speeches, but I would like to thank you very much, and I wish you a Merry Christmas and a happy and prosperous new year."

Though rough and dirty and dressed in the shabby clothes of a hermit, there came from the centre of his being a grace and eloquence that surprised and blessed all who had come.

Later that year as we got deeper into the Advent season, our under 50s group of couples (who met once a month for Bible Study) went carolling and in their travels also went to Helmar's home. They filled his little shack and with those great carols of Christmas he listened and wept as he joined in the singing.

My last visit with Helmar was just before Easter in 1977. Easter Sunday would be our last Sunday in this parish as we were preparing to move to take a call in British Columbia. It was late spring but we had a lot of snow and the roads to Helmar's home were blocked with snow.

One afternoon, I loaded a snow machine on the trailer. Bev had packed a care package for Helmar and I drove as far as I could, then unloaded the snow machine and went the last miles to Helmar's home by snowmobile. We had a wonderful visit and he appreciated Bev's gifts.

As I finally got up to leave, I informed Helmar we were moving to British Columbia and we wouldn't likely get a chance to see each other again. Helmar's health was fragile in his old age. Helmar rose from his chair, he took my hand with both of his hands, looked me in the eye, and with firm determination replied, "We'll meet again. We'll meet again."

This was my last visit before we moved. The last Sunday in the parish was Easter Sunday. There was no question of my sermon theme that Easter. It was the farewell message of the resurrection so clearly articulated by Helmar. "We'll meet again." This was a farewell of faith that reminds us that not even death can end that life of fellowship we have received through God's grace in Jesus and the great knowledge of the resurrection.

V.
Wrestling with the Need for Change (Spring 1977).

When I look back on those first years of ministry, I realize I was a runaway workaholic. Bev had a way of bringing some gracious and much needed perspective and wisdom in her quiet and quite articulate way. For example, one day I asked Bev why our oldest son, then four years old, never came to me when he got hurt. With incredible grace but inescapable clarity Bev replied, "He doesn't know you Dan. You are gone every morning before he is up, and he is long in bed before you ever get home."

Another evening, some time later, we were chatting at home.

Bev said, "You know, you would drop anything for anyone at anytime... and I guess I really wouldn't want you to be different, but there is something you should remember."

I asked her what that was.

She replied, "We are people too."

I think that is what you call crushing truth, but it was so graciously given I could only be thankful. How easy to think of one's family as oneself, and then to realize they are not "me". Family are also people who need commitment and care and that does not happen without awareness and time.

I wanted to find more time for our children. Our oldest son loved fishing since he was two years old. I had made him a short fishing rod and he would spend hours on the lake if his dad would take him. After my wife graciously opened my eyes I found a Friday night free in my schedule and I told our oldest son I would take him fishing.

Late that Friday afternoon I got a call from a family in crisis. I apologized to our son and stated that I had to go take care of this family, but we would go fishing the following Friday. He accepted the change of plans and was still enthused. The following Friday I was looking forward to fishing when I got another call: another family in crisis.

Again, I went home and apologized and stated that we could not go fishing because I had to take care of this family. I will always remember the look of discouragement. He walked away, and the next time I talked about doing something with our son he showed no excitement at all.

That great gift, which my father had understood so well, I had forgotten. The great gift of any special time is the anticipation, but anticipation once crushed, takes away that excitement and delight we need in our relationships to turn those special moments into wonderful occasions.

I heard the echo of Bev's wise words speaking softly and with some urgency, "We are people too." Thus began the struggle to change direction and also commit time and energy to care for the family with which God had blessed me.

I had made it my goal to be in every home every year and along with that I had many other commitments: I served as Chair of the Bible Camp Board; served on an Interagency Committee in the Health District; served the Board of St. Paul's Home in Melville; served for a time as President of the Lutheran Collegiate Bible Institute Alumni Association; served on the Board of the Saskatchewan Camp Association; and the last years few years of my service, I also served as President of the Yorkton Conference of our ELCC. At that time, I also took some grad-study classes in the spring term at the seminary. I did all this combined with regular parish work during those four years.

I drove over forty-five thousand miles each year. I often went for six weeks with three hours sleep a night. Of course it usually ended with sickness, antibiotics and a day of sleep. I recovered quickly. I guess I was still young.

Those years in that first parish were a wonderful education and I had much to learn. The parish was large. We had over six hundred members in an area of more than 3000 square miles. I had been serving Norquay Congregation as a preaching point for much of this time and this congregation seemed to have had a history of being caught in the middle. Norquay had, at one time, been a part of the Preeceville Parish. Then they were dropped, and later picked up by the parish in Swan River, Manitoba. Then, Swan River Parish dropped them. They were caught in the middle and were at the point where they hardly dared entrust themselves into any new arrangement.

We began talks of including them in the Preeceville Parish, which would also facilitate the possibility of hiring an intern to provide more pastoral support for the long term with the hopes of one day calling two full-time pastors to serve this large parish. During my last year, Norquay came into our parish alignment and with this expansion the parish also arranged to have a student pastor for assistance.

When our new intern pastor arrived, I took him through the parish to introduce him to each congregation. We were coming out of Norquay when my chest felt like someone hit me with a sledge hammer. I slumped forward and for a moment couldn't see over the dash while I was driving.

My intern was concerned; however, everything stabilized and I continued the course of the day. After this event I decided it was time to see a doctor. To this day I do not know what happened. The doctor didn't find any damage but he informed me it was time to slow down or I would be in trouble. I was only 29 years old.

Having an intern was a new challenge. It certainly took some pressure off but of course there were some adjustments in the first weeks as we developed our working relationship.

When I took our intern to Buchanan, he had his first adventure. As we drove, I was explaining where people lived and then as we approached Ralph and Pat's farm I informed him we were stopping for coffee.

He was uneasy about stopping in unannounced. I had told the parish from the beginning that I would likely drop in unannounced. If my arrival was inconvenient they should just let me know and I would move on. We developed a comfortable relationship and that was the way we operated in this parish. We walked up to the door of the house just as Ralph was coming out. He had a shotgun in his hand, "We're butchering" he said, "Dan, it's your turn to shoot him ..." and placed the gun in my hands.

I carried coveralls in my trunk, so I pulled them out and put them on. Ralph handed me the shotgun and we went into the corral. He pointed out the steer that was to be butchered.

This was not a comfortable moment for our young intern from Edmonton. To avoid the discomfort of the process, let's just say in a short time there were two halves of a healthy beef hanging from the front-end loader before we went in for coffee. I kept an eye on our intern. He paced back and forth at a distance and watched in glances and looked too white to be healthy. On the inside I know I chuckled.

Eventually we went into the house for coffee and stayed for supper. On the way home that evening, after our Confirmation classes were over, the intern sat in the car rather quietly. Then he finally asked, "Dan, do you have to do things like that often?"

I replied with as much seriousness as I could muster, "When you are in the parish if someone says butcher, you butcher, and you don't ask questions."

"Really?" he replied. And then the shocked silence was broken as I laughed until I almost drove in the ditch. The tension was gone.

That same fall, the Preeceville congregation had a financial crisis. They had an operating surplus when I arrived because they hadn't had a pastor for some time before I came and this had reduced their costs. Finances were always a sensitive issue in this congregation; people did not want to talk about it.

One day I visited a lady in an outlying area who was on our records, but I had not met in church. We had a wonderful visit and as I got up to leave she said, "Just a minute pastor and I will get you some money." I asked her why she would do that.

She answered, "No pastor has ever come here without looking for money for the congregation."

I was shocked and replied, "Well, you can't say that anymore because I did not come for money. I just wanted to meet you and let you know that you would be most welcome to come and worship with us anytime." I refused to take any money.

She started worshiping with us and when I returned some years later I was greeted by this wonderful smile from this gracious lady, now almost one hundred years old. She had found a home and fellowship where life was blessed.

There was a history with money that had created great sensitivities and much alienation in this congregation and it affected the congregation on so many levels.

In fact, in these years the Church Council in Preeceville did not even have financial statements at their council meetings.

Earlier, I had tried to encourage them to have regular statements but they resisted. After one council meeting I went home in frustration and told Bev that I had done all I could do to help them realize that they were going to run out of money. I pushed till they almost got irritated and I had to back off.

Bev asked what I was going to do. I told her I was going to do nothing. I felt I had done everything I could to help them see what was happening and now we would have to wait for the crisis. Then, they would have to be deal with the realities of their financial situation. They would be out of money by fall.

At the end of September that year the treasurer came and asked if it would be possible for me to wait another week to get the balance of my salary since they were out of money. I assured him it would be no problem.

That day I went home and informed Bev, "The time has come." Bev wondered what I meant. I told her what had happened and now the time had come for the congregation to deal with the real issues that surrounded their financial crisis.

On Wednesday of that week the chairman heard that they had not been able to pay my salary. He came into the coffee shop and asked me if it was true. I assured him it was. He was extremely supportive and felt genuine regret for these circumstances.

I suggested that it was not terrible at all, that difficulties will always arise and when they do we have to deal with them. We were now going to deal with some issues. He asked what should happen.

I told him that they would have to cut my salary since I was their biggest expense and they did not have the money to pay. I assured him that Bev and I had lived on a student's income for some years and we would survive. I also suggested that if it got so that we could not afford to live we would have to resign, but that was not a threat, just an unavoidable reality and I doubted that it would come to that.

I studied the history of the parish through the minutes of Church Council and annual meetings. I had also heard members talk about the past. Whenever there was a financial crisis, they would canvas both active and inactive members for money. It had caused many tensions and alienated many people over the years.

The chairman suggested that we would have to canvas the congregation for money and I told him I would resign. He questioned if I was serious. I assured him I was.

Then I explained why. If I read the history of the congregation correctly, it seemed to me that they had always shamed people into giving and avoided the crisis by doing this. However, I really believed the real issue was not the shortage of money. The real issue was that we were not sure if it was really important to have a regular pastoral ministry to be involved in mission and ministry and to have a place of worship and Christian education.

I suggested that these were the real issues. It seemed we always had money for the things that were important. If we were not sure that the life of the church was important it was quite natural and maybe necessary that in the stewardship of our people, under these circumstances, the church could be dropped in our people's priorities as they made decisions as to how they would use the resources God had given them.

The chairman asked if I would speak to the congregation. I told him that I wouldn't. I felt that congregations were tired of hearing pastors work only to secure their salary. I would rather take a cut in salary and take time to deal with the real issues. We talked further and he seemed to understand. I finally suggested that he should consider calling a meeting of the trustees who were responsible for the physical and financial matters of the congregation. I also suggested that the treasurer be there with a full financial statement.

The meeting was called. The outcome of this meeting was wonderful. The chairman decided that he should speak to the congregation. He arranged to take some of the sermon time on a normal Sunday and I was happy to accommodate him.

I think he gave the finest presentation I have heard on stewardship. He suggested that our problem was not that we were short of money but that we were not sure if the church was important to us. He then used a widow in the congregation as an example.

He took quite a risk, but he knew the grace of this lady and he humbly acknowledged the imposition he publicly placed on her. She had been widowed early and struggled to find the financial resources to raise her family. When she reached the age of sixty-five she received Old Age Security, which provided a luxury she had never known. She made cushions in her spare time and sold these cushions and everything she made she donated to the congregation. The chairman informed the congregation of the size of her annual contribution, which in proportion to the average giving of members of the congregation was huge.

The chairman reminded everyone that she did not do this to gain attention. She did it because she loved her Lord, and she found worship and Christian education and pastoral ministry and the fellowship of the church an important part of her life and the lives of others.

The chairman said that in considering what this lady had done, he found it necessary to re-evaluate what he was doing. He was going to make some changes in his own life to support the congregation because the ministry of the congregation was important to him, and he thought that everyone else should do the same.

Nothing more was done. In three months the congregation went from a large deficit to a surplus for the year. At the same time, worship attendance increased by 50 percent. Then, the trustees decided to do something about the need for maintenance of the parsonage and the Sunday School Centre beside the church. The crisis had helped the congregation focus on the real issues out of which they lived their stewardship. The lack of support for the church is often by default more than thought.

In early February of 1977 I was exhausted. I really could not see making it till spring. It was like staring into a black hole. I saw no way out and I talked about this with Bev. The next week I got an unexpected letter in the mail. It was a call to a small mission church in British Columbia. I had never thought about a call. It was like a gentle tap on the shoulder that said . . . "You need a change, a new start." Here was another lesson to be learned.

I loved these people and I had no desire to move. The experience of parish ministry had been invigorating, exciting and incredibly rewarding. But I also knew that there were other things that were important like living a lifestyle that one could survive and taking care of those holy gifts of life called family. By now we also had a new daughter with our two growing sons. Plus, I was blessed to have the most amazing wife whose grace and wisdom helped me see what I would never have seen.

We had so many deep friendships in the parish. The struggle was difficult. On top of all this, the Buchanan congregation had raised half the money they needed to build their new church and the Preeceville parish had just made plans to totally renovate the parsonage having asked Bev to make a list of what she wanted done (and she was not to show the list to me). They had plans to renovate their Sunday School Centre, and Norquay was just new in the parish and we had the new internship program for additional ministry support.

I could not decide. I met with the chair of the Buchanan congregation to try to sort out the issue of their building program. Was it responsible for me to leave at this time? I remember sharing with the chairman that it was the pastor's job to build the congregation, but if the congregation needed a new house in which to worship, that was their responsibility. I was confident that they would still build the new church if I was to leave.

Pastors sometimes push congregations into building and acquiring a huge debt, which congregations drag for years like a ball and chain after the pastor is gone. Other times pastors take credit for building those churches. It did not seem right. Was it responsible to leave a congregation and possibly jeopardize their plans?

I finally said, "I don't pride myself in much, but I do pride myself in knowing people. If I know this congregation you will not only build this new church but it will be paid for on the day of dedication."

The chairman replied, "It is nice to dream." Then with grace and compassion I will always remember he told me that if we felt called to leave, we had to go and they understood that. He also affirmed the wonderful experience we had together over those four short years.

After several days, I asked for a meeting with the parish council. I was stalling. I had no idea what the decision should be but I could not delay any longer. As I left for the meeting, Bev asked if I had made a decision. We had talked and prayed, but always ended up in stalemate. Bev's final words were, "You know that whatever is decided, we are with you."

The Parish Council had some business to handle and then turned the floor over to me. I did not know what to say. I decided I had to buy time to think. I would work through each congregation in the parish and try to describe where I felt each one was.

As I approached the last congregation, I looked around the table. What I saw came with such clarity. My inner voice said, "You think you are indispensable? Look at the quality of leadership around this table. They don't need you."

I smiled within myself. I finished my review and made an announcement. It choked in my throat, but came out, "I have decided to accept the call." There was stunned silence.

This was an incredibly difficult decision, but a necessary part of the journey. There is a time for change.

VI. THE SECOND CALL:
Nelson Evangelical Lutheran Church (1977-83).

After Easter 1977 we moved to British Columbia in response to the call to be the pastor of Nelson Evangelical Lutheran Church (NELC). We were called to a mission church that was almost ten years old. The Director of Canadian Missions told me that I should feel honoured to be called to the best Mission Church in Canada.

We moved into a beautiful home high on the mountainside overlooking the city of Nelson. At the bottom of the valley lay Kootenay River, an extension of Kootenay Lake. The lake ran for miles between Creston in the south, to Kaslo in the north.

The view out our dining room window provided incredible beauty every day and that first summer was an experience of adventure just living in the raw beauty of the Kootenays.

It would take time to get to know the people of this new parish and it would take time to get to know the larger community. The move immersed us into a new world of unknowns. In the midst of those unknowns we encountered people who once again provided security and fellowship to remove the loneliness of this new venture.

Members of the congregation lived across the street from us. Lincoln and Ida Sept were two people of the pews who were the first to see us and proved to be wonderful friends who made us feel at home and welcome.

Lincoln had an old boat and loved to go Kokanee salmon fishing at Balfour, where the Kootenay River flowed out of Kootenay Lake. We enjoyed many fishing trips. We could also fish from shore along the Kootenay River. Here was a place we could go as a family for outings since we did not at first have our own boat and the boys loved fishing.

It took a long time for me to see maggots as bait. I learned that maggots kept well in a cool fridge (but don't put them in if the package is not sealed . . . there isn't a wife anywhere that appreciates the results - I learned that too). Yes, one learns many things with time and experience.

Fishing provided many hours of family enjoyment with picnics and exploration of the many miles of beaches. It was also a great gathering activity over the years that followed, especially for the men of the congregation.

This congregation was a bold contrast to the congregations I had served. The total membership was just over 100 people, with one service held each Sunday and one set of confirmation classes. Most of the congregation lived in Nelson or in the immediate rural area. Some members lived as far south as Salmo and as far east as Balfour. Compared to my last posting, there was far less travel to see everyone.

Most of all this was a new beginning and in this new beginning I knew there had to be necessary changes to provide a sustainable ministry while still having time for our family life. How should things change?

My day off had to change. I began taking Mondays off, but in the fall our son was going to be in school. How much would I see him if I took Mondays off? I was worried about taking Saturdays off as traditionally I took Saturdays to finish my sermons. New discipline was needed. My sermons would have to be finished during the week.

Saturday became my day off and I set aside time for sermon preparation every morning. My goal was to have the sermon completed and placed on the right hand corner of my desk by Friday at noon. I set aside two hours a day for reading. Prior to this, I had not done much reading outside of sermon preparation. Then I announced my office hours: Monday to Friday beginning at nine o'clock with a work schedule until five o'clock. In the afternoons I would be in the office, if not visiting in the community or working on other matters of parish ministry.

Tuesday after dinner would be for hospital visitation; there was only one hospital to cover. That was different as well. Then there were mid-week Bible studies and Sunday morning Bible studies and all those other normal meetings. I joined the local ministerial association and got involved in providing services to two of the senior's residences in the city.

The chairman of our Church Council Fred Martin was a wonderfully gifted man. He followed basic protocols in running council meetings without a mechanical rigidity. Council meetings were one hour long, an hour and a quarter if things ran away.

We did more work in the hour than I had ever seen in longer meetings. It was an education to watch this man work and the grace with which he did his work. He was the head of commercial printing for the local newspaper and over the years I learned a lot from him about printing and publishing that only later I would find so helpful. We got to know each other very well and found great comfort working together for the parish.

That first year, we golfed in Castlegar on a regular basis. After a couple months the chairman asked me, "So what is your analysis of our congregation?"

Daniel A. Haugen

As a mission church, many people had come from a wide variety of faith backgrounds. Many had been unhappy with their previous church experience. This congregation had found ways to adapt and accept this broad spectrum of people, though this process caused some difficulties.

There were many things in the congregation which people were afraid to speak about. For those who came from churches that practiced "believer's baptism" it was difficult to talk about baptism without a fear of conflict. The head deacon was of Baptist background. At first he would not allow his children to attend Confirmation instruction and later had his teenage children baptized in the river at the base of our city by the Evangelical Covenant pastor.

The head trustee was a private contractor and member of a more charismatic organization of business people. It was not difficult to run into tensions.

Early in this ministry a group of people held prayer meetings that their pastor would become a Christian. Someone told me about this with great concern. I assured them that I would rather have people pray for me than against me. I assured them it would be all right and there was nothing to worry about. Their prayers for the pastor could do no harm.

What direction should ministry take in this new setting? I suggested to the chairman that this diverse makeup of people had not come to a common understanding of their faith. The only thing they could say without fear of conflict was "Praise the Lord" (so it seemed). They did not know each other, even in this small congregation. I was also convinced that due to the fragility of the fellowship, if anyone threw a monkey wrench into the works, the congregation would scatter to the four winds.

The chairman agreed with my analyses and said, "We can't live this way. So, what do we do?"

I replied that I thought we should enter into a serious program of adult Christian education and talk about the things we were afraid to talk about. I suggested that we not use any particular book as the source of our study and use only the Bible. That way we can all wrestle with the scriptures, which we hold as Lutherans to be the authority for life and faith. But I also cautioned him, that if we did this, we still might lose some members.

His response was simple, "We don't want to lose anyone, but if we have to, we have to, because we cannot go on living like this."

So began a new adventure in adult Christian education. In the midst of some problems, there was much strength within this congregation. A significant number of people attended Bible Studies and we had thirty or more adults who came for adult Bible Study every Sunday morning. We had a mid-week study that always attracted a large number of people. Several lay members were excellent study leaders. We varied the focus of the studies and the study leaders over time.

We took a new approach in how we scheduled adult education. We divided all our studies into groups of six to eight studies. There was a week break between each mid-week study. Every time a new study was to begin we informed people and let them know they were all welcome. We also encouraged people to make sure they felt free not to come if they had other priorities or did not find the study of interest. That was fine too. Over time we hoped everyone would find something to meet their needs. We planned the studies for the whole year in advance, so people knew what was coming.

Some thought it was backsliding to take a week off between studies. I encouraged them to enjoy the break and take time with family or friends as so many lives got over scheduled. We wanted people to have space in their lives for other things as well.

There were a few people who (at first) did not come to Bible Studies like they used to. Maybe they had come out of a sense of duty and for the first time found a chance to take a break. Maybe they really had not wanted to come in the first place but felt it was necessary to keep an image. With time, many came again just because they wanted to come.

We also found many people came to Bible Studies who had never come before. Was it freeing to know there was a gracious exit if they were not comfortable with this environment? One always wondered what life in the parish looked like through the eyes of this diverse group of people in order to serve them better.

The studies had a beginning and a gracious end. New people could venture in and have a gracious exit if it was uncomfortable. I often felt that some studies gave new definition to eternity. No one knew when the study began, and it was to never end. People had no gracious entrance or exit. To avoid the tension, they never started.

The process seemed to work. For six years in this parish we averaged close to 90 percent of our adults in one or more components of the adult Christian education each year. I had never seen that before or since.

As predicted, we had some struggles. Five families chose to worship elsewhere within the first two years. I visited all these families after they left. I wanted them to know that we missed them but that we also respected their decisions. The door was always open, but we would respect their decision and would not try to "get them back".

I wanted to be able to visit them because we were still committed to the fellowship we had shared. Sometimes we abandon, and even abuse people who leave our fellowship or treat them as simply disposable. I hoped that when I came to visit they would know I was not there to prod them into coming back but rather to continue to enjoy the fellowship we had together and to support them in their life and faith.

For those first visits they may have had doubts about the sincerity of this intent, but with time I think they realized that they could relax in their decision and enjoy the place of Christian fellowship they had chosen in which to worship, grow and serve.

Our trustee who left to join the Pentecostal Church in town was a dear friend and I visited him often. After he left our church he donated all the material to finish the ceiling in our church basement and also installed it as a gift to the congregation. Later, the congregation hired him as the contractor to build the new parsonage.

I remember the last visit to his home before leaving six years later. I stopped to have coffee and say farewell. As I left that day he shook my hand and said, "Pastor, I left your church, and you have visited me more than my own pastor. We have had wonderful fellowship. There must be something there."

Our congregation settled and there was a growing understanding of life and faith that provided a close fellowship in the congregation. My Baptist Deacon continued as a member of the congregation and we had many deep theological discussions into the wee hours of the morning. His teenage children (in the end) did come for confirmation instruction. He had a strong Bible School background that nurtured a strong and knowledgeable faith. He was an excellent teacher and shared as leader of our Sunday morning Bible studies along with a number of others. He and his family were wonderful gifts to our church and to our family.

Every congregation seems to be blessed with some outstanding servants. One of these servant people was Joan who worked with our Youth Group. She met with our youth on Friday nights and built a diverse group of 20 to 30 youth. They had Bible studies, played games and went on outings together. She worked hard to nurture these youth in life and faith and she seemed to have an unlimited energy. Hers was a formidable task.

I worked with a local Canadian Pacific Railway (CPR) policeman with a local Wolf Cub Pack through Boy Scouts Canada. After our first year of working together, he convinced me that we should plan a whole year's program before we began our second year. The planning covered every meeting and included the games we would play and what badges and projects we would do.

With some reluctance I cooperated. We both marvelled how easy it was after that. We didn't feel any pressure and actually looked forward to each night. We were both amazed at the results.

Our youth worker came to me and expressed concern that she was running out of energy and dreaded Friday Youth Group nights. After the experience we had with Cubs, I encouraged her to try to do the same with her youth program.

I understood her hesitance because I had the same reaction, but she was willing to try it. Some weeks later she found she had the same experience. She found Youth Group became a time she anticipated, and though she did the same things she had done before, it seemed so easy and stress free. She was amazed.

We were blessed to have this youth worker with us for a number of years till she took a new job in the greater Vancouver area. Through her ministry we had a vibrant and faithful group of teenagers who shared in the life of our congregation and community.

The Deacons started a monthly men's breakfast for our men and teenage guys. The breakfast was held in the church basement and the meal was cooked by some of the men. Our group struggled at first.

The turning point for our men's fellowship was through the CEO of Kootenay Forest Products (the largest employer in the Kootenays at that time) who was a faithful member of our congregation. He was a gracious presence in our congregation and community who embodied a quiet spirit, deep faith and a wisdom that was recognized through the whole community of Nelson.

At one breakfast he shared some of the experiences in his life where his trust in God had grown and made such a difference for his whole life. That event seemed to open all kinds of doors in the life and faith of our men. From that time on, our men's fellowship grew. The last years we had almost all of our men and teenage guys at our men's breakfasts every month. Our men discovered the gift of God's grace that came into every aspect of their lives and they found real ways to share it with each other. They had come to understand their life in relationship with God and others to the extent that they could talk about it in as real ways as they talked about anything else in life.

The men also held a men's fishing trip at Balfour (a small resort community on Kootenay Lake) on an annual basis. We put in our boats early in the morning and fished all day. At nine o'clock in the morning we docked our boats in front of the restaurant that hosted our breakfast event and each year we brought in a guest speaker. After our speaker was finished, we went back to fishing.

Of course there were prizes for the biggest fish, the most, and the best fish stories. We would present the prizes the following day after our regular worship. This event reached out to many men from outside our congregation as well. It built a strong fellowship for our men and teenage guys.

I had built a boat in my basement the first year I was in the parish. My son Tim was quite young but learned to drive hundreds of screws as we worked together. The boat turned out better than I could have hoped and provided many hours of enjoyment for our family on days off and most Sunday afternoons through the summer months. We fished and water-skied and took tours up the lake exploring the incredible beauty of the Kootenays on my days off.

One of the young men in our congregation didn't have a father. As a teenager he managed several revenue houses for his mother. This was a gifted young man who hung out at our house quite often. He was an active part of the church's Youth Group and often looked after our children when we were away for an evening.

He watched me build our boat, and came up with plans for a kayak. I helped him build it in our basement. Later, he wanted to build a little speedboat. So, we built that as well. He had quite a time getting the money to buy a suitable motor for his speedboat. It was the beginning of some struggles with tastes that exceeded his ability to pay. Most young people have to sort out these matters.

In his mid-teens an incident seemed to turn him down another path. He worked at a local ski hill and that year they hosted the local RCMP Christmas Party. At this event he saw things he never expected with the RCMP: the abuse of alcohol and drugs. He had held the RCMP in such high regard and it seemed to destroy something in this young man.

His disillusionment became mixed with his own growing up struggles and took him on a downhill road. It was hard to watch. I remember talking with him as I tried to help him see where the road would ultimately take him, but he could not see it.

The road he chose was rougher than one could ever have wished. I saw him several years ago on a visit back to this community and he is a grown man today. He has dealt with a lot of things. I still hope he will find the richness and vitality he once had.

This mission church had a different character from the aged and seasoned histories of my previous parish. The stable church with history sometimes frustrated me because they could be slow to move. In the mission church you sometimes wished for some of that stability and historical identity that held people together. This congregation was working to develop that identity and sense of belonging, and with it would come loyalty . . . all the qualities one sometimes took for granted in an established congregation that enjoyed a long history of service in God's kingdom.

This urban community of the Kootenays was quite different than rural Saskatchewan. I had to find new ways to get to know the larger community in this very different setting. Our church was up on the mountainside quite set apart from the mainstream of life.

I got to know the man who owned a local service station and he became a very close friend. I found out much later that he had been baptized in a Lutheran church. This man got me connected with a commercial hockey team in town. I had played hockey in my previous parish and missed it very much. The commercial hockey league was not a gentle league, but it was hockey. I finally had a connection outside the congregation.

Most of the guys in this league were in their early twenties. One of the members of the opposing team was a former NHL player. Though most of his career he played for a farm club of one of the major leagues, his presence added some prestige to the league.

It did not take long for everyone to find out I was a preacher. That happened of course with every team I had played with and they always got over it, but this team found it difficult.

I remember (after one particularly strained experience) coming back from a game and telling Bev that I might have to quit for the sake of the team. They could not seem to handle having a preacher in the dressing room and I was not sure what to do. I had never tried to "prove" preachers were normal people. Now, I hope we honour God and I hope our life style is not one that degrades life, but I am also confident that when people get to know us they have no trouble discovering we are still normal human beings.

To this day, I have no idea what happened in the chemistry of this group. The next game they greeted me like a long lost friend and from that day on I was "Rev". That is all they called me and we had a great time. They made the transition.

There was one incident that challenged the "Rev" to decide how "normal" he was. One of the teams we regularly played was the Molson Nighthawks. This was not a particularly gracious team on the ice and there were one or two players who were the most challenging.

One of the most difficult was like an animal on ice. He had little respect for anyone. During one game he speared me in the stomach which resulted in kidney damage that lasted a year. Cross checking, slashing . . . all normal skills he had developed and he seemed to like giving it to the "Rev" whenever he could.

One game I was coming out of our zone, with an eye on my winger who had the puck. I never saw "him" on my blind side till it was too late. He wound up with full swing of his stick and caught me on the side of the helmet. I remember the thump and the lights went out.

When the lights came on he was the first person I saw. He stood in a crowd. Even though he acted like an animal, he was still a human being who in God's eyes had value. Everyone thought I was going to kill him: I didn't.

After that game I told Bev that I did not know what to do. This was getting too dangerous. I could see only three choices: keep taking it (I ruled that out), tune him (wonderful picture, preacher beats on twenty year old) or quit commercial hockey (I did not want to quit). I did not know what to do.

The Molson Nighthawks came up on our game schedule again. I was sitting in the dressing room wondering how to deal with this young man when to my surprise he walked into our room. I have no idea why he came. He had never come into our dressing room before - it seemed divinely appointed.

I called him over and informed him the last game was the end of the road. I had never broken (and got in a fight) in all my years of hockey, but the last game was the end of the road and I would take no more garbage from him. So, I suggested we go out and just play hockey.

He left with no response. We got through the first period without an incident. During the second period I came in on their blue line ready to let go a slap shot and out of the corner of my eye I saw him coming. He was going to run right over me.

I let the shot go and just as I did I dropped my shoulder in time to catch him in the middle of his chest. I remember it in slow motion as his body stopped and his legs came up each side of me, after which gravity did its job and he hit the ice flat on his back. I chose to ignore him and went for the rebound (hoping to add my scorn to the incident . . . not very holy I know).

I never had trouble with him after that. I don't think the encounter hurt him physically. He was a pretty solid boy. The guys must have given him a hard time about the "Rev" cold-cocking him. He quit hockey for some time. We played against each other after that, but we didn't have any problems.

I have often thought about this incident. I believe every human life is "holy" by definition. Indeed there are many ways people profane life and treat it as a disposable commodity. But if life is holy how does one care for people? The answers were not always easy. If this young man had no value, I would have happily punched his face off. It is not always easy to know how to deal with some issues in life as we are called to love God and love people. I am sure the satisfaction I found was likely that quality in us called "by nature sinful". On the other hand, maybe something good came out of it. Today only God and this young man might know. I guess we leave it at that.

My friend who got me into hockey was a special gift throughout these years. He became a diabetic through an injury he acquired while he played hockey at Gonzaga University in his younger years. We had coffee together quite often and met for lunch as occasions arose. We golfed together, and on one occasion our families spent a couple days together in Spokane, Washington.

I met his mother when she was in the hospital. She struggled with health issues for many years and when she died he asked if I would preside over her funeral.

The morning of the funeral I was in my office putting the finishing touches on the service when my friend apologetically came into the office knowing I was busy. He said he just needed some time. I had never seen him in a suit. We talked about his mom and her struggles and then he said, "Dan, I don't know if this is theologically right or not, but I can just picture mom looking down on us and saying, I feel sorry for those who are left behind. I now have it so good." He was aware of the faith of his mother. He came to church on a few occasions but there were issues that seemed to be a barrier.

After we left Nelson and moved to Saskatchewan (summer of 1983), his trouble with diabetes got worse. First he went blind. He got his vision back, but had more health issues including a series of strokes.

He phoned me during this time and said, "I read my Bible every day and pray. You can't imagine how much it helps." In the years that followed his health deteriorated.

I would try to go back and visit him whenever I could. His wife told me I was the only person he would see. He had difficulty with his mobility and speech. He lived this way for many years and finally had to be placed in a care home. He died a few years ago. In my list of regrets in ministry, is the regret that I did not get back for his funeral, especially as his wife had asked me to come.

An Anglican pastor had helped his wife through this time and I thought it was more important for her sake that this Anglican pastor be her pastor since it could be an on-going relationship for her. Having said that, I still wished I had gone back. We thank God for forgiveness, and I will always treasure the gift that this man and his wife were to us.

My wife worked hard to teach me to say "No". I served for two years on the Board for Canadian Lutheran World Relief and I was also on the Board of Congregational Life for our national church for six years. For the most part I was not as involved in outside commitments and locally I served on a board for an agency that provided service as a halfway house for struggling youth. I was not very encouraged by what was happening so after two years I resigned. Nelson is a beautiful city, but behind the manicured beauty there was a huge dysfunction in the homes of the community.

Our two boys played hockey and soccer as they grew older. We also got involved with our children and met many people through the education system in our community. As we got connected, the telephone seemed to ring more every year. So many were crisis calls. It was not uncommon to get four to six phone calls over a supper meal from all over the community. Almost all were people struggling with life and it became overwhelming.

How could I keep up? How could I understand what was happening? I finally felt like I was down on the rocks at the foot of a cliff where a bridge was washed out and the whole mainstream of the community was coming over the cliff. On the rocks I tried to help salvage an arm and a leg of shattered lives and relationships.

I wished someone would go up on the highway and tell people this was the wrong way to travel, but that would be legalism and we can't have that. We are grace people. We let them run over the cliff before we care. I found myself becoming very cynical. I pressed on in the ministry and looked for ways to reach beyond the congregation, and sought ways to work with people and seek something redemptive.

Our boys played hockey and I served as an assistant coach. I enjoyed this involvement and it gave me time with our two sons. It also connected me with a reality that complicated life. Hockey was already out of control in Nelson. At that time there was an Atom team that played (if I remember right) about as many games as NHL teams were playing in a regular season. It was a tremendous cost to parents and it burnt out the children. One of the concerns in the community was that by the time the youth were playing midget hockey there was a huge "drop out" rate.

On one occasion I was asked to coach one of the midget teams still surviving. They had lost their coach. Someone called and asked if I could take this team to Castlegar for a game that evening. This was not much notice, even to think about the request. I was told that the team was difficult to coach. Apparently that was why the former coach quit.

In the end I was convinced to take this group to Castlegar. We were to meet at the arena and I had a van so I could take several of the team members. How I would get them all to Castlegar was unknown but I was told some of the guys had cars. I got to the place where I was to meet the team and nobody was there. I waited as long as I could, but none arrived. I concluded that they must have already left by their own means.

I drove to Castlegar alone feeling quite exposed to the liabilities of the responsibility I had taken for this team. I had never met a single player. They did not know me and I did not know them. When I got to Castlegar I found them in the dressing room.

They apparently had been told that the coach was a pastor. If I was a bit uncomfortable, it did not take long to see how uncomfortable they were. I passed around a paper on which they were to write their names, their numbers and the position they normally played. Then I informed them how I wanted them to play. I would not accept any fighting. I expected to see them play their position and play as a team and to show class and respect for each other and for the opposing team - at the same time I liked aggressive hockey.

After every instruction came the same reply, "Yes Sir." It was more fear and uncertainty than it was submission. I finally informed them that my name was Dan and the next person to call me "Sir" would be benched. They caught the drift. We worked out lines and positions and the game was on. The first period they played well. There was some good talent in these boys. Fear had actually provided some temporary control, though I expected that to wear off. They were ahead by the end of the first period.

During the second period they relaxed and became themselves. They tried to run guys down and provided several fights for the crowd. Several times guys came into the box swearing because someone had hit them. I would smile and ask if they were hurt. Of course they would deny being hurt. I was a little sarcastic suggesting they did a lot of crying for not being hurt and encouraged them to toughen up. Hockey isn't for whiners. Their play fell apart.

In the dressing room before the third period I tried to help them see that they had destroyed their own game. They had shown how skilled they could really be the first period and I had been quite proud of them. Yet, in the second period they just looked silly.

During the third period they pulled it together and played hockey in a way that any coach would be pleased and won the game. The next week I got a phone call informing me that the team asked if I could be their coach for the rest of the year.

There are times one regrets the decisions one makes. I felt I was really too committed to take on the team and later on I learned that almost every member of that team was in youth detention before the end of the year. The team ceased to exist. Had I closed the door on an opportunity that I might never have again? What opportunities had I missed in ministry to this group of young men? Sometimes we forget what is most important. I still often wonder.

As good as sports could be for young people, it was crowding out Christian education and worship even for youth with strong Christian backgrounds. I was convinced that this would result in huge consequences for the future. I had become convinced that this nurture in God's word, worship and Christian education were life changing and equipped people to live in this struggling world. What happens when there is no knowledge of God in the land? The prophet Hosea seemed to understand the functional consequences in the life of a nation:

> There is no faithfulness, no love, no acknowledgment of God in the land. There is only cursing, lying and murder, stealing and adultery; they break all bounds, and bloodshed follows bloodshed. (Hosea 4:1b-2)

The devaluation of life always seemed to end in its further abuse. When life has no value it becomes disposable and always seemed to result in escalating conflict and degradation of life. Was this part of the growing crisis in which one was already involved?

It seemed without any changes this could only get worse. How can we do something to break this cycle?

The intense schedules for organized sports were a real problem for anyone who felt a high commitment to provide opportunities for worship and for Christian education for our children and youth. I spent a lot of time raising the concern in informal conversations with people involved in minor sports within the community. We talked about it in the rinks and wherever one met families in sports. As Christian parents we were a part of the community. We wanted our children to participate in community life and have a commitment to it, but we also wanted them to have time for worship and Christian education.

The issue was raised in our ministerial association. We decided to put together a brief for our city council and requested their support in principle and that our city ask minor sport organizations to avoid scheduling sports activities on Sunday mornings when the major worship and Christian education times were held in our community. As chair of the ministerial, I arranged an appointment with the mayor and city council members in the council chambers.

We presented the ministerial brief and shared in the discussion. Some councillors really wanted to kill the proposal but did it by demanding the necessity to legislate the closure of facilities on Sunday mornings. The council could not come to a decision. Finally, the mayor stood and announced that as mayor he would encourage all minor sports groups to keep Sunday morning clear of organized sports and he would openly advocate such in the community.

Sunday mornings were cleared from organized sports for our children and youth. It was a most gracious and easy process. This lasted for a number of years and then eventually crept back.

Daniel A. Haugen

Sometimes we are too silent in our support of affirming actions within our communities, which help everyone find moderation and nurture environments that can support life and faith for others. It was a reminder of the need to pursue functional ways the Christian community can be "salt" and "light" that can benefit the whole community.

The problem persists in our communities, but this experience suggested to me that there are gracious ways to approach issues, and the community might actually surprise us if it is done with respect. It reminded me that the community of faith is a part of the community and as such has a voice that can be listened to as any other voice. We speak from within the community not as people from the outside. And hopefully we speak, not to condemn, but to pursue the goal of bringing something upstream and life giving, in a downstream world.

I have often rebelled when I hear people in the church talk about how we can get the church into the community. The reality is that we are a part of the community. Our members work and live and participate in all kinds of activities in the community. The more important question is how do we live our faith in the communities in which we already live?

A large part of the work of ministry is to nurture our parishioners in life and faith to equip them to live that faith in the centre of community. It should affect how we do business, how we care for employees, how we work for employers, how we coach teams, how we share in every aspect of community life. Communities need upstream people as much as upstream people need community. How do we put love for God and people into action? This is all part of the Great Commission and part of the journey of learning and doing that to which we are called. This was one of the great challenges and ventures where one needed to learn so much for the sake of the task with which we are commissioned.

I remember the ministerial meeting when the director for mental health spoke to us. He talked about the changing social environment of our community and illustrated it with a story ... the husband moved out on his wife and in with another woman and her children, and how they were coping quite well.

However, another man moved in with the wife and family that this man had left and they were not coping well at all. Then he said, "Your job as clergy is to help people learn to cope with a changing environment."

My response was instant. I had never thought these thoughts before but they came out of my mouth as fast as it focused in my brain, "You know if we sent theologians or sociologists down to the river when the fish were coming belly up we would likely have heard them say . . . 'hmmm, obviously fish that have not learned to cope with a changing environment' and we would pull them out, give them a group therapy session and throw them back into the river . . . and been a bit disturbed at the little success we had."

"Now," I continued, "if scientists were true to their philosophies of evolution, the scientist should likely say 'wow isn't this exciting, what we obviously have here is a changing environment and out of it will evolve a higher species of fish'. However the scientists set aside their philosophy and became more functional and decided that at least the fish cannot adapt fast enough, and they identify the conditions that support life, go upstream to find what is destroying them and then become very action oriented to bring change."

Scientist today are moralists. You can throw a piece of paper out the window of your car and get a thousand dollar fine. You can throw a person out the window of your house and (depending on the circumstance) may go unchallenged.

I asked the director, "Do you think we will ever consider the possibility that there are some conditions that support life? Will this motivate us to get into that approximating business to identify what those conditions are, and then go upstream to find what is destroying those conditions and consider again that there might be some things that are just plain wrong, and work for change."

I will always remember his reply. After a profound silence he said, "No I don't think we will ever go back to that again."

This to me was the articulated voice of our culture. It was also the voice of dysfunction. We would never function this way with the physical environment. Can we assume the human creature to be infinitely adaptable to any social condition that might arise?

From time to time, I read my wife's *Chatelaine* magazine to see what women were saying to women. I remember an article that talked about the accelerated breakdown of marriage and how this would evolve a new and higher concept of family. This was the flow of cultural philosophy. What was washing up on the shores of our community life, were quite different results. It was sobering.

On this journey of ministry I became more convinced that the faith community has so much more to bring to our world than "coping skills". The gospel can actually change environment through the leaven and salt that the faith community is called to live:

> *You are the salt of the earth. But if the salt loses its saltiness, how can it be made salty again? It is no longer good for anything, except to be thrown out and trampled by men. You are the light of the world. A city on a hill cannot be hidden. Neither do people light a lamp and put it under a bowl. Instead they put it on its stand, and it gives light to everyone in the house. In the same way, let your light shine before men, that they may see your*

good deeds and praise your Father in heaven.
(Matthew 5:13-16)

I got a phone call on a Friday night. This person had a friend who wanted to get married on Monday and wondered if I would marry them. I suggested that I would like to meet with the couple first, but I was informed that would not be possible since they were in Spokane for the weekend.

I told the person that I would have to meet them if they wanted to have me marry them. Finally over the weekend it was decided they would come to see me on Monday morning.

At ten o'clock in the morning an old green Chevy half-ton drove into the parking lot of the church and in walked a fascinating couple. They lived in the Slocan Valley.

We got introduced and I told them that since we had little time for formalities we had to find a starting point. They did not know me and I did not know them.

I suggested that words without meaning are like cans without food. It is really garbage. The one thing I wanted to avoid was a service of empty words since they deserved more respect from me. They also deserved that respect from each other so that they would not throw empty words (garbage) in each other's face and call it their marriage ceremony. So I suggested that we look at the normal service I would use and see if it was something that might mean something to them.

We began to work through the service beginning with, "Marriage is a holy relationship ordained by God and to be held in honour by all." As we proceeded through the service we talked about each part and what it meant.

Halfway through the process the bride-to-be suddenly rose to her feet and informed me that I was a self-righteous blankety-blank son of a so-and-so and she walked out of the office and back to their truck.

The groom-to-be sat transfixed to his chair, head down. I apologized and asked him if he felt I had really been self-righteous. I certainly hoped I had not.

He assured me that he did not think I had, and he did not understand what had happened. Then he asked what we should do. I didn't share my inner thoughts; however, I did suggest that I had no right to be a cloud on their special day so if we could not work this out I could not do the wedding. I suggested that he go talk to his bride-to-be and see if there was a way to work it out.

There was 20 minutes of animated conversation in the parking lot. I could see it from my desk through my office window. Finally, they both came back into my office. I apologized and assured her I had no intention to be self-righteous. We continued to work through the rest of the service after which the bride suggested that maybe we should have a civil ceremony and wondered if I would do that.

I assured them that I would support anything that moved in what seemed a good direction, even if it was less than what I might want for them. They were living together so I felt that their desire to get married was something that at least moved in a positive direction. So, I was with them.

They wanted to write their own vows, so we worked that out in a way agreeable to everyone. Then, they started to tell me what they wanted me to say. I asked if it was fair for me to ask that I also be allowed to share with them what was genuine for me even as they wanted to do that for each other. They decided that was fair and the wedding was set for Wednesday on a friend's farm in the Slocan Valley.

Bev was not too impressed with the idea, and on the day of the wedding she insisted I at least wear my clerical collar. As a concession to Bev, I did. I found my way to the farm in the Slocan, parked and walked into the acreage where there was a large crowd. My doubts grew as I walked in. Several young women, beautifully dressed were stretched out on the grass in several locations quite stoned out of their minds on drugs.

I got acquainted and met guests from England and many from the San Francisco Bay area. We decided where the service would be held and so it began. The bride was in an average length white dress, and groom in a suit with his eye patch removed for the day.

One of the witnesses was a quadriplegic from the San Francisco Bay area who made his "X" and had his name signed by a man in a white suit and hat, his chauffeur and caregiver.

After the wedding I spent several hours visiting with the guests. They seemed to treat me like a novelty, but I found them most interesting. It was getting late and I finally found it necessary to leave.

I said my farewells to the bride and groom. As I did, the bride suggested that I really had not done a civil ceremony. I apologized but told her she had asked for a pastor to do the ceremony and I assured her that I meant every word I spoke and hoped that there was something in what I said that might in some way become a gift to them.

Then I went to the house to thank the friend who had provided the farm for this event. As I walked into the house strange chills ran up and down my spine. It was immediate and I had no idea why I got the feeling.

I was surprised to find the house full of people I hadn't met outside. As I walked into the house I was met by a verbal barrage from people that expressed with great clarity how little respect they had for everything I represented. I did not know what to do, so I let it flow unchallenged. I found the owner and thanked him for his generosity and hospitality in providing the place for this wedding. I wished him God's blessing and I left.

I often wondered if I made a mistake in conducting this wedding. I talked to senior pastors in the Okanagan who had been my mentors for years. They thought I was crazy to perform the wedding. After thinking a lot about what they shared I still could not get by the thought that at least it was moving in the right direction. I concluded that I would support anything that moved in what seemed a good direction, even if it was less than what I might wish. I still hoped in some way that wedding day would still be special to this couple.

A year later I got another call from the Slocan from a couple who wanted to get married. I asked them where they got my name. It turned out they were friends with this couple I had married who had suggested they give me a call.

So, I had another wedding and in attendance was the couple I had married a year earlier. After the wedding, the bride of that earlier wedding took me aside and we talked for two hours. She asked if I knew she was a Buddhist when she got married. I told her I had no idea. She informed me that since the wedding she went back to her Anglican roots.

One never knows. I met this couple by chance many years later while visiting in Nelson and they were still happily married, holy lives sharing the journey of life together.

The daily business of ministry took one into the mainstream of the life of this community. Behind the manicured lawns and fine houses were so many lives which were struggling. The social dysfunction in community life was striking. The consequences tore at the heart of life. For many people, life lost its value and purpose.

I wrote a poem during this time titled, *The House Where Nobody Lives*. From the busyness of work to the consumptive lifestyles of self-indulgence everyone was on the run. Relationships were crashing, children were confused, and the destructive lifestyles simply grew without challenge except for the growing consequences from which most people ran and hid.

I remember a funeral, which reminded me of so many people who get lost in all the confusion of our time. A funeral home called to ask if I would do a funeral for an elderly gentleman who had lived in a senior's home at Kaslo (a neighbouring community). This man had no known family. The service was held in the chapel of the funeral home in charge. We waited some time, but no one came to the funeral. We found a couple men on the street to help move the casket to the hearse. At the cemetery we got a couple of workers to help us carry the casket to its resting place.

There, at the graveside, the undertaker and myself listened to the words of scripture that reminded us of God's love for our struggling world. I had never met this man who died. It seemed he was truly an abandoned soul. We placed his body in that final resting place with the words of the committal service and found peace in the knowledge that we could simply entrust the soul of this seemingly abandoned man into the gracious hands of the Lord of life. He alone knows the human heart. That was enough.

In my fourth year of ministry in this parish I felt buried in human rubble. During every meal I would get several phone calls from families and people in crisis. I could not keep up. There was a need to get out in order to regain some perspective.

I had always wanted to go back and study. We were in the era of 16 percent interest rates and we had been out of debt for several years, but in calculating the cost we realized that we would have to cash all our savings and RRSPs (registered retirement savings). We would have to sell our boat, our van, and on top of that borrow at least five thousand dollars (that was the most we could afford to borrow on our salary at the time).

Some people think faith is just plunging ahead with the expectation that God will provide. I guess that is fine for those who do. We felt that our job as stewards of God's gifts was to evaluate what God had provided, and to trust that as God provided, we would proceed. Until we could see clear to go ahead with what God had provided (including what we could reasonably carry in debt through the future provision of our salary) we would wait. By the summer of 1981 we felt we could go.

The congregation had developed a plan to sell the parsonage to pay off their debt and get off mission support from the National Church. I thought I should take some time to look at our options for buying a house when we came back. The mayor of Nelson at that time also had a real estate firm. We had become friends, so I consulted him to see what was happening in the local real estate market.

While in his office he thanked me for all I had done for the youth of our city. I was quite surprised, because I felt I had done so little. I thanked him for his generosity but I also told him how frustrated I was that I had done so little for young people. He talked at some length about his grandson. (And then I had that experience again of saying things that I maybe should not have.)

I called him by name and said, "Until we can deal with guys like you, youth ministry is like leading a donkey by the tail. First, you will not get very far, and secondly, you will take a good kicking in the process."

He was shocked and so was I. I continued, "Is it important for your grandson to go to church and Sunday School?"

He answered, "Of course it is."

I asked, "Why . . . grandpa never goes to church. And your grandson will say his grandpa was a successful businessman, and mayor of the city. Grandpa doesn't need the church, and your grandson will want to be just like grandpa and will leave the church as soon as he can."

A brief silence followed . . . I was appalled that I had done this. The mayor leaned back, put his feet up on his desk and replied, "Dan, that is the most obvious truth. How come I did not see it till today?" We had a wonderful visit.

In the years that followed this mayor retired. He wrote two books and he gave me complimentary copies of both. What a fascinating read that included a wonderful exploration of life and faith.

In the days that followed, our family prepared to step out for a year and regain some perspective.

VII. GRAD STUDIES:
Time out for Evaluation and Back to Work (1981-83).

With the continuing education program provided for clergy and with the blessing of the congregation we took a one-year study leave in 1981-82. I was fortunate to find a 22-foot moving van, which we bought for the move. We packed up our family . . . back to Saskatchewan for a year of study and rented a little house in Hanley, Saskatchewan a small town about 40 miles south of Saskatoon. This was my wife's hometown while she was growing up. We chose to live in Hanley for a number of reasons: rent was cheap; Bev could live in the community where she was raised; we could be close to her parent's farm; and the community had a good school for our children where they could also be involved in the community and affordable recreation.

The little house we rented was well furnished, but had its challenges. The windows were so poor we had to clean out the dirt that had blown in and covered everything. The house had been empty for almost a year (the owner was serving some time in a government institution). The deep freeze had been disconnected with some meat left in it. It was ruined. We had mice living in the heat ducts. We found that a vacuum cleaner worked quite well to remove most of them . . . *schloop* . . . got another one.

Daniel A. Haugen

I worked for my brother-in-law in his factory manufacturing grain boxes and hoists and installing them on farm trucks throughout the summer months of 1981. I pulled the van back off our moving van and hired my brother-in-law to shorten the frame and install a grain box and hoist on it. Another friend in Watrous sold the truck for me on consignment and we did quite well after expenses. I worked the evenings and Saturdays on the farm.

In the fall of that same year I commuted from the small community of Hanley to university in Saskatoon. Back in the classroom after eight years was a striking change. I think the mind is like other muscles of the body; if it's not used and exercised muscles atrophy. It took two months before I got back into the disciplines of study.

I had a mixed agenda. I wanted to do further studies in the Old Testament, but I also wanted to engage professors in discussion about ministry and the issues of life one faced in community. The memory of the director of mental health in Nelson and his commentary on social evolution dominated my mind. Was our pastoral task simply to help people learn to cope with a changing environment, or does the gospel provide a healing that is truly redemptive and life changing?

I shared this struggle and the parish experience that had made me feel buried in human tragedy with a professor. He could not believe things were so bad. We talked at some length and in the end I wished I could take him into my parish for a month, and after the month let him draw his own conclusions. So many parish experiences took the pastor into circumstances, which made the worst of afternoon soap operas look like child's play.

The year of study also allowed me to explore some of my struggles with evangelism programs. I took an evangelism course and did a study on Kennedy's Evangelism Explosion, which was one of the popular programs of the time. In the process of the study I took out the name of "Jesus" and put in "Electrolux." Then I saw something I had never seen with such clarity before. The program really took Jesus and made him a product to be marketed. The goal of marketing was to get people to appropriate the product and "choose Jesus". The process was the transfer of good North American marketing technique, which was adapted to market Jesus.

The Kennedy Program suggested that if there was not follow up with Bible study and Christian fellowship there was little follow-through on the part of those who chose Jesus. I guess that could be expected.

At first I was quite critical of this program, and then I began to realize, that though the process was flawed, the final need for Bible study and Christian fellowship was likely where there was real value. I remembered the words of the dean of the bible school I had attended as a teenager. "God works through imperfect things too, otherwise how would he ever work through me or you?"

The focus of my studies was the Old Testament and the theses on which I would conclude these studies, was on the Old Testament book of Hosea. The striking motif of this book is the image of harlotry. It was interesting to see how Hosea included in his writing a deep exploration of the impact of "harlotry" on the social, economic, political and religious life of the nation.

Though harlotry has normally been viewed as a sexual motif, it was interesting to explore the possibility that "harlotry" was really an economic motif. Israel sought her, security and well-being, not through her love of God, but through her love of "hire". (The Hebrew word for the harlot's "love" of hire, was the same word used for God's "love" for his people.)

Israel "used" God, used people, and used every aspect of domestic and international politics to seek to secure the life and wealth through which Israel provided for herself. The results were certain and identifiable in Israel's life. The bi-product of the life of harlotry in Israel resulted in a deep destruction to social life, political life (both national and international) and the religious life as identified by the prophet. There was no knowledge of God in the land. Israel had abandoned God and pursued her lovers instead.

What were our people doing in community? Was God being abandoned also as people pursued their first loves? Was the social carnage simply a stage we had to go through before we discovered the real benefits of the secular culture we were nurturing (one of the voices one heard in the journey), or is the world we are in simply heading the wrong direction totally consumed by its materialistic gods, and using life at every level to achieve its goals? What was the role of the Christian community?

This year of study stimulated so much thought as I observed the realities of the world in which we live. Never had the role of pastoral ministry been so powerfully affirmed. In a vacuum, the ideology of the culture seemed quite sound. The reality one faced in real human lives was so much more sobering. The two did not equate, but the teaching of the scriptures rang with truth and made sense out of the reality in which I worked and lived in ministry.

The year of study was a wonderful time; however, I messed it up some with my tendency to get overcommitted and involved in too many other things. I played senior hockey that winter with the local team in Hanley. I coached a 10 and under team on which our two sons played. I also served the Watrous, Young and Viscount Parish on a time-to-time basis. It began with some Sunday supply and became a regular Sunday commitment and grew to include an Adult Bible Study and Confirmation classes once a week.

The parish involvement also came with surprises. Just before Christmas the parish council met and put me on a half-time salary retroactive to the first of September for the services I was able to offer. This was a gift I could have never imagined and for which I found it difficult to offer adequate thanks.

Watrous was 50 miles away by gravel road from Hanley. My Camero developed a bad reputation for speeding as I fought with time driving daily to Saskatoon for classes, to Watrous parish (sometimes twice a week), and travelling to hockey games.

I also put in several weeks of work for the national church, working with a person who had a strong background as an educator. Our task was to evaluate the materials used in the Sunday School at Home Curriculum. This was a program of Christian education carried out with individuals in isolated areas through the mail. My co-worker proved to be extremely gifted and made this experience a great time of learning.

The texts used for Sunday school at home were largely the texts I had used in my Sunday school years. It was the first time I saw a possible reason for my disjointed knowledge of the scriptures. The courses jumped from one story to another based on various themes. Seldom was there any attempt to put the stories of the Bible into a context. This program produced biblical knowledge without a filing system. Historical context was one form for filing these stories. The only contextual file system was thematic. Biblical knowledge remained fragmented and had no historical reference which one could re-enter for study and thought.

That encouraged me, when I returned to the parish, to write a Bible Introduction Course that covered both the Old and the New Testament. The first study covered the whole Old Testament in six sessions. I called it an aerial view. It was intended to give context. A CPR truck driver in his 60s said he learned more in those six studies than he had learned all his life.

In the end, all that happened was everything he learned in the past for the first time was given a context and for the first time it fit together and made sense and became retrievable knowledge. In the following months he read the whole Bible. It was also the first time he understood the Bible as a library of 66 books shelved in its own peculiar way as to order. It is difficult to read the Bible as if it was a book. It was confusing and better to view it as a library.

I did another series on the New Testament, and later a third series of studies were developed as an attempt to give some clarity to the history and development of the Christian church with a contextual attempt to understand the variety of denominations we know today.

Every experience proved an education and brought new perspective for ministry, but the broad agenda put a lot of pressure on my formal studies. I neglected some courses. I remember memorizing Syriac vocabulary while travelling on the road and there were times (I must confess) I caught up on reading with a book resting on the steering wheel. (Where is the wisdom we have lost . . . in the pursuit of knowledge?)

It was a full year but I managed to complete all the courses for my academic master's degree. The theses would come later.

In the fall of 1982 we returned to Nelson, British Columbia. The intern who served the parish for the year provided pastoral leadership to our congregation while I was gone. He did an excellent job and provided wonderful pastoral care to the people. He likely needed the experience in ministry more than he needed my supervision though we stayed in touch throughout the year.

When we arrived back in Nelson, we moved into an apartment since the congregation, having sold the parsonage, decided to build a new parsonage when we were away, but had not completed the task. This was the result of a plan we implemented before my leave of absence in order to pay off the mortgage that was held with the Board of Canadian Missions. Housing prices were good at the time. The revenue from the sale of the parsonage was used to clear the debt held by Canadian Missions. This freed our congregation to find more financial resource for local ministry and the support of missions abroad. The surplus was used to build a new parsonage on a spare lot owned by the congregation.

Back in Nelson, I spent a lot of time to help finish the parsonage so we could move in. I was now a carpenter. This circumstance was disrupting and made it difficult to get settled back into ministry.

In the early spring of 1983 I received a letter of call from the Hanley Lutheran Parish. We had just spent a year in that community. Bethlehem Hawarden, the country congregation in this parish was Bev's home church during her growing up years. There were many reasons to be attracted to this call including the proximity to Saskatoon for the completion of my STM theses, but there were also some circumstances that made this a complicated call since many family members were also members of the parish. In the end we returned the call.

For many years I told Bev that one day I would love to teach in one of our church's schools. I always had concluded that statement with the words "but not yet".

In April of 1983, I came home from the office for lunch, I sat down at the table and informed Bev, "I'm ready."

"Ready for what?" she asked.

"Ready to teach at one of our schools," I said.

"So what made you decide that?" she asked.

"I have no idea, but I'm ready."

I had been sitting in my office and to this day I have no explanation for this resolve, but it seemed clear and that was enough.

I never thought much about it again and went back to work. The next week Bev called to tell me there was an ad in *The*

Shepherd (the national magazine of our church). The Lutheran Collegiate Bible Institute in Outlook, Saskatchewan was advertising for someone to teach part time in the Bible School Department and to do some public relations for the school. Bev reminded me that I was leaving on April 26 for Saskatoon for a two-week study leave to continue research for my STM theses. The school was only 100 kms south of Saskatoon. Why not call them and arrange for an interview? This was too good to be just coincidental.

On April 15, 1983 I wrote a letter to the president of the Lutheran Collegiate Bible Institute (LCBI) inquiring about the position and suggested if there would be any benefit in further discussion, I would be glad to come to Outlook during that time in Saskatoon.

The president arranged for me to come for an interview. I was impressed with this gracious and gifted man. During the interview I also became aware of the difficulties he had inherited at this school of our church. The interview went well, but it also flagged a number of issues of concern. The school was in trouble financially and the symptoms seen in facilities indicated the problem had been long term. If I considered this position, it would have severe challenges. Following the interview I received a letter informing me that they would like to offer me the call to this position.

This all seemed so quick. By May 25 we accepted and prepared for our departure from Nelson for this new venture in ministry. We had a wonderful experience in Nelson and had been very close to the people of the parish. The farewells were difficult. It reminded us of the rich gift of fellowship we enjoy as God's servants wherever we go. The call to "go" moves us on as others "come" who also hear the call.

During the summer of 1983 we prepared for the move. Packing again (the third time in as many years) had to be disrupting for our children. We bought another moving van and contracted our own move. This saved the school a good deal of money in a time they really could not afford much. We bought a 22-foot moving van on a GMC cab-over chassis. I spent a good deal of time on my days off checking this truck over and preparing for the move. The truck had not been used for a long time. This would provide some challenges on our move to Saskatchewan but in the end worked well.

We stopped in Cranbrook the first night. We were very tired. We had worked long hours packing and we had accepted so many invitations to homes and farewells with friends. There had been little sleep in the days leading up to our departure and on the road we had a difficult start; however, a little "on the road maintenance" before breakfast on the second day of travel and we were rolling again.

The boys and I were travelling in our moving van, and Bev and our daughter were following in our Camaro. The backseat of the car was full of plants. Late, on the second day when we were a few miles from Medicine Hat, I looked in my mirror and there was a car driving down the middle of the ditch on the left hand side of the road. I was fighting sleep and wondered why anyone would be driving in the ditch. Then I suddenly realized it was Bev's car. I immediately pulled over walked across the highway and waved her up on the road. She was driving perfectly down the middle of the ditch. Why the large plants in the back stood out, I will never know. It was part of the incongruity and fatigue that for a moment was humorous.

Bev drove up onto the highway and pulled up behind the truck. I asked her what happened and she informed me she had fallen asleep and driven across the highway into the ditch. Her eyes told me another story. I was afraid she would lose her nerve, so I just said, "Well you are awake now, let's keep going." I climbed back into the cab and drove. She had to follow.

Bev was upset with me for not being more sympathetic. I was so thankful that nothing worse had happened. We stopped in Medicine Hat and stayed in the dumpiest motel I ever remember, but we needed to sleep.

We had bought a beautiful 1600 square foot home in Outlook (we had made an earlier trip to house shop). This was the first house we saw on our buying trip. The need to buy a house was the crisis of this call.

I did not know how we could buy anything. When considering the call, the purchase of our own home had been the greatest obstacle. I talked with our youth worker in Nelson about this difficulty. Though we had just taken a year off that we had expected would deplete all our resources, we had ended the year without debt. In fact, we had a surplus; however, we had invested that together with one of my brothers and his wife to purchase a half share in a quarter section (160 acres) of farmland.

Our youth worker had stopped in the office one day to encourage me to take the call. She assured me that this had to be God's calling. She felt the call was perfect for us. Her excitement was greater than my own, but I did not know how we could buy a house especially with the high interest rates of the time.

She assured me that if I thought about it there would be a way. I finally told her about an uncle who had informed me that if I ever borrowed money from anyone else he would be offended, but I just couldn't call him. On hearing this she fed back the sermon from the previous Sunday on "pride". She suggested I should practice what I preach. Then with little means of escape, she informed me in no uncertain terms that I would make that call.

It was difficult, but I called my uncle. And in that amazing and quiet way in which most miracles happen, the obstacle was removed. We were offered an interest-free loan that would make it possible to purchase a house. The door had opened again. It always seemed that God opened doors and our job was to walk through to the new adventures of ministry that lay ahead for us in the service of God and the people to whom we were called.

In June Bev and I had made that trip to Outlook to find a house. It was a trying experience since a large number of houses had come on the market a short time before our arrival and then were pulled from the market the day of our arrival because the Saskatchewan Water Corporation had changed its mind about moving some offices out of the community. Suddenly we had little to choose from.

We looked at many old homes with crumbling foundations and old cast plumbing. There had been a home we saw when we first drove into the community which was very larte and had an attached garage, but we ignored it knowing it had to be out of our price range.

We finally made an offer on an 1100 square foot home with no garage. There were some real problems in this home but it was all we could find. Our offer was turned down.

Our real estate agent decided we should look at one more house. The house we thought we could not afford. This house was extravagant from our measures. It was only three years old. It was everything we could dream of and more. We did not want to take advantage of the generosity of the uncle who had offered us the loan.

If only we could sell the farmland we had bought, then we would feel better looking at this house. We had an agreement with our partners that if anyone wanted to sell the land it would be automatic. To push them into a sale one year after buying seemed unfair. I called another brother as we looked for options. I thought he might be interested in an investment, so I offered him our half-share in the land for what we paid.

Then came another surprise. The brother who was a partner in this land was visiting with him at the time I called. He had just talked about selling the land but did not want to push us into selling. The door was open even before we knew it. I could only smile and quietly acknowledge with thanks how the road unfolded. We felt free to look at this last house.

We arranged for an evening viewing. We were amazed. This was a 1600 square foot, three-year-old home. It had three bedrooms, a study on the main floor, a laundry room on the main floor and only one finished room in the basement with attached garage. This was everything and more that we had talked about in our wildest dreams for a home. The backyard was 100 feet deep and 75 feet wide. It seemed too good to be true after a very discouraging day. Late that evening we made an offer. There was some conflict over selling and the deal fell through.

We were discouraged and decided that night we would have to buy a lot and build our own home. We felt abandoned in this new decision to move. We really did not want to have to be involved with building a new house while starting a new job, but we saw no other choice.

The next morning we returned to our real estate agent to recover our deposit and arrange to buy a lot with plans to build a new home, but the agent was out. We waited for some time for him to return. We were tired and had to drive 600 miles back to Nelson. It was hard to wait.

While we were waiting, the phone rang. The people selling the house had decided to sell after all. We were overwhelmed. It was a much better house than we had ever dreamt of and virtually the same price as the smaller house we had fortunately not been able to buy. We closed the deal and went home to pack.

On arriving in Outlook in July of 1983, it was hard to believe we actually owned the house into which we unloaded our possessions. Would this ever feel like home?

What lay ahead was beyond our imagination. This would be the place our household would find shelter and share life for the next 19 years. God always seemed to open doors and provide all that was needed and more wherever we had been. This new place for life and ministry had opened up for us in ways we could not have imagined. Ready or not, we were here.

VIII. CALL NUMBER THREE:
Lutheran Collegiate Bible Institute (1983-1985).

Life at the Lutheran Collegiate Bible Institute in Outlook, Saskatchewan was a whole new world for me. August 1, 1983 I officially began work. There was no office space available for me, so we found a storeroom I could clean out. It was in the basement at the far end of the hallways that led back to the main offices. After cleaning out the storeroom we collected furniture. I dug through many other storage areas and as I recall we had to buy a few items. I built some shelving for books and in the end I had a good working space, though it was like working in a cement bomb shelter being solid concrete with no windows. I had one month to get ready for work.

During this time Bev helped our young family get acquainted with the community. There were neighbours to meet and new friendships to initiate and build. A new congregation served our family, and Dad was not the pastor. This was a significant change and we could sit together for worship. This was a wonderful experience.

The boys were old enough to enjoy golf. The home we had in Hanley two years earlier was right against the golf course and the boys had learned to golf that year. Now in Outlook we golfed together, and they found new friends who liked to golf. There was also a new school with which to get acquainted, the third transition in three years. It must have been difficult for our children and for Bev although the move was softened because we knew so many people from this area. In a way it was already home.

LCBI offered the last three years of high school, and also had a Bible Department that offered one year of post-secondary Bible School education. My job description was in two parts: to work in public relations for the school and to teach part time in the Bible School Department.

Pastor David Kaiser was the Dean of the Bible School. Together we worked out the courses I would be teaching. Preparing for these classes was a formidable challenge. I had always loved teaching adult Bible studies in the parish but this was normally one class a week. Preparing to teach several classes at once on a daily basis Monday to Friday was a whole new experience. I had a lot to learn.

As I got to know the teaching faculty at LCBI I gained a whole new appreciation for the training teachers receive and the professional skills they develop. As pastors we got virtually no training to develop teaching skills.

Doing lesson plans on a daily basis was new to me. It was hard work, though I found it quite enjoyable. Of course in one month I did not complete the lessons planned for the whole year. Later this would catch up with me, and I had a lot of evening work to stay ahead of things.

The Bible School was very small but that did not change the work required to prepare. Reading assignments; however, was a much smaller task than the faculty had in the high school department with much larger classes.

I had another area of new work. Doing public relations on an informal basis was a normal part of work in the parish. Now, to formally be responsible for a public relations program to connect with a broad constituency to promote LCBI and to recruit students was a whole new world for which I was not prepared.

A part of this job included publishing *The Beacon*, a monthly mailing into our constituency. On September 21, I put together a plan for the publication of *The Beacon* for the coming year. The process in those years was complicated. The content and pictures were produced at the school. The material then went to the printers with instructions for layout. After they had put together a draft, it would be checked and if necessary suggestions made for change. After changes were made it was edited a final time before going to print.

The printer was in Saskatoon. If I did all this by mail, the process was very long. The alternative was many trips back and forth (100 kms one-way) to Saskatoon. When everything was finally printed, there was another trip to pick up the five-thousand copies that still had to be addressed and mailed out.

All that I had learned about printing from my first chairman at Nelson, who was involved in commercial printing, was a particular gift that came in very handy in this new challenge.

The process was relentless. One mailing was completed and immediately you began all over again. Years later the advent of the computer and email made this process wonderfully easy in comparison. Everything but the printing could be done on site with full layout and pictures included before it was sent off for printing.

I always loved working with teenagers. LCBI was a delightful environment in which to work. Students came from across Canada. We also had a significant enrolment of students from Hong Kong. The student body was a cross-section of our communities. The majority of the students were from Lutheran backgrounds, but close to 40 percent of the student body, in those first years were non-Lutheran, and some students had no faith background. We had chapel Monday through Friday and all the staff participated. Chapel provided a daily encounter with the whole student body. The majority of our students lived in residences on campus. This added a whole new dynamic of community to the education process.

When I began work at LCBI there was one thing that seemed terribly evident. The school was in financial trouble. I could see the consequence of this in the physical plant. The buildings were badly in need of renovation and repair. It is very difficult to maintain a campus without adequate financial resources.

The same was true of the academic programs. The shortage of funds resulted in limited resources for education. It also meant that the salaries were quite minimal. This was most recognized in the teacher's salaries as they were considerably below the grid provided through the Saskatchewan Teachers' Federation. Other salaries were even worse, particularly our residence staff.

LCBI had wonderful people on staff, but among the staff there was a deep sense of frustration. Financial resources are like stored energy. It seems when an institution is short on financial resources it tends to suck the needed energy out of its people. The cost was very high on staff morale and I am certain also resulted in the loss of that fresh ability to be creative and innovative. The shortfall also limited the number of staff available and tended to remove free time that could allow for creativity. At the same time the staff worked very hard and did good work in the circumstances.

This environment of financial pressure, deteriorating facilities and staff morale problems, combined to produce a very difficult time for leadership. Upon arrival at LCBI it was clear from the beginning that the future might be difficult.

When Bev and I talked about accepting the call to LCBI we also talked about the fact that we would have to accept the possibility that the conditions at LCBI may mean our stay might be as short as one year. We knowingly took that risk when we accepted the position.

With all the uncertainties ahead, work began. My biggest struggle was in the area of public relations. I remember some of the first times I took potential students and their families on tours through our campus. In the girl's dorm (Old Main) the rooms had been painted with left-over paint in every wild combination of colours one could imagine. There was plaster falling out of the walls. It was like walking into a ghetto.

In the boy's dorm, though a much more modern building, the furniture was not only in bad repair, but was used in every possible way, sometimes a bed on end as a room divider. Drawers were missing; the carpet was damaged and dirty; and the doors in various states of disrepair. The conditions jumped at you as you walked through the campus especially when touring potential students and parents.

I was equally unimpressed with the environment of the classrooms. I saw students in one class lying on the floor during classes and there seemed to be a general lack of order.. I reminded myself that I had no previous experience in education. There had to be some way to get perspective that might help provide a better evaluation of what was happening. It certainly was a different environment than I remembered from my own high school days.

In that first year I became very frustrated. I met with the administrative staff and shared my observations and the difficulties these circumstances provided for promoting our school. If I was to do public relations, I needed something to promote. We are all at our worst when frustrated. I am sure the new guy on staff was not always a gracious presence. It was a difficult time.

I took every opportunity to speak in churches and I attended every gathering of pastors in the four western provinces that I could fit into my schedule. School displays were at every conference gathering and every Synod Convention in the four western synods. Sometimes I was given a few minutes on the floor to talk about our school. Sometimes we were just allowed to set up our display and be present. I tried to visit everyone who inquired and went to their homes if they could not come to the campus.

The major public relations event for that first year was a joint fund raising and promotional event which the Dean of the Bible Department and I put together. The Dean was a great jogger and wanted to do a major walk. We decided we could make it into a major promotion. Everyone on staff saw a need for something to happen since our enrolments were half of what they should have been and we needed a major change in fundraising.

I was reading in Exodus one day and came across the time when God's people were caught between the Red Sea and Pharaoh's armies. The circumstance seemed hopeless. Moses' message to the people was:

> *Do not fear! Stand by and see the salvation of the Lord which he will accomplish for you today . . . The Lord will fight for you while you keep silent."* And the message of God to Moses was *Why are you crying out to Me? Tell the sons of Israel to go forward" (another translation "to step forward").* (Exodus 14:13-15)

The proposed promotion we titled "Stepping Forward". We planned a 500-mile walk from Edmonton Alberta to Outlook. Every night we would do a promotion event in congregations on route. We also set out to raise pledges for each mile of the walk, as a fundraiser for the school.

Upstream Living in a Downstream World

The Dean of the Bible Department was going to do the walking. We had donations of shoes and apparel from a major sporting goods store. Another person donated the use of their motor home and we placed a large sign on the top of my little Camaro as a pilot car driven by Kevin Grant, one of our Bible School students. We asked people to pledge for every mile walked.

We drove to Edmonton and began "Stepping Forward". In the second day we learned the consequences from the combination of hot asphalt and flexing shoes. It produces heat that affects the feet. Dave's feet broke down early. Large blisters developed till he could hardly walk. Kevin and I took turns to give Dave's feet time to heal. Each evening we presented a promotional event.

We were amazed how we adapted after the first few days. The time went quickly and the miles were crossed "one step at a time". We had to extend our journey on Highway 11 south of Saskatoon to Craik and back before heading into Outlook from Keneston on Highway 15 to make the full 500 miles. For the last miles into Outlook the three of us decided to run together and were joined by the LCBI student body for the last distance from the town of Outlook to the campus.

This event was very successful. We raised $50,000 after expenses and the promotions each night began the development of a school presence in the minds of a broader constituency.

In retrospect I believe the greatest success was the therapy of walking 500 miles. How do you walk 500 miles? You take one step at a time and keep your direction. Many times I remember sitting in my office several years later reminding myself that we were on a journey. The journey often seemed hopeless, but if you kept taking one step at a time and kept direction, one would arrive at the destination. This was combined with a slogan that came out of this experience: *As God provides, so we will move.*

Student recruitment was a challenging task. The inertia of low enrolments would not change quickly. We worked at recruitment, but the results would be delayed without significant results for three years. The school was still struggling and the fall enrolments had actually got lower.

On October 18, 1984 the Board of Governors met. Boards like to be positive; however, sometimes being positive is a way to avoid facing real problems. I remember my growing frustration and asked to attend the board meeting.

I informed the board that they had some major problems that had to be dealt with if there was to be a future. I shared my observations of needs within our school from a development perspective, and some observations on the financial realities of which they were quite aware.

There was a need to address some problems. Some things had to change. One of the changes I suggested was that they terminate my position because finances were a problem. They had to cut expenses, and I was the last person hired so I had to be the first to go.

I was convinced that if they did not have the courage to terminate my position it was evidence that they were not prepared to face they had problems. If they refused to face they had problems, nothing would change, and if nothing changed I did not believe there was a future for the school.

One realizes that as human creatures we do not like to face problems. As Lutherans who hold to a theology of grace it seems strange that acknowledgment of problems should be so difficult, but we are still people. By reflex we "hide in the garden" and feel it a crime to have problems. It is even worse for us and for everyone else when we cannot address problems because there is usually a price to pay. Problems sometimes go away with time . . . and some fester and become worse.

Upstream Living in a Downstream World

Our Lutheran perspective on confession and forgiveness places us at the foot of the cross. When we can acknowledge problems, we can live with forgiveness, and be freed to move on and look for solutions to some of those problems and for new directions through which new life can follow as we move on under God's guidance.

Many times I have looked back on this time and wondered how pretentious my comments must have seemed. I admired the people I worked with and the board who were the overseers of LCBI. I also believed that there had to be changes in the light of the many problems that were growing at our school.

After my frustrated offering I asked to be excused and went home for the evening. This was a Thursday. I had to preach at Hague and Rosthern on the weekend so there was a lot to do.

On Friday morning I came to work like normal. The chairman of the Board was at the door as I entered my office. He asked if he could talk with me and we went to the staff lounge. I could tell he was disturbed.

The chairman informed me that the Board had met till three o'clock that morning. It had been a most difficult meeting, but in the end they had decided to give me the 30-day notice and that my position would be terminated. Tears were in his eyes as he told me. They were not happy with the decision, but did not know what else to do.

I assured the chairman that I was happy to hear of their decision, not because I did not want to be at LCBI but because I believed that the Board was formally recognizing that there were problems that needed to be addressed and they had shown courage in doing that. Their difficult decision gave me a new confidence for the future of the school.

This was good news. There were some personal uncertainties, but Bev and I had discussed the consequences. I was still confident that something good would come out of this for the school.

The chairman was most concerned for Bev and our family. I appreciated his concern, but I assured him that God seemed to have taken pretty good care of us over the years and He could likely handle this too.

This decision was the acknowledgment that our school had problems and it seemed important to allow that to stand. I also explained to the chairman that I had been worrying about how I was going to complete my Master's theses, and this would provide me with time. The finances would work out in some way.

We had taken a year of study leave two years earlier which had shown us that it was possible to live on less. I remember sharing with Bev what a huge dilemma this would have been if we had not taken that year for study and found we could survive.

The Board asked if I would serve as Business Manager for that last month since they had no one to do that job and they needed time to fill the position. I accepted the offer.

As Business Manager I got to see the financial matters more closely and I also became more acquainted with the problems we had with the facilities. The equipment, heating systems, and water and sewer infrastructure were in bad repair. There was need of a major overhaul at every level. This would require some serious resources.

I remember clearing my office at the end of that month. I felt guilty leaving while the rest of the administrative people and staff had to continue in the struggle. I felt strangely selfish. I was free, though there would be some issues that had to be worked out.

The consequences of the decision had a bit of a delay. We had one last paycheck, which would carry us one more month. I applied for unemployment insurance (EI) through the federal government, as this would at least put bread on the table. Bev was providing babysitting services so there was some additional income. It surprised us, but we seemed to make it through one month at a time and I went to work on my Master's theses.

Word got out and people seemed to feel sorry for us and I got a lot of preaching assignments. Unfortunately, anything they paid me had to be deducted from my EI so it did not really help much financially, but it provided many wonderful opportunities for ministry.

Two very special and unrelated events followed that first month of unemployment. The first was to preside at the wedding of a young man who had once lived with us while we were in Preeceville Parish. I had met him during the time I was visiting his grandfather in the hospital.

He had lived with us from January 1974 till the following summer. He had also attended LCBI in the years that followed and was an important part of our life. Even when we lived in British Columbia he would come and spend Christmas with us. He was working in Saskatoon and met his bride-to-be, a waitress, in a restaurant. Their wedding at Zion Lutheran Church in Saskatoon was a wonderful celebration and certainly one of the highlights of the year.

The other great gift of that time was a preaching mission the third week in November. Pastor Harold Engen served the East End and White Valley parish. The days spent in the Engen home were one of those fine memories of blessing and fellowship that I will never forget. The Engen family had spent many years as missionaries in India.

The humble life of faith that they embodied in their home was a gift that reminded me again that we live in God's constant and real care and provision. Those words Jesus so often spoke were well worth trusting, "Do not be afraid." The Engen family embodied this real and confident faith in God's continual care. Their joy in life with all its challenges was a constant inspiration.

These experiences affirmed the wealth of life that we shared even in those days of unemployment.

On a visit to the seminary during this time I spoke to a professor who wanted to assure me that I should not feel less a person for being on EI. My first thought was a question. Why would I feel less a person? I was so thankful for EI. Without it our family would have had to move the fourth time in as many years.

I thought about this for some time and began to realize we live in a society that believes our personal worth is determined by our ability to earn and provide for ourselves. No wonder people get confused when some become handicapped or retired or unemployed. We teach people that their worth comes through position and power and ability to earn, and then tell them the opposite when circumstances change.

During this time I was concerned that the circumstances in which we lived were so unfair to my family. They should not have to go through this time of drought because of me. The situation produced some difficult times, but God has graced me with a wife and family that have been so supportive. That is also a part of that richness of life and I could not escape. The reality that we were richly blessed gave deep and real reason to be overcome with gratitude even in these difficult times.

The deadline for my theses was the end of March: it was coming too fast. During this time the Board was struggling with issues at the school. They brought in an outside consultant on student recruitment and asked me to attend a meeting in Saskatoon where they continued their pursuit to find solutions to the problems they faced at LCBI.

The Board asked if I would do several important public relations events and then after the March deadline for my theses, come back full time to the end of June in recruitment. They offered to put me on a full salary beginning in February if I would agree to work till the end of the school year. This was a generous offer that I could not refuse. I hoped it would be of real benefit to the school as well. Meanwhile, I made it known that I was open for a call to a parish.

Between trips I made for the school and my struggle with circumstances around my Master's theses, the time went very quickly. I finally found it necessary to apply for an extension on my theses, something I always tried to avoid.

I went to work full time for LCBI for the rest of the academic year and during this time I was pleasantly surprised to receive a Letter of Call to serve as pastor of Bethlehem Lutheran Church in Outlook.

This seemed a wonderful God-send. To date we had moved our family in the summer of 1981 to go on study leave; and again the summer to 1982 to return to the parish in Nelson B.C.; then in the summer of 1983 we moved to Outlook to serve at LCBI. In the fall of 1984 I was unemployed and had assured our family that we would not move for at least a year. I told them that even if I had to sell shovels at Home Hardware in order to remain we would not move.

The call to be pastor in Outlook would be stability; no moving and the chance to serve a wonderful congregation.

It was a weight lifted from our lives. The day I sat down to write the letter of acceptance, I received a phone call from the chairman of the Board of Regents of LCBI. The chairman heard I had received this call and asked if I had made a decision. I told him that I had planned to write the letter of acceptance that very day.

There was a momentary silence after which he informed me that the board was looking at some possibilities that would bring some changes at LCBI but they needed time to sort out some issues. He wondered if I could hold off the decision for a week or so. I had no idea what was going on and I was not sure if it was fair to the congregation to delay our response to their call. I said I would talk to the chairman of the congregation to see if a delay would cause further problems for the parish.

Later the chairman of the Board notified me that they would like to ask me to consider a call to be President of LCBI. There were many sensitive issues around this but the grace of those involved allowed for consideration of this call.

The conflict of the two calls was difficult. The parish represented security and stability and a place where I felt some experience and a degree of confidence. The call to LCBI represented insecurity, instability and a venture into a new challenge for which I had little transferable experience. It seemed pretentious even to think of accepting this position.

Bev and I talked about the calls, and prayed about them. One day she asked me what I was thinking. I told her the call to LCBI was like being asked to step onto a sinking ship. I believed there was a year of life left in the school, maybe two with a miracle. And I asked her, "Do you really want to step on a sinking ship?"

Bev's response had that normal deep grace and thoughtfulness, "It seems the doors opened for us to come here in a way we could never have done. It seems this is where you should be. Why not give it the best you can. The worst thing that could happen is that the school closes, but life will still go on. If it survives, thank God."

Bev always could cut through the clutter and focus issues. Along with the fear of being "over one's head" was the fear of failure. My father's words came back, "You have to sort out what gifts God has given you. Then develop those gifts and find a place where you can use those gifts in a way that honours God.

In whatever you choose to do, put your best into it. If you have given your best, even if you fail at what you are doing, you never have to be ashamed."

There was great apprehension in accepting this call, but it seemed that was where we were supposed to be. Before doing anything decisive I thought it would be a good idea to meet with all the staff. I asked for a meeting where the staff would be informed of what was happening.

In meeting with the staff I wanted to outline some of the risks in this proposal. I wanted the staff to know that if I took this job I would work for some significant changes and that any time there is a movement for change there are many risks. I reminded them that nobody finds change comfortable.

I suggested to the staff that if I took this job we would work for changes in how we handled the academic program and academic disciplines. I suggested that we would work for changes in how we handled social discipline around residence life. I also told them that we would work for major changes in our facilities and how we handled our finances.

I was ever so aware that I was the new boy on the block. I was only 38 years old and many of the staff were my seniors and almost all the staff had more experience at LCBI than I had.

I assured them that they would not work very long with me before they would realize I was a highly imperfect human being. (I personally did not find that threatening, because only the Pope had to be perfect, and I was not running for Pope.) I also suggested that I would likely not work long with them till I would realize that they were imperfect as well. So I suggested that we would have to live graciously with each other and work it out together.

There were a couple key things I wanted them to think about seriously.

First I suggested that if they were not willing to take the risk of working for change, they would not want me to be President of LCBI. Secondly, I suggested the only way we would survive the risks was if we kept everything on the table, good, bad, or indifferent. Without open communication there would be no hope to work things out. If they were not prepared to keep everything on the table (good, bad, or indifferent), then they would not want me to take this job.

I asked them not to answer these questions during that meeting. They should think this over for a time, and in the next several days, come at their convenience and let me know how they felt. To complete the meeting we then discussed in more detail what changes I would propose.

Over the next several days all the staff came individually and assured me that they were willing to take the risks and would keep things on the table. They wanted me to take the position and so began a new upstream adventure.

IX. A NEW CHAPTER:
President (1985-1991).

With great apprehension I accepted the call to be President of LCBI. I remember trying to sort out all the issues that lay ahead. It was more than formidable. This new journey was filled with uncertainties. Was it pretentious to accept this task? Was the task even achievable? Was this a journey doomed to failure? In those days ahead, the promotion campaign "Stepping Forward" came back to my mind many times. How does one face the insurmountable journey? It started with that first step, and then one step at a time and the need to keep direction.

There was comfort in knowing that the call of God for His people was sometimes to step forward in the face of what seemed hopeless circumstances. The power was not in God's people, but in the One who went before them, and who was with them in the journey.

And how do we function with all our limitations? We move the same way we walked 500 miles. We walk one step at a time, waiting for God's provision and seeking his guidance to keep direction. When your feet blister, others will have to step in. When you are out of energy, you rest and go at it again another day.

I don't remember much detail of that first year. My first formal encounter with the staff was the Fall Staff Retreat held September

1-3. It was a fearful time as we worked to prepare for the soon to arrive student body. I tried to outline some of the vision and goals I saw for the future and we set out to organize ourselves for the coming year.

I was still trying to learn the basics of administration and thankful for the many opportunities I had in the past to serve on various boards of the church and in the community. I discovered I had gained some transferable knowledge for this new administrative work, yet I still had so much to learn.

When I look at my daybook for that first year, the schedule was very full. We hired personnel to cover the following positions: a new director of public relations, a bookkeeper, and a person in charge of student recruitment. Our new bookkeeper was a tremendous help in the formal area of bookkeeping. She was skilled in an area about which I knew very little.

Working with our staff we set in motion a process to develop a new structure for operations with departments and department heads. We designed the financial chart of accounts along the lines of the organizational structure and set up procedures for budgeting and for budget controls.

This process was refined over several years and later incorporated into a formal *Staff Policy Manual.* Over the years the staff became very skilled and professional in their involvement in program planning, budgeting and carrying out their plans. Of course there was never enough money for all their wants, and there was always a little tension with each new change and development plans that came with the years.

The systems we were able to put in place produced a keen awareness of what was happening and allowed us to target the adjustments that were necessary to stabilize the financial realities of our operation. We began looking for resources to upgrade the facility and infrastructure. We had major work to do on heating systems, new windows, and a deteriorating sewage system and general repairs and upkeep. There were many spaces in the facility that needed to be reworked and the campus itself was a parched ground in the summer that barely supported grass.

On the learning curve I remember a visit with the manager of the bank who handled our financial needs. The manager asked me to provide a cash flow of our school's operations.

I did not want him to know that I had no idea what a cash flow was so, I returned to my office, sat in my chair, and spent some time in deep thought. What was cash flow? I thought through our financial statements. Income, and expenses . . . some months negative, some with surpluses . . . finally the picture of cash flow seemed clear. I checked my conclusions with our bookkeeper (I could have begun there, but pride is a strange thing).

In the end I produced a program that calculated our cash flow automatically with a few minor adjustments each year. This was a wonderful tool that worked well with minor adjustments for many years.

While working on the school's needs, there was also work to do on our private finances. We had been fortunate to have an interest-free loan during the first years of home ownership. In the third year, interest rates had dropped so we could afford a regular mortgage through the bank. So, as not to presume on the generosity of the interest-free loan, we took out a mortgage and paid off the balance of the personal loan.

We were so thankful for this gracious act of kindness. It seemed we should have done more in appreciation. This generosity had made it possible for us to purchase the home in the first place. It was good to be able to finally afford to be on our own and able to share our home ownership with the bank. Our overall mortgage had been significantly depleted in the meantime. This would become more important for us later.

Daniel A. Haugen

The pressures of the years of struggle had left the staff deeply discouraged. They wanted to hope, but daily encountered challenges that could become overwhelming.

Our enrolments had come up to 100 students that first year, but a number of the students struggled with many life issues. From my perspective the general lack of discipline over the years had not provided a stable base to work from and this made it even more difficult to deal with students who struggled.

We wanted reverence in chapel, but seemed to do everything to create irreverence; sometimes standing on the pews singing action songs, and tweaking cheeks (though not certain which cheeks to tweak). There was a general thought that one needed a lot of "raw raw" to keep students interested.

I had seen this in many Bible Camps over the years and seemed to observe that youth are not afraid to be serious at times. My philosophy was let's play when we play, work when we work, worship when we worship and try to enjoy the difference. I was not very successful in convincing others to experiment with this until much later. We had our struggles together as we wrestled with change, and where we should go with change.

We had half a million dollars of accumulated debt on our books. An even greater liability existed in the depleted salaries of staff and the liabilities of deferred maintenance of our facilities. Operating budgets demanded a high level of donation support and capital funding was non-existent. We had a great need for people who would provide financial resources over and above our basic operational needs.

This was the time when computers were in the early stages of development and LCBI had to begin this transition to assist in reaching our constituency. Computers provided a new resource that made many tasks more achievable though there was a lot of work to get set up for it.

First we had to enter all our documented data on alumni and donors into a database. This was a massive task for our secretary who did not like the transition to computers though she valiantly set to work on it. Our records were not very complete and up to date so there was a huge amount of information gathering necessary in the process.

We wanted to find more personal ways to take care of our donors. We had normally accumulated the receipts for donations over the whole year before sending them out. We decided that we would work to have a maximum of one week before a letter of acknowledgment would be sent along with each receipt for gifts received. This allowed for more personal contact. I signed every letter, and would also often write notes to people in our constituency. That correspondence expanded over the years and took formidable time.

The advent of computers provided new ability to print our own receipts and at the same time build our database of supporters. From this database we could merge letters and maintain regular communication. Each step made it easier to communicate in ways we simply could not do before the age of computers.

Though we were in trouble, people stood with us. I often thought this a miracle in itself. Something we did not do was to seek ways to convince people that everything was wonderful. We freely acknowledged our problems and requested people's patience, prayers and support. We had to address one thing at a time. Our motto became more defined in our day-to-day reality, "as God provides, so we will move". Our task was to be stewards of every gift, to the best of our ability, and to use these gifts to work and respond to the long term needs of our school so that we could provide our church with a dynamic and strong place of Christian education that met the needs of our students.

By the spring of that first year we began looking for blueprints for Old Main. This facility was in great disrepair from years of strained budgets and making do. In March of that year we found a government program that assisted us to hire students for the summer months. We set out to hire eight students and began a plan to work to upgrade and clean up our campus and facilities.

In April of 1986 our principal resigned to take a position at Camrose Lutheran College. This was a huge loss. Our principal's knowledge and expertise were my security blanket. He was the source of knowledge for our academic program about which I knew very little. He was also a model for administration, much my superior but a wonderful mentor.

We set up a search for a new principal. By fall we had retained the service of Mr. Arlin Ryan who had extensive experience in education.

Pressure was on to recruit more students while we worked to make the facilities and campus more serviceable and provide a better working environment for the staff and a better environment for the students. We had to continue to seek creative ways to complete the work needed with limited financial resources.

In the fall of 1986 we encountered a major operational crisis. We were running to the maximum in our line of credit before the school year began. The fall spike in revenue through the student fees barely filled the financial hole from the summer months. What little was leftover was consumed in operating costs with the beginning of the school year.

To compound our problems, the Department of Education decided (for the first time) not to pay any of our operating grant until November. This created a major cash flow problem. By the end of September we had again maxed our line of credit: there was no money for October's payroll.

The staff at LCBI was still suffering from the years of struggle. They had a lot on their plates. I did not have the heart to tell them that there was no way we could make the October payroll. This was a very lonely time. We needed $50,000 in 30 days. Where were we going to find $50,000?

The Dead Sea and pharaoh came back into my mind. And those words to Moses, "Tell the people to step forward." I had quite a few discussions with God that seemed pretty one-sided.

I was not a fundraiser, but I had to try to do something. I informed God that for me to be a fundraiser was like asking someone who is tone deaf to be a choir director. I thought God had a rare sense of humour to suggest this was my task.

I had to do something. So I thought of people I knew and identified some people I might go see who could help. I booked a ticket to Calgary, Alberta, and then to Kelowna and then Vancouver in British Columbia.

I chose not to buy cancellation insurance since I was sure I would find an excuse to cancel if the option was available. I reminded God (as if God needed reminding) that this was going to take a miracle. I am sure he was tired of hearing the frantic call of the floundering president/now fundraiser. The time waiting was a nightmare of apprehension.

The day before departure I was in a certain city having dinner with a person I knew quite well. We often got together. I don't really know what we talked about. I was just deeply in need to visit someone in this lonely time. As I was getting up to leave this person, in the spur of the moment suggested he should send a check back to the school and might as well give it to me. He pulled out his check-book wrote on it and slid the check across the table.

I had never seen a check for $50,000. I was completely overwhelmed. I then told him of the dilemma of our finances and the payroll crisis. He smiled and assured me that we should use it where most needed. He was delighted to help out.

I am sure I sputtered like the fool I felt I was. How do you adequately say thank you? And how do you adequately apologize to God for the nagging and panic of the last weeks? And how do you get out of a trip for which you bought no cancellation insurance? It did not seem right to simply waste that much of the schools money. I was trapped. I still had to go.

I learned something in that experience. We often say that God will provide. We just have trouble to believe that this is more than a slogan. Over time I became convinced that this is a reality over which we do not need to be in control. It is the heart of the Good News that God loves us sinners:

> *Therefore I tell you, do not worry about your life, what you will eat or drink; or about your body, what you will wear. Is not life more important than food, and the body more important than clothes? Look at the birds of the air; they do not sow or reap or store away in barns, and yet your heavenly Father feeds them. Are you not much more valuable than they? Who of you by worrying can add a single hour to his life?"* (Matt. 6:25-27)

I knew this in my mind. I began to realize this was much more than words. There would likely be less gray if we could always rest in this certainty. I have found, even after my fretting, it keeps proving to be true.

I left the next day on the journey of terror. I had no idea what to do. I knew the school had a need and I simply asked some people if they had the ability or the desire to be a part of the work of our school through their financial support.

Upstream Living in a Downstream World

I did make one contact with a society that had a $500,000 surplus they had to give away since they were a non-profit and had finished their project with this surprise surplus.

I felt guilty suggesting that they might consider giving this total surplus for the support of LCBI, so I suggested that they might consider splitting it between LCBI and Camrose Lutheran College (another college of our church in Alberta). In retrospect I felt guilty that I had not included Luther College, another of our church schools.

This turned out to be a wonderful visit. Later we got word that they had decided to give the total amount as a 50/50 shared gift between LCBI and Camrose Lutheran College. It would be distributed in the spring.

This was exciting news for our small school. This was likely the largest financial gift we had ever been offered.

Beyond this visit, I think we received enough to pay for my airline ticket. At least it did not cost the school for me to take this trip. I smiled but chocked it up to education.

And that large gift . . . well, it had been invested in a company that by spring went bankrupt. About $70,000 was salvaged and given to LCBI and Camrose Lutheran College. We received approximately $35,000 each.

An old saying of my father came to mind . . . "Don't count your chickens before they are hatched." (In my last days at LCBI I should have remembered this simple wisdom.)

When we received this additional gift in the spring we encountered new challenges and with it more education. How should this gift be used? Should it be used for badly needed furnishings in the residence? Should it be used for classroom equipment and resources? Should it be used to upgrade transportation for students since the old vans were really not dependable and therefore not safe? Should it be used to upgrade low salaries? Should it be used to reduce debt? Depending where you stood, the needs were different because everyone had different priorities.

This experience was the first introduction to the thought that every issue has at least six sides. If you haven't seen at least six sides you likely haven't seen the issue. No matter what decision in the end was made, from someone's perspective it would be wrong. So, how do you decide? All the needs were real. One could not meet them all.

It became clear that in administration you have to learn to understand the many sides to every issue and respect where people are coming from even when you cannot satisfy everyone. Of course one would wish that the staff could also understand this, but that seldom happens for any of us.

This is not to discredit staff. One has to respect that the focus of their responsibilities did not always allow them to see with the same clarity the many dimensions of the whole school operation.

This confirmed the need to operate with the administrative process we had developed which helped us discuss issues from a broader perspective and at the same time with sensitivity to the needs of all departments.

Mr. Ryan had helped move our education program forward. When he was ready to retire we were fortunate to have a gifted teacher who was hired for this position, Mr. Gerald Langner. This teacher was well known in our constituency for his wonderful work in choral music through the concert choir that he directed and took on tour each year. He continued the work of bringing changes into the academic program and helped in shaping the character of our school.

To try to keep some balance in administrative decisions, we had formed an Administrative Committee made up of the principal, Dean of Campus Life, and the chaplain. As president I chaired this committee and chose not to have a vote unless there was need to break tied votes. We met weekly. I was also the business manager so I brought information from that side of our operation.

This committee made all the day-to-day operational decisions that were passed on to departments and brought a broader perspective to administrative decisions. We could at least view more sides of issues. It was more difficult to make decisions, but I believe we made better decisions. It also gave the key departments of our school a direct input into key decisions that affected the front lines of our work.

I attended department meetings only if requested. Each department had their guidelines and the department heads worked with their staff to carry out their programs. The department heads reported to the Administration Committee and shared in the decision making process.

The committee filled another need. The president was required to be away from the campus to keep in touch with the church we served, with the Department of Education in Regina, with alumni and congregations of our church and with those who gave financial support to our school. The role as business manager compounded the time away.

Before the development of the Administrative Committee, I could not be away for a day without a number of calls waiting for me wherever I went. As the Administrative Committee developed over the years I could be away for much longer times and there was no need to call. When I was away the Administrative Committee functioned with the principal as chair and decisions were made and recorded in the minutes. This committee became very skilled over the years and ran the school well in the absence of the president.

We were fortunate to have a very committed Board of Regents who also opened doors for us. One of our board members found a federal government program that changed our campus. Through this program we hired people on EI. As a part of this program we could top up their EI benefits to provide reasonable salaries to our workers. We hired a foreman who would oversee the work. The president/business manager would oversee the projects and handle the purchasing.

We used this program over several years. The first project was the renovation of the chapel. We also did major renovations to the girls' and boys' residences. By accessing this and other government programs, over the next several years we were able to do approximately $800,000 in major renovations to the campus usually finding three dollars of government grants for every dollar we spent.

We had good resources in other friends of the school who brought expertise in many other areas and trades.

In 1986 the Board made the difficult decision to close the Bible School Department. The Bible School was very small and was highly subsidized by the high school. The new management philosophy of that era in business was to downsize for efficiency. Our program was not only expensive, but also very weak with very few students. Now this was not in itself a reason to discontinue a program for it could also have been a good reason to strengthen the program.

In the discussions with faculty and staff and with the Board of Directors of LCBI and people throughout our constituency, it was observed that the Canadian Lutheran Bible Institute in Camrose was struggling for students. If we encouraged our students to attend CLBI, it would strengthen their program. Their program was a considerably broader program than we could offer. At the same time it allowed us to pour our energy into providing a stronger high school program and to include a stronger component of Christian education. It was a case of seeking to narrow our focus in order to do a better job and a means to direct more resources to achieve these goals. There were also significant financial benefits to help stabilize our operation.

Enrolments continued to grow. By 1990 we had 130 students in our high school and concurrently the Board became involved in a serious strategic planning process. LCBI was beginning to look beyond survival: this was a healthy milepost in the journey that seemed so hopeless in the beginning.

In the first years as president I also had the opportunity to teach the Grade 11 Christian Ethics Course. This was a wonderful challenge. I usually had around 30 students in this class. I had chosen a book by George Forell titled **Ethics of Decision** for this class.

It took some time to find an approach that served this diverse group of students. They were all in grade 11 but that was the only common ground one had. The students were about 50 percent from Lutheran backgrounds, and the rest from a broad spectrum of church backgrounds, but a significant group had never seen a Bible let alone read one. These students were indeed a broad cross-section of our culture. I also came to realize how much they were a product of the culture.

I had one series of questions I asked each class every year, "Why do you want to get a good education?"

Every year the answer was the same, "So I can get a good job."

My second question, "Why do you want to get a good job?"

"So I can make a good living."

And the third question, "Why do want to make a good living?" Their answer, "So I can have a good life."

I marvelled that it was the same every year. In these years I read everything I could that came from the Department of Education. It was always interesting to see the connection between the goals of education and a prospering economy. We were teaching these students well.

Forell emphasized that one of the qualities of adult life was the necessity to make decisions. He suggested that one needs values to weigh issues in order to make decisions. His big question was, "From where do you get your values?"

I had a particularly large class the year we had the most students and likely the most struggles with students. I shared information with them from a study I had read. This study was on the socialization process of youth. One of the study's conclusions was that 90 percent of the socialization process of youth came through television and peers, and 10 percent was shared through home, church and school (traditionally the primary institutions in the socialization process).

I suggested to the students that if this were true, there was likely a television show that would best represent the values of the culture in which we lived and as such would be the best parable expression of our society. I asked what that would be. (Remember, this was in the late 1980s.)

The students responded immediately, "*Dallas.*" (Some will remember the series.)

I asked why the television series *Dallas* was the best parable expression of our society.

Their answer, "Big acreages, beautiful houses, Lamborghinis and Maseratis, macho guys and beautiful girls." They felt this was pretty attractive.

Then I asked them what they saw in the social life of *Dallas*. The response was immediate, "That's hell."

I then asked if what they call "hell" might be the consequences of the transference of that value system into the day-to-day decisions of life.

What followed I will never forget. For the rest of the period I watched these grade 11 students take the mask off our culture in a way that I could have never done.

In another class as we continued the discussion on the socialization process that was shaped primarily by television and peers; a student from Edmonton replied, "What do you expect? I never see my parents. All I have left is television and peers."

I asked the student why she thought this was happening. She said, "They are doing what is most important for them . . . making money, they don't have time for me."

I asked her if she thought her parents were abandoning her intentionally. She did not think so, but she said, "They are doing this so I can get a good education, so I can make a good living . . ." and did not finish the statement. You could have heard a pin drop and in the minds of the students; I believe there was a ring of truth.

I think we all began to learn something that day.

A couple years later I was asked to speak at an event in Vancouver, British Columbia. The topic was *Christian Nurture in Our Society*. Following the last presentation, a professor from Simon Fraser University talked with me. He said, "That was the most intriguing presentation I have ever heard. Where did you get your information?"

I smiled and told him, "My grade 11 students taught me."

It was true. The material I had used came from those experiences with teenagers as I sought to walk the teaching of Jesus into the real world in which these young people had been nurtured. The thoughts of the scripture were quite different and nurtured some very different thoughts, which over time became even more convincing.

Jesus' pedagogy was powerful and freeing. I always told the students "Don't you dare swallow everything I have to say, and feel free to question it. I would not teach it if I did not believe it to be true. My goal is to put some things into your brain basket. But I want you to sort it out, take it into the middle of your life and test it out. If in the end you consider it of no value . . . deposit it into the appropriate container. If you find it to be real . . . take it into life. God does not need me to defend him. And I will bet you will find that he understands us, and our world better than we could ever do on our own."

I had to quit teaching. There was just too much to do and I had to be away so often it did not seem fair to the students, but I missed this time so much.

The Director of Education had to supervise my teaching since I was on a temporary teaching certificate with the Department of Education. He sat in on several classes and looked at different assignments. When his evaluations were complete he came to my office to share his observations, "Do you realize you are teaching these grade 11 students at a first year university level?"

I chuckled and did not reply. Then he observed that these students had no problem handling it and were doing amazing work. I must say I was proud of these students. It seemed if I could provide them with some tools, they could do some amazing things.

At LCBI we dealt with so many aspects of student life. We still had to work for a new approach to guide how we dealt with students who struggled. When I first came to LCBI, it had been quite a standard practice to expel students with some ease. I was concerned about this. If the Gospel is about God's love for sinners and the work of redemption, then it seemed to me that the goal of a Christian school was to get seriously involved in that work of redemption. Simply kicking out students with problems seemed to be a strange way to live out the gospel.

As we pushed to walk further with students on a redemptive path, we seemed to believe that secular counsellors were more equipped to help the students than we were. This often excused us from getting involved. There was tension as faculty and staff looked for a workable environment with students in crisis. Expulsion always remained a last resort, but where that boundary should be was the subject of much debate.

I think there is a lot to learn from those who work outside the community of faith as professional counsellors. I also believe that our Christian heritage provides a rich resource that reaches much deeper into human lives and has a lot to bring to the redemptive process through the gospel we teach and live. We have something that would also greatly enrich the thought world of secular counsellors.

Over the years I tried to impress upon our staff that each expulsion was a declaration of our failure. If our goal was to help students flourish in life and faith, and that goal was not achieved, then it was fair to also accept that we had failed to achieve our goal. It was a more humble perspective, but it took away the enthusiasm to have students expelled.

However, sometimes expulsion was necessary. I always wanted students to know that this was not a punishment but a "punctuation" that they had some issues in which we had failed to help them find workable solutions and that for their sake they still had to deal with these matters. They had to go home and with their parents or guardians, seek help to work out these matters. I also assured them that our staff would continue to hold them in our prayers and that having dealt with things, we wanted them back. This approach was a bit "upstream" and could be very challenging.

As we worked through the issues, all discipline up to and including short term suspensions were turned over to the departments concerned. The High School Department handled academic discipline and Campus Life handled the social disciplines. Should there be recommendations for expulsion; the departments after having followed their own processes to their limits would write a recommendation to the Administrative Committee who would approve the recommendation, and if not, would themselves become involved in seeking remedial action.

Each department developed their own policies and these policies were then printed in the *Student Handbook*. Each year there were revisions and each year that approximating business which sought ways to handle the work of the school and care for students struggled with its limitations and wrote and revised policies as we learned together.

I remember the first student expelled and later accepted back as a student at LCBI. This student was a clinical alcoholic in grade 10. We had managed to get him through grade 10, though his marks were minimal. He came back for grade 11. The decision to accept him back had not been very popular and before the Christmas break it was evident that the student still had to deal with his problems and we had failed. The student had to be asked to go home and deal with his alcoholism.

The next summer a rumour ran on campus that this student was planning again to apply. A number of faculty members came to my office to express their unhappiness and wanted assurance that this would not happen.

I assured them that if a student applied they would have the right to an interview if the Administrative Committee decided there might be basis for evaluation. If the student was accepted, through the processes we had in place, then we would ask them for their support of that decision and work to care for the student.

The feared event happened. The student came on opening day and had an interview: he was accepted back. The decision almost resulted in a small mutiny. The good news was that the student did well in grade 11. He came back and graduated, and went on to a Lutheran college for undergraduate work.

Several years later I got an email from this student. He was married with a family and was beginning his studies in law. He wrote that he did not even want to imagine where he could have been if our school had not hung in with him. He concluded that email with these words, "Keep hanging in with kids."

Sometimes we were successful, and sometimes with our best efforts we did not succeed in helping students find a way to function in our community. When students struggled it demanded a lot out of our staff.

How does one balance the care of one student over the needs of the other students? Of course a parable comes to mind. There was a Good Shepherd who left the 99 sheep to search for one sheep that he had lost (Matthew 18:12-14). This was upstream thinking that stretched us.

The following year, 1990, was the celebration of the 75'th anniversary of the opening of Outlook College. In the fall Rev. Dr. George Evenson was retained to write the school's history. Dr. Evenson had been the President from 1939 when the school reopened after the Great Depression as a Bible School, until 1951.

Dr. Evenson lived with us during this time and spent considerable time on campus. In the time he was with us I am sure he got to know every one of our students and all the staff. Dr. Evenson's presence during this time was a gift to our campus and was a personal inspiration.

Beginning the new academic year 1990-91, I was exhausted. We had journeyed through many renovation projects, and some staff transitions. The struggle to develop new skills to handle student issues was coming and overall, we were experiencing some new glimmers of hope. We had bolstered our student recruitment by hiring an excellent person who worked in recruitment and public relations. We saw significant results.

As numbers were growing, so were the pressures on the staff. We were also involved in residence renovations during the school year. This resulted in a very strained environment for our students, but seemed the only way we could improve our facilities and still operate.

Major sewage problems dominated the opening of school and caused great disruption on our campus that fall. I spent many evenings in the trenches digging out and laying new sewage lines with our new maintenance staff.

Maintenance could be a lonely position on our campus. One wanted to do whatever was possible to lend some support. In this same time the renovation projects also brought tensions between our maintenance staff and the workers on the renovations to Old Main. This circumstance escalated already existing problems and pressures that finally got out of hand.

There were other currents at the time that, in my naive way, I was not aware of. By the spring of 1991 I made it known to the Board that I was exhausted and if I was to continue I would need to take a leave of absence. The Board was very affirming and offered me anything I needed. I was not aware of any major concerns.

A month later the regular spring board meeting was held on the same weekend as graduation. I was tired. The board meeting began on a Friday and as we approached the supper hour, the chairman of the board observed that I looked tired. He suggested I should go home for supper and rest for the remainder of the evening since the Board had nothing particularly pressing on the agenda.

I appreciated the consideration. As I was leaving, the Bishop asked if he could use the phone in my office to make a call to let people know he would be later than planned. I took him to my office to use the phone.

While in my office the Bishop informed me with a rather passing comment that there were some people who thought I should not be at LCBI. I assured him I was certain that this was true as it is of any people who hold different positions in the church. Nobody works beyond criticism. I went home for supper and a quiet evening.

As I spent the evening at home, I waited up since the chairman of the board was going to stay in our home that night. As the hour got later, my naive mind returned to the Bishop's comment. Something began to stir my awareness that indeed something must be going on.

The board meeting continued early that next day. It was Saturday and graduation weekend. The first item on the agenda was the announcement by the chair that the board had decided to terminate my position as president of LCBI at the end of the academic year. What I remember after that was a blur.

Lightning out of clear sky would not have been more shocking. I told myself to sit quietly and say nothing. Maybe by the end of the chair's comments I would understand.

Finally the chairman turned the floor over to me for comments. There was not much to say. I told them that only a month before they had suggested that they could not afford to lose me, but something had obviously happened in the interim that I had not been privileged to be a part of. I did not know why this decision was made, but I informed them that at this point that was academic. They had terminated my position. I wanted them to know that I accepted their decision and would not challenge the decision.

I did want to know in writing the reasons for this decision for my own peace of mind. I assured them that they would not need to fear any formal or legal action for the decision. I also suggested that the Board should not announce this decision until after the weekend, because graduation was the highest celebration of our school and should not be overshadowed with this news.

On the other hand, come Monday I expected the Board to announce it to our staff, since it was not my decision but theirs. I also asked that I be allowed to share this news in confidence with my family at noon since I did not want them to find out after the fact. This having been resolved we continued with the regular agenda.

X. FIRED:
And The Aftermath (1991-2002).

This was a strange experience. From my perspective the purpose of our school and its business in Christian education was really important. Therefore one could continue with the meeting even after the announcement. My mind was on a rollercoaster. I had been there for eight years.

I went home for lunch. This was our son David's graduation weekend and we all sat in the living room with a buffet lunch. I had told Bev what had happened before the family gathered.

I shared with the family that I had been fired that morning. The personalities of our three children reacted immediately. Tim was instantly upset; sensitive David bled internally; and Amanda just seemed to take it in stride as she did everything. The support of our three children was incredible.

I assured the family that everything would be all right. God had taken care of us over the years so much better than we could ever ask, and He would take care of us again. So, I suggested to our family that for this weekend we were going to just celebrate David's grad. A day at a time and we would see where the road led. Most important, we could know that we are never alone and life would go on.

My father's words came back again, "If you have given your best, even if you fail at what you are doing, you never have to be ashamed." I knew I had given this job the best I had. I am sure others could have done it better, but I had given this job everything I could.

In looking back I have caught glimpses of how exhausted I really was. I am sure I was in no condition to be the parent I should have been. Our children were all in their teens. We had a wonderful relationship, but I am sure they saw that their dad was under awful pressure. And I can only imagine the burden this was for Bev. The whole family was an amazing support.

On Saturday night we had the graduation banquet and I don't remember a lot about the evening program; although, I do remember standing on the sidewalk by the office and classroom building later on that evening. I looked across the campus envisioning where things were eight years earlier and recalling in my mind some of the things we had achieved in program and facility. I felt quite satisfied. I knew there was still a long way to go for LCBI to be the school I felt it could be, but we had come a long way.

As I stood there our oldest son came out of the chapel. He saw me in the distance and came straight to where I stood. His words were an incredible gift, "Dad, quit worrying about it. You know you have done a good job. Everyone else knows you have done a good job. If the Board does not know, that is their problem."

The words meant a lot, but even more to have your 20-year old son take such initiative to come to support his dad was the greatest gift of all. The Board had shared their decision with the chaplain and principal that Saturday. The chaplain and principal came to the house to see me in the afternoon. They were shocked by the decision and offered support.

The chaplain asked if I would like to have him take over my responsibilities in chairing the grad exercises the next day. I thanked him for that and spent the day as "Dad" for our son who was graduating.

On Sunday morning I was mystified by the changing emotions from quiet satisfaction to deep despair. It was difficult to understand how quickly one's emotions could change. I needed some help to keep perspective and I did not want to end this time with bitterness.

So, I called my good friend who was president of Augustana University College in Camrose, Alberta. I began the conversation with these words "A funny thing happened to me on the way to work yesterday. I was fired."

It took a while to convince him of the reality. I told him that I had accepted the decision and did not want anyone to work to change the decision, but I needed someone to do two things for me. First, in the chaos I was experiencing I needed someone to help me keep perspective, because when one has lost all orientation the best decisions one makes can be dumb as a sack of hammers.

Secondly, I needed someone who would help me come out of this without bitterness because life was too good to be trapped in that way. I remembered another situation where a person who had gone through a similar situation could never escape that bitterness.

I appreciated his support. A week later he drove from Camrose and spent the day with Bev and myself. There was nothing particularly significant in what was said. We just spent the day together. He took us out for dinner. That simple act of friendship meant so much to both of us.

Monday morning after graduation weekend, I went to work with a deluge of thoughts. As I thought about what had happened

I became convinced that the best thing I could do was leave immediately. I was afraid that I could do so many things (which unintentionally) could make things worse for the school. I also felt that I had to get out so the Board could take responsibility for their decision and get things in place for the future well-being of the school. As yet, the rest of the staff did not know what had happened.

I calculated the days of holidays I had coming. I was several days short of the termination date of June 30 and I decided those days would be my sick leave.

I asked the chaplain and the principal to meet in my office and I explained to them why I felt I should leave immediately, being ever so aware of my confusion and the difficulty to function without the danger of causing more problems. And secondly I felt the board needed me gone so that they could take responsibility for this decision to prepare for the future. I was concerned that my suggestion would put added pressure on the Administrative Committee, but I was confident they could handle it.

We discussed the circumstances and in the end, the principal and chaplain agreed this was a good decision. Given our administrative structure there was no perceived problem for the day-to-day operation since the administrative committee was familiar with running the school in my absence.

I rose from my chair; shook the hand of the principal and announced that he was acting president. I shook the hand of the chaplain and informed him that he was the president's advisor. And as for me, I was going fishing.

I called two of my brothers who had also gone through some difficult circumstances at the same time. We set up a fishing trip for the following week.

In the meantime, I received a call from the chairman who suggested they might have made a mistake and wanted to put the decision on hold. I was upset. I informed him that the decision stood. That decision had to be in the minutes, and my acceptance of the decision better be in the minutes and if it was not then they were in trouble.

My reaction was strange. It was spontaneous, but I believe that behind this reaction was the fear that it would remove the only thing that anchored me and gave me a fixed point that gave orientation to my life. I was finished. If that was taken away I was totally adrift. I clutched by reflex to this, my only certainty and anchor in the circumstance.

In the following weeks life was wild and confusing. The Board finally called in an evaluation team. They spent three days on campus interviewing staff and others as they attempted to find out what had happened and to evaluate what had been done. After this process was complete the committee came to our house to show me what they had concluded. The report was generally affirming, though it also included criticisms of the president. They asked me what I thought.

I read the report carefully. I was impressed with the frankness and accuracy. As to the personal criticisms, I assured them that there were times I was not happy with the way I handled things so I was not surprised that there were legitimate concerns. When frustrated, none of us function at our best. Sometimes we are frustrated because of false expectations. Sometimes frustration is caused by an inability to address problems effectively. Whatever the reasons for frustration, one thing is certain, at those times we are not at our best.

On the whole I was amazed at the thoroughness of the evaluation. The committee concluded that there was ultimately no good reason for the decision that was made. They recommended a severance package or that the president should be rehired. They also suggested that should the president be rehired, there be a significant increase in salary and benefits. The Board evaluated the report. After the evaluation, the chairman suggested to me that they wished to reverse the decision.

I did not believe this was a good idea for them or for me. It seemed that if there was any possibility of proceeding from this point it had to be through clear decisions. If the Board wanted me back they had to look at it carefully and make it a clear decision of the Board. If I was to accept any proposal, it had to be by a clear decision from me as well. There seemed to be far too much risk to try to continue without some clearly thought through decisions. I also informed the chair that it would take a miracle for me to accept any offer, but I lived in a world of miracles and I supposed that could happen too.

In the end, the board voted to offer me the position of president and business manager. This was a difficult offer to consider. Bev and I talked and prayed about it at great length and after some time, she informed me that I should continue to think and pray about it: and whatever I decided she was with me.

A week later she asked how the decision-making was coming. I informed her that it was not going well. So, as only Bev could do, she clarified the issues by asking, "So, is the work less important than it was before?" Her silence demanded an answer.

I replied, "No, I guess it is just as important."

Then she asked a second question, "Do you feel less called to this work than you did before?"

"No, I guess I don't."

"So, what is the problem, is it pride?"

"You bet your life it is!" And then the two of us laughed until it seemed silly. When we were done laughing pride set in again and I said, "But I am not going back till someone talks to me."

I arranged for a meeting with the chairman of the board in Saskatoon. The conversation was most gracious and deeply appreciated. Shortly after this meeting I informed the Board that I would accept the call.

The end of that academic year had many tensions. The staff and students gathered for the regular awards' night celebration. We all gathered in the campus chapel for the ceremony. Bev and I felt very special with our graduating son sitting with us.

The graduating class gave out cards to the staff. When I opened up mine, no one had signed the card. I smiled and put it in my pocket.

Our son leaned over in consternation, "Dad, nobody signed it."

I quietly suggested it was okay.

Later, when the evening was over, our son pulled back my suit jacket, reached in, took the card and left. The next day he came and gave me the card. He had got seventeen grads to sign it.

I was in tears. To have a son with such courage and compassion for his father overwhelmed me. I thanked him and marvelled again at how rich life could be.

A student later came and told me he had never seen such courage as our son had shown. The students were still struggling with all that had happened.

One faculty member, upset with the board's decision, chose to resign. He made the announcement in the middle of his chapel presentation. I had been delayed in my office because of a phone call and some staff members came back to inform me of the uproar that had happened in chapel that day and the accusations. This staff member was well loved by many students. Several staff members assured me it was fortunate I had not been in attendance.

I found out later that this same faculty member had taken his attacks into the classroom for a number of months before all this happened. Many students became upset with the president. They were friends with our son. My son had sat through this without mentioning it to me. When I found this out I took him aside and reminded him that he should not blame the students for what adults had done, and that he should still feel free to be their friends.

Of course that was easier for a father to suggest than it was for him to do. I think this was the first time I experienced anger in its worst form. This anger was mixed with regret. Why should my son be put through this by an adult who should know better, and why should he have to endure this experience because of his father? This was the greatest burden of the whole experience.

The experience left its scars. I was surprised that by reflex I drew back from the open abandon I once had with both staff and students. I became much more distant than I had ever been. I always loved being close to teenagers. Out of respect for the dislike of so many, I felt the need to give them some distance so they could freely continue their lives. They were still fine students and deserved respect. I never did recover the close relationships I had once enjoyed with young people. Maybe part of that was also the process of aging, but I would like to think it was not.

It was also difficult to have friends outside the school who were quite convinced by this discontented staff member that something was amiss. The destructive nature of gossip ceased to be theory. It was real.

The Board and a representative of the national church offices thought there should be a written submission to the Canada Lutheran (the national publication of our church) as a means to control some of the damage done. In discussion on this matter I suggested it be brief and to the point. In the end we would be judged, not by our defence but by how we fulfilled our calling to provide the church with the best quality Christian education we could provide. It seemed the more defence; the more one would cultivate doubt. Maybe it was similar to what William Shakespeare penned in Hamlet, *The lady doth protest too much, methinks.*

Life had to go on. We had work to do and that work was still important for the lives of our youth and the care of our staff. We finished the year, but not without further consequences. With the confusion at the school our donations stopped. We ended the year with a deficit; and we began the new academic year with a huge drop in student enrolment. Many students shared the confusion of the time and did not come back. We should have cut staff to balance our budget, but after all the confusion it would have been viewed as vindictive. The fact was, we had staff who were more skilled working with young people than they even realized and the school could not afford to lose them. We made a conscious decision to run a large deficit so we did not have to cut staff.

The net result of this incident on our operating budget was the loss in excess of a quarter of a million dollars, between the loss of donations and the following year deficit caused by the drop in enrolments. It took some disciplines to set resentment aside and keep the focus on the ministry we had to the students and the care of our staff. The focus was a source of freedom.

The summer of 1992 was the worst summer of my life. The financial crisis was overwhelming. How could we meet the demands of the bank and assure that we were not going to run both students and faculty into a dead end? There was work to be done to project our needs for the coming year. I worked out the most realistic budget I could with projections we could make for the coming year. The results were difficult, but clear. We had to refinance $320,000 of the operating deficit we would incur.. We assured the bank we would pay the interest and 10 percent of the initial balance on an annual basis for 10 years and assure them of a balanced budget. They had to commit to stay with the school for a full academic year since students and staff could not be abandoned mid-year. If they could not we would have to close the school. I laid out the realities on the bank manager's desk. The cash flow for the year was also graphed and a red line drawn through showing the deficit we had to cover with borrowed money. I suggested we needed an answer within two weeks. Two weeks later I got a call to meet with our bank manager: they agreed to the proposal and assured us they were with us for the whole year.

By September 30, 1992 we had to submit our enrolment numbers to the Department of Education in order to apply for the operating grant we would receive from the government. We worked on the revised budget. There was no way we could find to balance the budget unless we cut two staff members . . . or cut the president.

There seemed to be no other option. We could not cut the frontline people. What mattered was what happened through our ministry of Christian education offered to our students. This was the frontline business we could not compromise. I recommended to our Administrative Committee that the president take a leave of absence without pay.

The Administrative Committee considered the proposal. In the end they saw no other option but to accept my recommendation in order to balance the budget. Bev and I had talked this over and felt it was possible for us to live with this decision. Besides, I was very tired and needed a break.

The recommendation went to the board and with reluctance the board agreed to the proposal. Because of the structure we had with our Administrative Committee, the school would run well. I assured both board and staff that I would drop by and try to give support as much as possible.

My leave of absence began with my health breaking down. I was overcome with severe abdominal pain that left me helpless and bed ridden. The days ahead were filled with tests and visits to doctors that ended in the diagnosis that I had Irritable Bowel Syndrome (IBS) which, I was informed was stress related and chronic. I had to learn to live with it for the rest of my life.

Knowing what it was seemed to help and I returned to my time of leisure. I went up to the school several times a week to see what was happening and to give support any way I could. My leave of absence put some stress on our personal finances. With our limited income, we decided to refinance the house as the mortgage came due. This gave us some financial space to survive.

I had always wanted to get my pilot's licence. I had a brother who got me interested and had taught me a lot about flying. You can borrow money, but you can't borrow time. I now had time, so I signed up in Saskatoon for flying lessons.

I wondered if my Clergy Continuing Education money could be drawn on for this venture. One does not know if one does not ask. So I applied for this fund held in my name in Winnipeg. My application was deemed "professional development" and the fund was provided in full. I did not have to borrow any money after all, and soon I was travelling to Saskatoon to learn how to fly.

I also got involved with four other people and began a new company in Wynyard, Saskatchewan. Much of our time was spent developing the business plan, renovating the offices and working with the four partners to equip and open a machine shop. We also built a small plant to produce liquid ammonium sulphate; an adjuvant used with herbicides. I found this a rather enjoyable enterprise, though it took me away from home for some time.

In the meantime, things were turning around at the school. With strong support from our constituency and stabilizing finances, by spring 1993 the Board suggested I should come back to work and shorten the planned leave of absence.

Daniel A. Haugen

I returned to LCBI in the spring of 1993. The pressure was off and life was good. That same spring I found what seemed like a good deal on an airplane located at Moosamin, in eastern Saskatchewan. My brother flew me over to have a look. It looked like a good purchase. I phoned the bank manager and arranged for a line of credit. He told me to come in the next working day and we would fill out the papers. I wrote a check and flew it home.

That trip home was a memorable experience. Once airborne I looked out at the wings and the earth below. This was freedom. I remember suggesting to God that I was a rather spoiled pastor to have this privilege. As I flew home I floated above the Earth, and got a broader perspective. The world seemed at once smaller but the context was so much larger. The first article of the Apostle's Creed came to mind.

Floating in this massive universe, the ball below was the product of God's crafting. That world below was an environment designed for that crown of creation, people. I remember looking down and thinking . . . there is a farm, I wonder if they know that they are living on the face of God's world and that same God deeply loves people? Then a small town or a city passed below and I saw people, gathered together to form a community on the face of God's world. When you have worked with people, you know that from the outside one does not begin to understand what happens inside those homes and places of work. Life issues seemed to fit into a larger context and at once became more focused as well.

Even the work at the school took on new perspective. Ministry was all about loving God who created it all, and loving people who walked and lived daily on the face of God's world. Loving people was not a simple equation. Sometimes love moved hearts to respond with generosity as undeserved kindness. Sometimes kindness was saying "No". Sometimes kindness required that issues be confronted to seek something redemptive. Jesus even called us to love our enemies. Now that was a radical upstream thought. It was no longer theory. On the face of that world in which we lived, was I prepared to do that?

There were many circumstances that had been a part of the crisis of 1991 and most of that had found some resolve. But, the faculty member who had such difficulty with the president had not finished his attacks when he left the school. This former faculty member continued to write letters to politicians, church leaders and individuals within the constituency. I received copies of some of these letters from the board chair. I was told I should take legal action for defamation but I was not interested. It seemed to me that this person needed help more than there was need for litigation. I was always disappointed that no one seemed to get involved to help him sort out the issues. Did no one care about him? Justice is so much easier than reconciliation, because justice does not have to care.

On the other hand, was there anything I could do? I finally wrote a letter and tried to assure this person that I held no grudge for what he had done and was continuing to do. I also suggested that whether he knew it or not, he was wrong and that I wished he could find someone who could help him sort out the issues. I assured him that I did not find his accusations a threat but I was concerned that he would do more harm to himself than he would do to me. I also assured him I would continue to pray for him and that one day, I hoped we could find a basis for reconciliation. After this letter I felt I had done what I could do and life had to go on.

The years that followed were intense - but delightful. We immediately set plans in place for a total renovation of the area under the chapel to convert it into a large student centre with canteen, recreation areas and lounge. What made this project particularly satisfying was that the Student Representative Council (SRC) took on the cost of this project. Our faculty advisor to the SRC had produced an entrepreneurial spirit in our SRC. They ran the canteen on campus and vending machines and found many creative ways to raise funds. It was amazing to see.

I remember some of the frustrations we encountered to meet deadlines on this renovation. One day I came out in my suit and the workers were having trouble with the jackhammer we had rented. They had to cut a door size hole in the foundation that was poured in the 1950s. Apparently there was no shortage of cement back then. After half a day there was only a small hole into the very thick wall. The workers had not used a jackhammer before.

I remember taking off my sport coat and tie. I picked up the jackhammer and did not set it down till the rough door opening was complete an hour later. It felt good to do some hands on stuff. It was not very good for the pants and dress shirt, but they dusted off quite well. I put my tie and my sport coat back on and went back to the office for the rest of the day. I am sure my wife would not have approved. I must admit, I don't remember telling her when I got home either. There was likely some reason.

The student centre was a wonderful addition. This "campus living room" provided space where the students could socialize, play games, watch TV and enjoy the fellowship of our campus. With time students from the Outlook community found a welcome place to gather and shared the fellowship of our school and we saw more day students applying. We had to be careful with this since we did not want to cultivate tensions between the public high school in town and LCBI since we had a growing relationship that was mutually enriching. The added students helped our enrolments; provided a new dynamic to the ministry of our school; and built a broader and deeper fellowship within the local community.

We also made plans to build a new classroom facility, which we needed so badly. We received a very generous estate that provided a significant resource to set in motion a fundraising appeal to complete this project.

Watching the staff work together with our architect in a wonderful process to plan this facility was a fascinating time. Here again, the corporate gifts of architect and staff crafted a plan for a facility that tied together our existing classroom complex and the existing gymnasium. This total renewal of our instructional space was completed with much celebration and thanksgiving. The day of dedication this new and renewed facility was paid for in full.

At this same time, we began a private Internet service company in the town of Outlook. A number of businesses in town got involved to form a company in order to provide Internet services. LCBI was one of the partners. This allowed our school to be on-line some years before the phone company and others provided a broader coverage. Forming this joint internet service was an interesting new experience and affirmed our relationship with the business community.

LCBI also joined the Chamber of Commerce in this time. The Chamber had been struggling. We worked with the local business community in order to renew the local Outlook and District Chamber of Commerce. In the years that followed, I served a number of years on the Chamber executive, and as president of the chamber for five years.

I remember attending a provincial Chamber convention in Estevan, Saskatchewan. At first I asked myself, "Preacher, what are you doing here?" The longer I was there the more comfortable I became. I met many business people who had a strong Christian faith and we talked about the relationship between business and the task of being stewards of the resources God provides in our communities. We talked of how business can be a means through which one can honour God and care for people as various goods and services are provided, and people are employed.

How do we use the resources in our communities to care for the lives of our people? This was Christian stewardship. This was a part of the calling of God that was to be guided by our love for God and our love for people. The purpose of stewardship was not just accumulation for the sake of accumulation. The resources we worked with were resources for life lived in community and equipment we could use to serve others.

I enjoyed this involvement and I wondered how we could bring some dimensions of these thoughts into our education program. I talked with one member of the community about bringing the Junior Achievement Program into our school. Pressures of other demands seemed to crowd it out and we never proceeded.

There was also a need for a new airport in town. There were three aircraft owners at the time, but a growing itinerant traffic with oil pipeline activity in the area and new demands in aerial spray application was created by a growing potato industry. We worked together with the town to build a new 3000 ft. turf runway with a terminal building and automatic runway lights.

I am sure this was one of the best turf runways of its kind in Western Canada. Part of this was due to the soil we had to work with. With a slight crown on the runway, there was little problem with the strip due to rain or those times of the season when there was melting snow. The grasses we used stood up well to the climate and provided a wonderful cover. The town gave us good support to maintain it year round, with snow removal in the winter and grass cutting in the summer.

LCBI worked with all the private schools in Saskatchewan as we tried to form a common organization of private schools.

The Saskatchewan Association of Independent High Schools was formed in late 1995. This was the first time such an organization functioned on behalf of all independent schools in Saskatchewan. I served several years on the executive committee of this organization and as president of the association. The diversity of the schools in this association and the existence of several other organizations that represented some of the schools had already made it difficult to work with a common voice. Overall it was still an important time for all our schools as it broadened perspectives on what was happening in private schools. The information helped soften some of the prejudices we all shared.

At the same time I served on the executive of the Federation of Independent Schools in Canada. It was helpful to be in these organizations to learn what was happening in other parts of our country. This helped bring context to issues we worked with in our own province.

The Board of Regents had instructed me to be involved with the annual gathering of the Lutheran Educators Conference of North America. This conference brought together the chief executives of all the Lutheran University Colleges and Seminaries in North America. Every second year this conference was held in Washington D.C. In the between years, it was held in numerous American cities and was hosted twice in Canada at Banff, Alberta and Vancouver, British Columbia. Bev and I felt privileged to attend and became acquainted with many of our Lutheran educational institutions over the years.

At one of these conferences held in Washington D.C. we were given a tour of the Capitol by the chaplain who was also a Lutheran pastor. He took us into areas of the Capitol few ever got to see.

One of the most significant memories of this trip was a comment the chaplain made. The chaplain played racket ball with President George Bush Sr. on a regular basis. He spent his time working with politicians of every stripe. He observed that when one gets to know elected officials personally, regardless of political persuasion, he found people who generally had far more depth and character than that which was portrayed through the media. He said that when you know these people personally, and see the image portrayed in the media, there is seldom a similarity.

His words seemed an important reminder that we need to be much more careful in the superficial judgments we impose on public officials. Since that event, I have often thought about this need for caution. I think I also needed this counsel especially when dealing with concerns related to church leadership. I hope I am learning from it.

Prejudice is the shortcut to conclusions, which is uninhibited when there is little or no information. The media can manipulate this very well. Information often produces a much more complex picture and good information is sometimes difficult to attain. One begins to think that organizations have a real need to provide accessible information to provide an avenue to explore the ill informed prejudices that can grow like mushrooms when there is no light. The best way to maintain prejudice is "not to know" and the best way to perpetuate it is "not to inform".

The conference of Lutheran educators, though a wonderful experience, finally became so expensive that we decided it was not a good use of our school's money. It appeared that the major colleges and seminaries in the United States operated on a much different budget.

A new adventure came in 1997. I responded to a communication from the ELCIC requesting someone with a background in Old Testament study to be a resource for the Lutheran Church in Colombia, South America. Each year they held a continuing education program for their clergy and lay leaders in Bogota, Colombia.

I did not consider myself very qualified, but saw little harm in applying since this challenge had strong interest for me. I had earned an academic masters degree in Old Testament some years before and I hoped I might have something to offer. Sometimes one wades in and is stretched by the adventure. It was a surprise to be chosen and invited to participate in a two-week education event in Bogota.

The church in Colombia requested lectures on two topics: *Torah for Today* and in the afternoons to provide presentations on youth ministry. These presentations were given over the two-week schedule from Monday to Friday when the Lutheran Church in Colombia brought all their pastors and lay leaders to Bogota for this annual education event.

This was a formidable challenge and another time in my life when I wondered if I was going in over my head. It was difficult to find preparation time with all the business of the school going full speed. Bev and I finally packed up a box of books and took some holiday time at our recreational condominium by Lake Diefenbaker, less than an hour's drive from Outlook. We had bought this as a retreat place some years before. This was also the time Bev was working on a course on drugs for her return to work as a nurse at the hospital in our community.

We had a wonderful week, each of us in our own world of books. I got my research completed, but had a lot of the final preparation to complete after arriving in Bogota. We both studied Spanish at the University of Saskatchewan in Saskatoon in preparation for this trip. We were far from fluent, but we found later that we would have been very lost without this time to become somewhat familiar with the language.

We were wonderfully cared for by the Lutheran Church in Colombia. The first Sunday we worshiped in a Lutheran Church served by an American pastor. The service was in Spanish. We followed along, and joined in the singing as best we could.

The contrast between wealth and poverty struck us. The pastors often talked about the struggle they had with this reality. Issues of "justice" were strong in the Lutheran Church of Colombia. In the meeting room at the church offices "justico" and "derecher" dominated the posters.

The Lutheran Church of Colombia is a small church. At that time it had less than three thousand members. They had an active Christian education program and sought to build schools along with their congregations. While in Colombia, the president of the Lutheran Church in Colombia took a Saturday to help wheel cement as they were building an addition onto one of their schools. It was obvious that this man saw Christian education as a primary need for their people and for their church leaders. There was a passion for ministry that was inspiring and fresh.

On the weekends our interpreter took us into the countryside to visit a number of communities. One weekend we drove down the mountain from Bogota to attend a women's retreat held in a facility much like some of our bible camps. The setting was beautiful and though everything was conducted in Spanish, we felt the fellowship and the grace in this community of faith.

Our interpreter took us on another weekend day trip. He informed us it was very dangerous for North Americans to visit the countryside since hostage takings were too common; however, he also said we had come too far not to get to see their country. During our time in Colombia, we visited a number of villages and walked the village squares and saw many Catholic churches. We were always graciously welcomed.

In one community they were holding a Vacation Bible School in a large Catholic church. Groups of children were gathered around numerous lay people who were teaching them in the sanctuary. We felt quite at home. It reminded me of our own childhood experiences at Vacation Bible School.

One of the most striking experiences of this trip was a visit to a theme park just out of Bogota. A wealthy citizen, as a gift, built this theme park for the people of Colombia. He wanted to provide a place where everyone could come to a place of peace. There were shops of every kind, restaurants and rides for adults and children alike.

In this theme park also stood a sculpture of a massive hand rising from the centre of the park, and in that hand was held an even larger globe of the world. In the midst of the poverty, conflict and the destructive realities of political conflicts, stood this reminder of the One who holds this world in his hand. In the crisis of the drug trade, conflict of armies, and the many struggles to find the basics of life this park was indeed a place of sanctuary.

The testimony that rose from the centre of this park reminded me again of the first article of the Apostles Creed and the wonderful message of the Gospel of Jesus. One could almost hear in the background:

> *For God so loved the world that he gave his one and only Son, that whoever believes in him shall not perish but have eternal life. For God did not send his Son into the world to condemn the world, but to save the world through him.* (John 3:16-17)

It brought me back to the cross in the corner of my office. This world that is the product of God's mind is still loved by God. God loves this world so much that Christ would die so people could live. The need to hear this message and to find in it that new and life-giving change of direction for living was as real in Colombia as it is around the world.

There were more adventures ahead. In the spring of 1998 I remembered a man who came to LCBI from Australia in 1966 when I was in Bible School. He was a pastor from Australia who came to North America to study what was happening in Lutheran education. He looked for new ideas to take back into the ever-growing Lutheran education system in Australia.

I decided to search the Internet to see if I could find the person responsible for the Lutheran education system in Australia. I sent him an email introducing LCBI and myself. I asked if he knew this pastor who had visited Canada and explained the encounter we had in 1966.

His response was immediate and affirmative. At the same time the Director of Education informed me that he was coming to Canada in July and wondered if we could meet. He would be in Edmonton about the time we had planned some holidays at a retreat place in the foothills of Alberta a short distance north west of Pincher Creek.

We arranged to meet the Australian Director of Education in Calgary on July 3. We had a wonderful dinner together and learned more about the Lutheran education system in Australia. When our visit was completed, I could not help but want to learn more about the Lutheran schools in Australia.

After he returned to Adelaide, I received another surprise. In the fall of 1998 I received a formal invitation to attend an International Lutheran Educational Conference that was to be held on the Gold Coast of Australia from September 26 to September 30, 1999. He also offered to arrange a tour for me of Lutheran Schools in Australia following the conference.

In conversation with the board of directors of LCBI, I arranged to use some of my study time to make a three-week visit to Australia in the fall of 1999 in order to attend the International Lutheran Education Conference and to visit some schools. This was also a wonderful opportunity to visit some district offices, and also the national offices of the Lutheran Church in Australia that were located in Adelaide.

On September 22 I departed for Australia via Hong Kong. Since I had to overnight in Hong Kong I arranged to meet with several Hong Kong alumni of the Lutheran Collegiate Bible Institute. One of our alumni members was now operating a business in Hong Kong. He met me at the airport and took me by rapid transit to downtown Hong Kong where we met my sister-in-law's brother who worked in a bank nearby. I stayed in their home that night.

In the morning I met with another alumnus who took me on a tour of Hong Kong that included several Lutheran educational institutions including a seminary and a high school.

We travelled on the Star Ferry, which crossed the Victoria Harbour from Hong Kong to the Island of KowLoon. This ferry has been in operation for over 100 years.

Then we took the tram to the top of The Peak, from which one can view the coastline of Hong Kong. We also, quite by chance, stopped in at the offices of a Lutheran organization involved in Mainland China. We stumbled on this place quite by accident. We had the address, but on arriving there was no indication on this walled facility of what kind of a place this was. We rang the bell at the gate, explained who we were and were admitted. It was indeed a Lutheran mission, but even after our visit it remained a bit of a mystery.

At noon my tour guide's sister joined us at the Peking Restaurant where they provided me with a wonderful dinner.

She had also graduated from LCBI and was now working for her father's engineering firm. One of their company's projects was a contract for the rapid transit system I had travelled on from the new airport in Hong Kong.

Finally, in the evening they invited me to attend a Chinese Moon Festival at their grandparent's home. This was a Buddhist festival. There were over twenty family members including children. What a fascinating evening with a glimpse into the family life of another culture. Since there were only three of us who understood English, it was difficult to communicate but the universal language of children playing and the pride in the parents' eyes said these lives were special.

I had a midnight flight from Hong Kong to Brisbane. The two sisters insisted they drive me to the airport. It was good to experience the far-reaching fellowship of our school and the wealth of life it nurtured.

The flight out of Hong Kong was late because of mechanical problems with the aircraft. I remember waking up briefly as we flew over Indonesia, and then I slept soundly until we were well down the east coast of Australia before landing in Brisbane.

The International Lutheran Educators Conference was a wonderful introduction to Lutheran education in many parts of the world. There were representatives from Australia, Indonesia, New Guinea, the United States, Hong Kong and Europe. This was the first time I came to realize how many Lutheran churches around the world have viewed the need for Christian education. These churches were very serious about developing their mission in Christian education. The event concluded with an International Lutheran Leaders Day when there was an exchange of vision and information on Lutheran schools around the world.

I could not help but wonder even more why we in Canada struggled to find support from our own Church leaders in

Christian education when it seemed to be such a central part of so many Lutheran Churches around the world. That mystery continues to this day.

After the conference I began my tour of Australia. I toured many Lutheran schools around Brisbane and spent some time with a number of school principals. The enthusiasm for Christian education and its role in the life of the church was infectious.

While in Brisbane I spent a day in the Queensland District Offices of the Lutheran Church of Australia where I interviewed many church staff throughout the day. I was intrigued by the broad use of lay people in leadership positions within the church offices. This seemed to be a common characteristic of the Lutheran Church of Australia.

I took a bus two hours inland from Brisbane to Toowoomba in order to tour Concordia College. After this tour the chaplain drove me another two hours inland to a bush camp where Concordia College offered a fascinating outdoor education program. All the students were required to spend several weeks at this bush camp as a part of their Christian education. They were also taught other subjects and trained in survival skills.

From Toowoomba I returned to Brisbane for my flight to Adelaide. While in Adelaide I met the President of the Lutheran Church of Australia and spent some time in their church offices meeting and interviewing people to learn more about their church in Australia.

One of the practices of the Lutheran Church in Australia was to attach congregations to their schools. The families represented in their schools became an expanding part of the focus for their ministry.

I returned to the church offices for a tour of a number of schools in the Adelaide area. One of the interesting new schools was in a new city that was still being built. The Lutheran Church was developing a Lutheran school located on a new university campus in this new city. The school was designed like a shopping mall, with a major anchor building at one end currently occupied with offices and classrooms. The next stages of development would create classrooms spread out like a shopping centre from this main building and would end on a huge new chapel complex that would serve as chapel for the school and as a worship centre for a new congregation in this university community.

From there we went into the Bourassa Valley, a major vineyard and wine production area of Australia where the Lutheran Church had several large educational institutions.

In one school they had a huge auditorium where they gather their school body for worship, and also where they hosted major concerts and conventions. This commercial enterprise was set up to generate significant profits that were put back into their education program.

The innovation and dynamic ministry of Christian education in Australia was striking to experience. All this, was growing in a church that was about the same size as our Evangelical Lutheran Church in Canada. We often have thought we are too small to do much. This experience reminded me that it is likely time we "step forward".

My wife had a cousin just out of Adelaide so her husband picked me up at the national church offices after my first day of interviews and I spent the weekend in their home. Her husband drove a Fiat Spider convertible that was reworked for racing. As we were walking to the car he tossed me his keys and said, "You drive."

With right hand steering, and left hand gearshift there were some adjustments: and that was the easy part. Driving on the right hand side of the road and navigating Australian "roundabouts" (traffic circles) demanded careful thought to know where to go and what to watch for. It all went well, and driving up the mountain with those winding roads was an inspiration for a closet race car driver.

During the weekend I was able to do a few tourist things. I also met a number of other relatives and had a refreshing break from a heavy schedule.

I departed Adelaide October 13 for Hong Kong. I had not booked accommodation for that night and the cheapest room I could get was about CAD$400. I decided to pass on that idea. At that price I would likely not sleep anyway. I slept in the airport that night with my daypack as a pillow and my legs hung over the arm rest in a public seating area. When I awoke all the floors were scrubbed around me, yet I had heard nothing.

My departure was not until eleven o'clock so I had lots of time to meet people in the airport. I spent a good deal of time visiting with some people I met from Vietnam and Pakistan. Their stories were interesting and I almost hated to leave for home.

I arrived in Saskatoon shortly after two o'clock in the afternoon. My own airplane was at the airport, so I loaded the plane and flew home to Outlook and finished the day at the office. I felt rested and delighted to be home. The memories of Australia continued to linger in my mind and their excitement about Christian education was inspiring. For a small church they had ventured into an impressive array of ministries.

I have thought about that experience ever since. In conversations with the Director of Education and other church leaders in Australia something became strikingly evident to me. This church used the gifts of its people and used education to add knowledge for the use of those gifts. I was reminded that people's gifts would never develop if leadership does not use the gifts that are there. As people use their gifts, their gifts and knowledge develop and they keep on producing. No one begins with excellence. You start where you are and excellence grows from the learning and the use of our gifts.

Years later I was speaking with a former president of one of our church schools in Canada who was a member of the congregation I was serving, and he said, "Dan when you began your work at LCBI and when I began at Luther College, did we know what we were doing? Of course we didn't. But over the years we were allowed to work and to learn and when we were done, we at least knew a lot more than we did when we began and developed some of our abilities more than we would have if no one allowed us the chance."

I wondered if we have not lost so many gifts in the people of our church because we do not want to give people the chance to grow by allowing them to take on new challenges for which they might have wonderful gifts. I am confident we have as many gifts in our Evangelical Lutheran Church in Canada as I saw in the Lutheran Church of Australia. Maybe we live with a lack of excellence, because we do not give people opportunity to learn by doing, which is an important part of education.

Of course, this is also a reminder to pastors and congregations. The "priesthood of all believers" also will not develop unless they have opportunity to use their gifts and abilities in the work of the church. How do we help people discover their gifts? How do we step back and let them develop those gifts even if for a time someone else might be able to do it better?

Plunging back into the work at LCBI was fun. We had struggled with finances for years and cherished the partial funding we received for our Saskatchewan based students from the Government of Saskatchewan. In the spring of 1999, quite by accident at a meeting of the Saskatchewan Association of Historical High Schools, we discovered that two of the eight schools in our organization had been fully funded by the government since the early 1960s. This had been a secret arrangement that on an annual basis was masked with the assurance that all the Historical High Schools were treated the same. The new information was a shock. How to deal with this new information was a challenge.

We did not want to lose the good relationship with the provincial Department of Education, but there was a need for some correction of this secret historical inequity.

In October of 1999 I put together a brief for the Minister of Education. For several years LCBI had become an Associate School with the Outlook School Division. This provided a major new source of revenue since we received the full cost of education grant for all of our Saskatchewan students through this arrangement.

LCBI and Rosthern Junior College (a Mennonite school in Rosthern, Saskatchewan) always had a very close relationship over the years. RJC did not have the opportunity to be an Associate School as we did and so did not receive the same funding as we received. Our fees for Saskatchewan students were much lower than they could afford. It was good for us. It was not as good for them and it did not seem fair.

I asked the principal if he would be able to join me for a meeting with the Minister of Education at which time I wanted to present a brief and also articulate the concern for the inequity of their circumstance. We were now drawing students from their school since our fees were necessarily lower because of our funding arrangement. His presence at the meeting would give some added reality to the presentation.

The Minister of Education agreed to meet with us. I presented the brief and we discussed the growing inequity throughout the Historical High Schools and punctuated it with the circumstances of our two institutions to give it reality. The Minister seemed to hear us. We had no idea what the outcome would be.

Daniel A. Haugen

In the spring of 2000 the Department sent a letter informing us that all the Historical High Schools would receive the full cost of education grant for all Saskatchewan Students on the rolls as of September 30 of each year. This was a total surprise that we celebrated. Few believed we would ever see this day.

There had been others meeting with the Minister of Education at the same time. Who deserves credit for this milestone? I frankly think it makes no difference at all. Remember, it is not about us. There is a need for Christian education and that is the reason we work. What really matters is that this new reality made our schools more stable. We do best to simply give the government credit for making this happen.

The year had been very full. A friend of ours had planned a three-week trip to Hawaii with members of their family. Because of circumstances the family members were not able to go so they asked us to come along. We spent a week in Maui, a week on the Big Island and a week on Kawai. This was a wonderful occasion, with lots of beach time, some golfing and just doing tourist things. My health was not good and the rest was needed. Bev and I celebrated our thirty-first anniversary in Hawaii with a wonderful supper on a roof top restaurant where we could watch the tour boats and a wonderful sunset over the ocean.

There was a lot on my plate in 1999. I was still very active in the local Chamber of Commerce and I was still working with the Organization of Independent High Schools in Saskatchewan. It was becoming more evident as time went on that it was difficult to bring together this independent group of educators. They represented very different perspectives in education and also operated under other umbrella groups that maintained a separate course of action and communication. These differences deflected them from a committed involvement to this fledgling organization.

I was also the treasurer for the Kinasao Board of Directors of our Lutheran Bible Camp at Christopher Lake. I also had a soft spot for the old log building that was on the property when it was purchased in 1939. The building had need of major renovation, yet it seemed a good setting to provide office space for our camp directors. The Board agreed. We were fortunate to have an architect who always put together excellent plans for any facility. His plan for this building provided a wonderful addition to the camp and made for a much healthier working situation for the camp director and staff.

This was also the year our principal Tony Peter retired. He was a wonderful principal. I had known this man since my first parish. He was the principal in Rama, Saskatchewan when he joined our congregation in Buchanan in the mid 1970s. I had tried to get him to LCBI on several occasions. He brought a wonderful professional ability and experience to our school and a deep faith that he shared with students and staff.

As one person of experience stepped out, we were able to hire one of our teachers who had not had experience as a principal but had taught with us for some years. Phil Guebert began his time as principal in the fall of 1999 and brought an array of gifts to the position and a lot of energy. I think he found the job quite a transition from teaching in the classroom but he was equal to the task.

With changes in board members there was a time again of growing pains. I remember experiencing a push and pull with the new board in a number of areas. It seemed there was an uncertainty of the relationship between the board and myself. I finally invited the new board chair to my office to raise the concern.

I assured the chair that I was not interested in a power struggle. We had an important service in Christian education to offer youth and we had some very gifted staff to care for. We had to find a way to work together. The chair informed me that there were some people in the constituency who thought I was an autocratic leader.

I replied, "I am certain that is true. But the real question is what do you think? You see, if you think I am an autocratic leader then I expect you to come into my office and help me through some changes. But if you do not think that I am an autocratic leader then it would be at least supportive, if you would let those people out there know what you believe to be true."

I then encouraged the chair to take some time for evaluation. I asked him to take time to talk to students and staff and others. After doing the evaluation I hoped he would come and let me know what he decided and deal with the circumstance accordingly. In the meantime, we had to get to work and together care for the students and staff and lay foundations for the future development of our school.

From that day on I found working with the new chair a most gracious experience. We sorted out some of the issues we had to deal with and got into new strategic planning. The gymnasium was painted in July of 1999 and we were again looking to the future.

We still had a continuing discontent with the issue of how to deal with struggling students. There was a growing impatience. The thought prevailed that students should simply be sent home if there were problems. This issue always seemed to flare up from time to time. I always felt the staff did not realize how good a job they did with students and the gift they were in their work with those who struggled.

This issue took on more focus a year later. Just before Christmas in 2000 Bev and I attended the Barn Playhouse north of Saskatoon for a dinner theatre. We did not know anyone and sat across from a man at dinner that had been a social worker in Saskatoon his entire working career.

When he found that I was from LCBI he commented, "You must feel privileged!" He went on to explain that over the years he had watched so many young people from Saskatoon who had gone to LCBI with many difficulties in life. He told how he saw these young people come back totally changed.

He said he had worked in social services for his whole career. He distributed money, manipulated some psychology but in all his years he said they were never able to change a life. He was amazed at the success of our school.

It was difficult for the staff to step back far enough to see how successful they were in their care of students. I brought this message back to our staff and they did not seem able to take the compliment seriously. Yet they were likely some of the most skilled and caring people I have ever met in youth ministry.

The staff seemed to struggle with their professional relationships though I expect that is common wherever gifted people serve with high commitment in a small staff. Everyone in a small staff can get to know each other extremely well. They get to know each other's strengths, but they also see each other's weaknesses. I became convinced that it takes more skill and professional discipline to function in a small, highly gifted and committed staff than in larger institutions.

Sometimes I believe we also had problems because our staff did not have a broad enough experience in other public schools to keep perspective. Too often the staff felt that their lives were totally different from that of any other school. I am certain there were differences, but we also had much in common. And in some sides of this many-sided issue, we likely had opportunities public school teachers never have.

Daniel A. Haugen

Students are people wherever you find them; but one difference might have been that we got to know students better because of residential life. We had to provide a broader spectrum of care. In part, we had a parenting role. Of course that is also part of the reason the program was sometimes more challenging, and also why it was so successful.

I remember a certain grade 12 student that struggled with us. I got word that he had a set of keys belonging to the school. I invited him to my office and told him I had reason to believe he had keys that did not belong to him.

He denied having any keys, so I told him I was concerned because I heard he had keys, but since he told me he didn't have keys I would have to accept that. What was most important was he knew the truth and we would leave it at that. He left my office.

About one o'clock the next morning I woke up and could not sleep. I do not like accusing people on hearsay. I also wanted to clear this issue for his sake and for the safety of everyone. He would not keep the keys in his room since the residence staff might check. In that case, where are they?

I omit a part of this story to protect the guilty (me) but I did find the keys ... so we pick up the story the next morning. After staff devotions I invited him to my office and asked him if he liked to play poker. He looked a bit confused but said he did and I offered to play one hand with him. If he won, he stayed in our school, and if he lost he packed his bags.

I asked if he still wanted to play. He was confused, but agreed. He asked how we played. I explained, "I am going to ask you one question. If you lie to me, you pack your bags. If you tell me the truth, you stay." He would have to consider if I was bluffing. I cautioned him that I was serious, and wanted him to answer carefully.

I asked him if he was ready to play. He agreed. So I asked, "Do you have any keys that belong to LCBI?" And again I cautioned him to answer carefully.

I felt a little bit evil. He struggled. Through his eyes you could almost see the questions flashing through his mind . . . "He knows? He doesn't know? He's bluffing . . . or not?"

Finally he answered, "Yes, I have."

I was so relieved. I really did not want to lose this student. I thanked him for being honest and let him know that I really wanted him to stay and discover that one can live with honesty. I also suggested that he should not sign his name in a locked space and date it. That is kind of an official confession. (I had found his name quite by accident one day while checking some items stored in a locked area.) I assured him he was forgiven and we were glad he was one of our students. Plus, I hoped he would learn to live honestly.

When we were done, I shared with the student my confession and I placed all his keys on the table between us. I apologized for how I had gotten the keys and asked for his forgiveness. He forgave me. We shook hands and he returned to being one of our students. I hope it helped him explore some new direction.

Residence life provided the need and the opportunity to deal with much more than the formal program of education. We also had the task of helping students deal with life outside the formal program.

A young female student came to my office one day. She was having a difficult time with life. Her life style was totally destructive. I asked her how she could so abuse this wonderful gift of life God had given her.

She looked at me with all seriousness and said, "Pastor Dan, life has no value, and so what is the big deal if you trash it?"

I asked her how she could say that.

Her response was sobering. She said she felt like a recreational vehicle, used and abused and thrown away on the garbage dump with other used vehicles. Her life style of promiscuity had taken away all sense of human value, and the reflex response simply accepted the road and accelerated it.

I pointed her to the cross in the corner of my office. That cross was a reminder that every life has value in God's eyes, and her life (in God's eyes) was also worth dying for so she could live. God's forgiveness offered a new beginning, and the holiness of life gave her a new treasure to care for in herself and others. She seemed to find new hope.

There was a similar circumstance with another student who had experienced horrible abuse. We visited and talked about a lot of things. I always wanted our students to remember the cross. Forgiveness is the only freedom from the past. It is a gift we receive in the gospel because God has a deep love for us and gives us new beginnings. I met her twenty some years later; married with a family. When she saw me, she ran up and gave me a big hug. She talked about how life was becoming good again and then she said, "It began the first day I stopped in your office."

There are hundreds of those stories I could share, but they are personal and just a normal part of the business of ministry where one sees the power of the gospel and the instruction of God's Word and the work of God's Spirit that has the power to reach where human wisdom cannot reach, and to bring healing and new life where nothing else can.

We had so many students whose lives were rich and full. Maybe 8 to twelve percent of our student body would have severe struggles at times. They needed to see models that encouraged them to believe that life could be holy and good. They needed life support people. If you have lived all your life in a destructive environment, it is hard to believe that life can be good. When some students saw examples of flourishing life, they often were convinced it was not real, because it was so far out of their life experience.

Over the years I remember many students who came with the same question "Pastor Dan, why do I love it here and I hate it here?"

I suggested that they like the benefits of being followers of Jesus where life is holy and cared for . . . but the human heart seems to fight with the source of that life which is Jesus. Something in the human heart wants to do everything "my way" and we pay the price as we fight this losing battle.

One will always find the consequences when we go "downstream". The longer one works with people, the more those consequences seem quite predictable.

By the end of 2000 I was feeling so much healthier, but the fatigue from the years was starting to grow deep though my family was more aware of this than me. A job interview just out of Minneapolis in 2000 started some thought about the possibility of moving on. My wife's comment one day also made me think. She said, "At one time you were the most patient man I have ever known . . . now you are not."

The '90s was likely the most difficult time we had in our personal lives. We journeyed through the crisis of our school; from the struggles of 1991 to the wonderful celebrations of a new era of hope and anticipation of the future for our school. Woven through this same time our personal lives seemed to face one difficult time after another.

In 1992 we took a leave of absence in order to balance the budget. With this leave also came health problems. For a time I could not get out of bed for pain. These problems made any physical activity difficult. Every step walking was painful. I could not bend over to pick something off the floor without going to my knees. When we did the survey for the new airport, I could not walk between survey stakes.

The turbulence of 1991 continued with strained friendships. People who were treasured friends got caught in a lot of gossip and the struggles of some who were not happy with me as president. I saw wedges being driven into relationships. There was a deep sense of loss. I worked to find ways to accept the circumstances and respect the doubts that some nurtured. I still respected those who drew back and tried to allow the space that they seemed more comfortable with. It was still freeing to remember, that the ministry of the school was not about us. The work and ministry of our school and the nurture of our students in life and faith was the real priority.

In the summer of 1993 my father died. Bev and I were on vacation at our condominium on Diefenbaker Lake when he took a bad turn in his health. We went to be with Mom while Dad was in the hospital. He died very shortly after we got there. It was a hard time, but in many ways a holy time with mom.

Dad's funeral was a time of wonderful worship as our whole family gathered. As a family we requested that the service be a time of worship and thanksgiving to God. The days that followed for Mom were naturally difficult and we all lived so far away. But by God's grace mom walked those lonely days and we shared as many days as we could with her whenever we could visit. There was a deep sense of loss, which was mixed with a rich portion of memories that brought so much for which we celebrated and gave thanks.

Our oldest son was engaged in the fall of 1993 and his fiancé was working as a nurse in Uranium City. In January of 1994 he was in a horrible car accident coming out of Grand Prairie where he was working. The roads had been shear ice and an oncoming vehicle went out of control and met him head on. The injuries were severe.

He was flown to a hospital in Edmonton. We spent a month in a hotel in Edmonton and we got to know our amazing daughter-in-law-to-be as she spent the whole time with us; every day by our son's bed as we waited to see if he would survive this ordeal. His injuries were many.

We finally had our son transferred to Saskatoon where he required emergency heart surgery, a result of the accident. Those were long and difficult days but by the grace of God each day brought new hope. In late March he was released and came home for a couple days before he had a relapse with major blood clots in his lungs.

However, eight days before they set their wedding date, our son came home. April 2, 1994 we celebrated the gracious gift of his life in a wedding service held in the chapel at LCBI. How many miracles had taken him through these difficult days we will never know. We can only marvel at God's grace.

These were hard days for our whole family. In this same decade our last two children graduated from high school. As they were looking at plans for their future, they walked through all the confusion of the time. Sometimes as adults we can get so caught up in our own struggles we easily forget the effect the same times have on our children. We did our best to care for and understand what was happening for them, but came to realize that there is so much, that even when we are looking we do not see.

In 1998 we hit heavy waters again when a nephew attending our school took his own life. He was such a gifted and special young man. He used to stop in my office often and just loved to visit. When this horrible day happened our larger family went through a most difficult time. How do you care for this extended family, parents and grandparents? How do you help a whole student body walk through these days? How do you handle this in your own home?

It was impossible to feel adequate to all the circumstances that converged. It was good to have such a faithful and faith-filled staff that stepped forward with grace and wisdom as they cared for the whole student body and for family members. The funeral was held in our gymnasium where hundreds of family and friends gathered. In the middle of life's darkest times one turns again to the cross and recalls God's love for a sinful and struggling world. We do not mourn as people who have no hope.

The '90s was a decade of turbulent living in an upstream call. I often went back to a book I received from Dr. Otto Olson who was the President of the Central Canada Synod when I served my first parish. It was a small book titled **Meditations of a Radical Christian** by Leslie F. Brandt. He writes about how we tend to look for a quiet harbour in life. He reminds us that there is finally a quiet harbour, but in the meantime Jesus called his people to be his servants in the midst of the storm. That book has become quite worn over the years.

Indeed the decade had worn heavy on me. I believe Bev was right. I was likely becoming less patient. Maybe my skin was wearing thin. Maybe I was just weary. In the spring of 2001 I suggested to the Board that my term would be expiring in just over a year and I thought it was likely wise to talk about the future. I asked for an evaluation. Following this, the Board offered me another four-year term commencing the summer of 2002.

This offer provided a time of deep struggle. The experience at LCBI had been intense, challenging, and yet incredibly rewarding. I had learned a lot about administration. In working with students, I became aware that a study of youth is the study of the bi-product of the adult community. It was a good way to come to learn a lot about the culture in which we live and the values that we put into practice in the daily decisions that we make in community. It was a good place to discover the power of the gospel and the gift of God's instruction that equips people to function in our struggling world and to bring something redemptive to those who struggle.

Back in October of 1998 I had an invitation from the Rotary Club in North Battleford, Saskatchewan to speak on the topic "Working with Youth in our Culture". It was a memorable event. My presentation suggested that what we see in youth today is indeed the by-product of the adult community. At the end of the presentation over two-thirds of the people attending came to talk to me.

The Director of the Youth Detention Centre asked if I would spend the rest of the day with him. He gave me a tour of the detention centre and we spent several hours in conversation. We found so much in common and shared similar observations. It was a great afternoon.

Though I felt that so much of what was happening at LCBI was so positive, I really felt that the "old blood" was weary. I believed LCBI was ready to fly. We had full funding from Saskatchewan Education for Saskatchewan students. Our instructional facility was an excellent place for staff and students, and the overall campus provided a beautiful setting. We needed an addition on our boys' residence to make our campus serve a balanced offering for guys and girls with 150 students as the average enrolment of resident students. At 150 students we would have a significant operating surplus. This would allow a new freedom to maintain and develop our program. This was a key to the future.

In addition, I always felt LCBI needed a hockey program. In 1990-91 we had put together an AA midget hockey program for a year with the community of Kenaston. It showed the potential for this program and it left me with no doubt that this program would give us a wider door for recruitment that we dearly needed.

I could never get support from the staff at LCBI to move in this direction. There was a fear it would take away from basketball and that always mystified me. My interpretation of this concern was that hockey would be too popular with the students; therefore, we shouldn't have it. I did not understand.

In 2000 I met a man who offered to bring an AAA midget hockey program to our campus. He brought in about thirty American students for his AAA program. They did not play in a league so all the games were on weekends. He was looking for a school. He had shown his clients and parents information on several schools and the consensus from the parents of students in his program was that they wanted LCBI and the values we held. We would negotiate with the community and surrounding small towns for ice time. All we had to do was provide education. The hockey program would be totally taken care of.

Here was a bonus of almost 30 students we would not have to recruit: our school would be full. This program would also be open for Canadian students. Indeed it would change some things on our campus. It would be a great attraction for hockey fans.

However, it did not fly. It just seemed too difficult for our staff to consider. I think this was when I realized it was time for me to leave. Recruitment was the key to a stable future. From my perspective we needed this wider door and I had failed to achieve it. Without the broader window for recruitment, the enrolment pressures produced administrative pressures I could no longer endure.

In the spring of 2001 I turned down the offer for another four-year term. The Board would have a year to get involved in a search for a new president. It seemed it was time after 19 years at LCBI to pass the torch.

Upstream Living in a Downstream World

This was a rather satisfying time. Our residence staff had been on stipends more than salaries in the early years. All our staff had been on Saskatchewan Teacher's Federation salary grids though the last years of enrolment put pressures on this. We could afford these salaries on the long term with stable enrolments over 132 students.

We had worked hard to control spending and to build without debt. If the school could maintain balanced budgets it would be totally debt free by 2007. There seemed to be a real opportunity for a stable and healthy future.

A new president could help bring depth and strength to a creative program of Christian education that would place LCBI in a very healthy position and provide our church with a powerful source for Christian education if it could find the key for student recruitment.

The last year proved to be a very strange and difficult year. In the fall of 2001 I was invited to talk to a person who was interested in supporting LCBI. He wanted to know what LCBI needed to complete its facility.

In our strategic planning the Board had identified the need for a new cafeteria, chapel and addition to the boys' residence. Our strategic planning process had all this in place. The cost was estimated at two and a half million dollars.

I showed this potential donor the plan and the projected cost. After a few questions he informed me that he could provide the full amount needed and he wanted us to proceed with the plans. He informed me that all the money would be in our hands that fall.

I was shocked. This was unbelievable. I wept. This was my last year and suddenly out of nowhere this dream could be completed. This could give LCBI the campus it needed to take care of 150 students. This would provide stability and the resources to support the on-going development of a strong program of Christian education. I was hesitant, but the donor was confident and told us to start working with our architect.

The Board formed a building committee. We worked on concept plans with the whole staff, and began the process to bring the whole development into focus.

In the meantime, the money was delayed. I spoke to the donor every few weeks and was assured the money would be there. The deadline for arrival kept changing. We kept planning and finally had floor plans and elevation drawings in place. LCBI would have the most beautiful and serviceable campus one could find.

As I came to the close of my time at LCBI the money still had not come and I heard less and less from the donor. Slowly the realization came that for whatever reason, this money was not going to arrive.

It was hard to know how to handle this with staff and constituency. I could not provide any adequate explanation of what had happened since we did not know. The dream evaporated, and on that note, I left LCBI.

It was like leaving under a cloud. It was a small thing that my hopes were crushed. The staff that remained at the school shared the same dream with such excitement that turned to disappointment. It was mostly hard on those who were left behind.

This experience reminded me of the wisdom of our earlier approach to gifts. No gift is a gift till it is in the hands of the school. "Don't count your chickens before they are hatched." My father's words came back. I often thought after how this would have spared us much embarrassment and disappointment.

My time at LCBI was a rich and rewarding experience. The last years were an affirmation that my earlier expectations for LCBI were not fanciful. LCBI could be a thriving institution that could live on a plain well above "survival". All the foundations were in place. The future hinged on 132-student enrolment and the ultimate goal to average 150 students in residence.

When I left there wasn't a replacement. The Board opted for a part-time interim president. This was at least a good decision in the absence of a permanent position, but it was not the way to meet the future. Many good things happened in this time, but there seemed a loss of momentum. Maybe that had begun before I left. Whatever the case, it was hard to watch from a distance.

I was talking to one of our now adult sons on the phone one day and I commented on some of my concerns about the school.

He replied, "Dad, n ... m ... d."

"N ... m ... d" I asked, "what do you mean by that?"

He replied, "Not my department!"

It was his gentle reminder that affirmed this was no longer my responsibility. His simple but wise counsel gave me freedom. It was time to let it go and get on with the new responsibilities of the day. I smiled and was thankful for his advice.

Those three letters pop up in my mind quite often since, not only in relationship to the school, but sometimes in relationship to other matters as well. God calls us to different places where we are to serve. One person plants, another waters, but it is God who gives the increase. The realization that we are all parts of the body of Christ also reminds us that there is a larger picture of which we are just a part. It is not just about us. This realization allows us to give everything we have to the task at hand, but once we move on there are things to let go, and there are new tasks and responsibilities to pick up.

I had resolved through the last year that I wanted to work full out to the moment I turned in my keys. The last day of work was a full day. At five o'clock I remember picking up my keys. I walked out the door and as I closed it, there was that finality of the click. The door was locked. I handed in my keys and went home. It was no longer my office. I was now an alumnus like so many who had been a part of the life of this school.

I went back a few times after I left to visit and have a cup of coffee. It was good, but I began to realize it would be best for the school to step away to avoid misunderstanding. The new administration was in charge. My presence could become problematic.

For 19 years I had been gifted with such varied opportunities to serve God at LCBI. Through the service and ministry of this school so many lives were influenced and nurtured in a life-giving way. The ministry has not ended.

I was told recently of an alumnus who made a comment to this effect, that LCBI, even at its weakest still changed lives. Students come from a huge variety of backgrounds and this microcosm of community encounters God's Word daily in the message that is shared and the lives that are lived. And God works to bring the surprises of new life and learning in the joys and struggles of community. What a gift to have been a part of this place of service in our church.

So began a new chapter in the adventure of ministry. I had let our church leadership know that I would be finished work at LCBI by the end of June 2002. I had also wanted a couple months off before taking another call. We sold our condominium on Diefenbaker Lake the previous summer when we knew we would likely be moving. We had also purchased a cabin on Bells Beach at Christopher Lake together with our oldest son and his wife, so Bev and I decided to go to the lake for some time away.

The Saskatchewan Synod Convention was held in Swift Current that summer. There were rumours that I was a likely candidate in the election process for a new Saskatchewan Synod Bishop. This was not good news to me.

Every pastor makes an annual report to the Bishop. Over the last years I wrote many times that I felt like a square peg in a round hole. I had little in common with the leadership of the church, but, my great freedom was to go back to work.

Why did I find little in common? Church leadership seemed more concerned to make political statements than to do ministry. Political correctness dominated practice and policy. As Lutherans we have held high the themes of "grace" and "mercy" in theology and practice. "Rights" and "justice" had become the new dominant themes and I lived in wonder that even the Pauline greeting of "grace and peace" was replaced with prayers for "justice and peace". The church that for so long had scorned legalism returned to legalism through another door. Social ethics had been abandoned. In a materialistic world; however, socio-economic issues took on a new and central role. Socio-economic issues were viewed through a lens of "human rights" and "justice". The new *modus operandi* for functional theology was political activism. This was the new source of life's redemption.

For want of a better term, the new standard of operation for church leadership is what I would call "politicized theology" which no longer found so much guidance through the scriptures and our confessions as it did through the friends found in the culture with whom we adopted a common ideological voice in socio-economic issues. The voice of church leadership sounded no different in its prime issues than our national radio broadcaster, the Canadian Broadcasting Corporation and the politicians who govern our country.

Theologically, we massaged the muscles we strained to bend in this direction by reworking our exegesis and hermeneutics. Any focused opposition was silenced, by claiming biblical and confessional ambiguity for the topics of choice. We of course do not use the same exegetical and hermeneutical reworking of scripture and confessions for sacramental practices, about the only teaching that was left. (Yes, a little overstated but intentional to stir thought.)

This new environment hallmarked by "rights" and "justice" had produced a progressively deteriorating fellowship. The new environment produced an adversarial environment that caused a breakdown in conversation and fellowship. The new template shifted from the authority of scripture to the authority of human rights. The template for functional theology shifted to the use of strategic power and political activism to produce "justice". And the Micah text is read, not in the light of "doing justly" but in "demanding justice" from everyone else.

Leadership people now seemed to be "right by definition" and found support in secular human rights legislation: challenge was silenced and meaningful conversation came to an end.

How does one debate that which is now "right by definition"? Anyone who questioned the direction of the church leadership was viewed as "troublemaker". They were spoken of and treated as outsiders. Fellowship ended. Opposition was either crushed through strategic political manipulation, or through a strategic shorthand, which labelled all opposition as "right wing" or "pietist" or "fundamentalist". People, so labelled were people to whom there was no need to listen or respond.

These are strong indictments. Similar ideology permeates our Western culture and produces adversarial environments where meaningful discussion and debate are mostly eliminated. The same environment has largely enshrined the transcendence of human evolution as its own authority. The great humanistic philosophers have prevailed.

The character of the Christian community in the Western world since the middle of the last century; seems to be hallmarked by insecurity and uncertainty. Many of our current leaders were trained in the academic community of the 1960s when the push was to "become relevant". It was not difficult to get caught in the flow of the culture and when in the full flow there is the allusion that finally we have caught up. This may be what one could call "downstream living in a downstream world". This is likely not a conscious act of faithlessness but one in which God's people through all history have been vulnerable as we drift and respond to our inner reflexes and seek to affirm our own ways.

The breach of fellowship produced a growing cloud of discontent within many mainline churches. This breach of fellowship has been condemned by leadership but not seriously evaluated. Many people have abandoned the struggle and left the church and some have sought out fellowship in other Christian denominations. Some are pushed out of the mainstream as political outcasts, but hang in hoping and working for a change of direction. Whether a new day will come before we tear the rest of our church apart is yet to be seen.

When one looks around in the broader spectrum of the Christian church in the Western world, it seems the "secular" infection has resulted in a progressive atrophy of those churches that accelerate down this channel. Will one find many mainline denominations washing up on the shore if one looks downstream? Time will tell.

The first summer after being at LCBI for nineteen years was a confusing time. The Synod Convention fell in the middle of the summer. In all my years of ministry, to this time, I had never missed a National Church Convention, and I had never missed a Synod Convention.

I wrestled with the whole issue related to the position of Synod Bishop for some time and prayed about it. In the end I informed God that I was Jonah and it would take a prairie whale . . . I was not going to attend the Synod convention. I would do nothing to encourage people to vote for me as Bishop. Bev and I would spend the convention at the lake.

I did not feel very responsible but that was where I was. I got a phone call early in the convention process to inform me I was high in votes on the first ballot and should be prepared for the possibility that I would have to come to Swift Current to make a presentation to the Convention with the other candidates still on the ballot. This was not good news. The next day I got called and told I had to come to make a presentation.

Bev and I left for Swift Current. It was a long drive (almost 400 km. one-way) with much time to think. I was petrified of the thought that there was even a chance I would be elected. If putting on clerical garb was a crisis before my ordination, the thought of a Bishop's paraphernalia and the image that went with it was too much in itself. I love ministry and I would love to work with pastors and congregations to seek to be faithful stewards of the gifts God has provided to equip us to fulfill the Great Commission, but this was not the time or environment and I was not interested in becoming a bishop.

Whether it was right or wrong to feel as I did; the environment of the leadership of our church was not a place I found comfortable. The issues which dominated discussion were not issues I found key to the life of our church or its calling. It seemed our ELCIC had so much to offer. It seemed we offered so little. We seemed more concerned to play church politics and exercise power than to be God's servant people in the world God deeply loved.

I remember walking into the convention already feeling like an outsider. This was enhanced by the result of my own decision to not attend. Here I was, called to speak and I was not even registered as a delegate. I had nothing prepared.

How should I address the Synod in Convention? I had three primary thoughts in my mind. I broke out several sub-points under each. I had nothing written down. I am afraid I consciously phrased what I had to say in a way that would likely offend some of the clergy. This was half the vote at the average convention and I felt this strategy would assure my defeat. (Yes, this too is politics.) I was very brief, but I was successful in my goal.

On our drive back to the lake that same day, I tried to find some area of regret. I thought at least my pride should be hurt even though I did not want the job, but I could not find any wound - even on pride. One thing I did feel was guilt. Was this really an act of faithfulness to God or simply my own stubborn heart? I prayed that God would forgive me.

The summer of 2002 was very dry, so the crops in our area were very poor. Our oldest son farmed between Outlook and Kenaston. He asked if I would be willing to take off his crop. He had been offered a job on the pipeline just south of where he lived and this could supplement the farm income on a bad year. It was an ideal circumstance for him because he did not have to leave home and it was good timing for me.

XI. THE CALL TO MESSIAH LUTHERAN:
Joy Under a Cloud (2002-2010).

As the summer of 2002 passed I began to wonder what we were going to do after harvest. Originally when we turned down the four-year term at LCBI we thought we would move to Kelowna, British Columbia. My mother had been living in Kelowna since 1967. After Dad died in 1993, mom was under some pressure to move since there weren't any family members who lived there.

She loved her life in Kelowna. Bev and I decided if we did not accept another term at LCBI we would move to Kelowna so Mom could stay. We thought we would buy a business and run it together. We weren't sure what business, but we would work that out when the time came. If a parish opening came up, then I would see if I could go back into the parish. We thought of it as another adventure.

Our plan changed when Mom decided to move to Saskatoon in the summer of 2001; before we had made our decision. Through the year we had not come up with alternatives, so I decided to notify the synod that I was open for a call.

A call hadn't come throughout my last year at LCBI. I finally found out that there was a new process where no one got a call without filling in a document called a "Mobility Form". I guess I was negligent in keeping up, so I asked the Synod office to send me the form. I filled it out and sent it back to the synod office.

As harvest progressed that fall there were no calls coming. Our income was not as significant after my last check came from the school. Bev was working full time as a licensed practical nurse at the hospital. The crunch was going to come.

Late in the fall I was informed that Messiah Lutheran in Prince Albert, Saskatchewan was considering me as a pastoral candidate. I went for an interview and later received the call.

There was a lot of time to think while sitting on the combine that fall. I had heard of some concerns about this parish.

Each day passed quickly as harvest continued and I realized it was time to make a decision, but there were some growing questions. After receiving the call, I had been warned by several phone calls from different church leaders that this congregation had problems. That I would get such calls itself was a strange experience. As I thought about this, I became more concerned. If this congregation had problems, it might be good to know those problems before making decisions.

I had my cell phone with me on the combine so I called my Bishop. I asked if I could meet with him to talk about this call. He was very busy and did not know when he would find time but in the conversation I found that he was leaving for Regina that evening.

My son's farm was a short distance from Kenaston, a community on the highway to Regina. I suggested I buy him a cup of coffee if he would be able to take time on route to meet me there. I appreciated his willingness to accommodate me in his busy schedule.

There was no suitable dress available for the occasion. I needed fifteen minutes to get to Kenaston from the field where I was working. I ran the combine as long as I could, got into my truck and drove to Kenaston to meet the Bishop in my best coveralls and ball cap, which had an appropriate amount of grease and dust well embedded in them from the previous days of work. My dress was less than formal wear.

I asked the Bishop what issues he was aware of at Messiah Lutheran in Prince Albert. There was some difficulty to really identify any specifics. He shared how the congregation had gone through some difficult times and had lost many members. In the end it seemed he could not really identify what the problems were.

It is not new for congregations or any other human organization to have problems. As human beings, we prove again and again that we are indeed by nature sinful. I thought about the circumstances for some time on returning to the field. I guess it is one of the snares of life. We sometimes get caught up in particular personalities and labels, and forget to deal with the real issues. As Lutherans we talk about how we are all by nature sinful. Strangely, when we see it in congregations (and in leadership people) we get upset.

How often we forget that the church is a fellowship of acknowledged sinners who live by God's grace. How often we beat our people up for being less than what they ought to be instead of taking the challenge to work for reconciliation and renewal.

It reminded me of Bonhoeffer's book titled *Life Together*. Bonhoeffer wrote about many pastors, who, seeking to build the ideal fellowship often become the accusers of their people, and in so doing destroyed everything they wanted to create. This is one of the easiest snares in which we can get caught in ministry at all levels. In the end, we decided to accept the call. I am afraid it was a decision, at least in part based on the fact that we really had no other options.

We sold our house in Outlook to our future son-in-law. We then went to Prince Albert and found a beautiful home just a block and a half from the church. The house was only a year old with a partially completed basement and two-car garage attached. We had occupancy set for December 1, 2002.

I moved to Prince Albert on November 1. My oldest brother and his wife generously provided me with room and board until we could get into our new house while Bev continued to live and work in Outlook until we got occupancy.

It did not take long to settle in and begin the adjustments to parish ministry. I had never been fully away from parish ministry even while at LCBI. At LCBI I had been involved in supply preaching and had served several interim positions. I had served interim ministries for two years in the Hanley/Bethlehem Parish, two years in the Davidson/Skudesness Parish, and I had supplied Zion Lutheran in Weyburn twice a month on two occasions for most of a year. I was interim pastor at Bethlehem Outlook also for a short time.

I went through the church directory of congregations and found that I had preached in over 100 congregations since ordination in Saskatchewan alone. I had also preached in more than twenty congregations in each of the Manitoba and Alberta Synods, and in many congregations of the B.C. Synod and most of these while serving at L.C.B.I.

While I was involved in these various opportunities of pastoral ministry I was very concerned to keep the work at LCBI my first priority. I would not use office time for prep, but kept that to evenings and weekends. If I ever had to do any funerals or weddings on working days at the school, I would book those days as holiday time. Because of these involvements in parish ministry throughout my time at LCBI moving into the parish was, for the most part comfortable.

The biggest change was the loss of the broad range of involvement that I had at the college. I missed the administrative challenges. I enjoyed the business side of the work at LCBI. At LCBI I worked with government people, church leadership, and alumni across our country. Suddenly life was quite simple. My people lived in Prince Albert and the surrounding area. I was no longer an administrator. In fact, it was important to encourage people in the congregation to take on the administrative leadership of the congregation.

We have not had a clear focus of the relationship between pastors and Church Councils in our congregational life. This was a chance to try to work it out with more clarity.

I took the Constitution of the congregation and the Letter Of Call that all pastors in our church receive, and began to craft a proposal for an operational model that was based on these two documents. Together with the Church Council we worked to refine this structure and then put it into practice. This was a good exercise for both pastor and church council.

I was now a pastor, no longer an administrator or businessperson. In those matters I had only an advisory capacity. The adjustments were more comfortable than I expected.

When I was at LCBI I remember sharing with the students on many occasions that only boring people get bored. In my early days at Messiah I worried that I was becoming a boring person. I had lost that passion for each day. There was a lot of work to do in the congregation but I had some difficulty to ignite again. This was not the fault of the congregation, but it became their liability.

In December of 2002 we were just nicely settled into our more sedentary life when I got a phone call from Phoenix, Arizona. A church in Phoenix was in the process of expanding their educational program. They were looking for an executive director to oversee their schools. They had a pre-school with 450 children and their K-8 program had over 300 students. They now wanted to build and develop their overall educational programs to about 1700 students with the addition of a high school program. They asked if I would send them a resume.

I was not looking for a change since I had just begun work in this congregation. They still wanted me to send a resume, so I did. There was something rather exciting in the possibility, but it seemed unlikely that anything would come out of it.

In February they called again and asked if Bev and I could come down for an interview. This was a surprise. Bev and I have always operated on the basis that we have never set personal goals other than to seek to be faithful wherever God called us. It seems that God opens doors and we walk through. God closes doors and we move on. That had been the way we had lived out our ministry to this time. In the end, we accepted the offer for an interview and flew to Phoenix.

I was impressed with their interview process. We had opportunity to tour the existing schools and meet with the principal and the staff. We also met with the management group. The church had a broad ministry and had set up a number of different organizations within its corporate structure.

We spent several days in the interview process and researched the overall operation examining the various structures that made up this rather large complex of ministries. I was quite convinced that if I were to take this job there would need to be some changes in organization.

I suggested that I would like to see the school set up as a separate corporation. It seemed in the present structures that it would otherwise be quite impossible to operate. The governance board was open to this if I were to accept the position. They were in the process of looking at modifying their corporate structure and suggested they would like some help in shaping those structures.

We spent a wonderful week in Arizona exploring this position. I remember at times thinking that it was too good to be true. If I could have written a job description I could not have defined it more favourably. There were some quiet concerns overall, but that seemed normal in any situation.

I remember thinking about our visit on the flight home. One question dominated my mind: why was it, that each time I got that burst of adrenalin with that sense of excitement about this possible new challenge, it was always followed by a sigh?

Before we arrived home I began to understand. My years at LCBI had drained me of energy. Our children and Bev had often told me years before, that it was time for me to leave LCBI. I again caught a glimpse of what they had seen. I was tired.

In early March I received the formal offer from Phoenix. We had to make a decision. Bev and I talked about the situation at length and prayed for guidance. It seemed so unfair to the Messiah congregation to have accepted their call to ministry and then consider a change so soon. Was this a new doorway?

I had kept in conversation with the Church Council about the contact from Phoenix ever since the original enquiry. I did not want it shared with the congregation in those early stages (this uncertainty would be a disruption), but I also did not want to have anything happen behind their backs. I used to tell students that "trust" is the fragile gift of relationship. It was important to keep that trust.

When I had the call, it was time to formally announce it to the congregation. I wanted them to know that my consideration of this call was in no way an expression of unhappiness with the congregation. The congregation seemed to understand and were most gracious in the process; they even assured us that if we felt this was God's call that we should not hesitate to go.

Daniel A. Haugen

One Saturday morning a man came to our door. He had just started coming to church and asked if he could talk to me. He informed me he was not used to talking to preachers so he did not know how to do what he was about to do. He assured me that he would keep coming to church whether we were there or not, but he wanted me to know that he hoped we would not leave. He also graciously assured us that if we did leave he would also understand. That was a very special visit and affirmed once again the holy journey of ministry and the care of people who are the focus of ministry.

There was a certain appeal of glamour in the call to Phoenix. I had felt rather unchallenged in the early stages of adjustment to Parish ministry. On top of that the call was very affirming at a time when I was not feeling so sure about anything. I tried to sort out the issues. Which were important issues, and which were fanciful? The bottom line, I realized was my fatigue.

From my experience at LCBI I felt quite confident I could do a reasonably good job for the people in Phoenix. On the other hand, if I did not have the energy for the task it did not matter if I had the ability.

In the end I turned down the offer. It was doubly hard to do because I was 56 years old and realized this kind of opportunity would likely not come again. Some doors close. Life goes on.

The work at Messiah moved on. I found it necessary to discipline my days and for the first time in my ministry the church council informed me I was to take two days off each week. This was a radical experience.

I took Saturdays and Mondays off. The weeks seemed so short. I set regular office hours from 9:00-12:00pm and if I was not elsewhere I would be in the office from 1:00-5:00pm Tuesdays through Friday. Any work scheduled in the evenings simply filled out the work week and compensated for Sundays which might be a shorter work day on occasions. If the normal hours got longer than a normal 40-hour week, I considered that no different than the volunteer hours offered by members of the congregation. If I had to work a half-day on my days off I seldom recorded it, but if I had to work a full day I would sometimes book it as an EDO and add it to my accumulated holidays.

Messiah also insisted that every month where there was a fifth Sunday, I was to take a Sunday off (though it could be taken any Sunday). They also liked this because it gave lay people a chance to lead worship and developed the gifts of the priesthood of all believers.

I had trouble from the beginning to see this congregation as a difficult congregation to serve. I had never experienced such generosity and as I got to know the people I was impressed at the diversity of people who shared the fellowship of this church.

I thought about this more in recent times after the editor of the ELCIC asked to do an article on Messiah as our national church leaders worked to encourage "diversity" in our ELCIC. What struck me is that Messiah did not have a program to become diverse. Messiah people lived in the community of Prince Albert and area. The area had a very diverse population. Messiah's goal was to serve God and the people they lived among. Diversity was not the goal. Given the diverse community served, it was one of many results. I shared this with the editor and they decided not to write the article.

Life in the parish was a gracious experience. There was huge freedom in the congregation to explore and pursue the challenges of ministry. They had gone through some difficult years. There were wounds and there was uncertainty and a degree of distrust of clergy. I had to accept the timeline for healing and new life.

Life flowed very smoothly in the parish. I spent the first weeks seeking to become familiar with the congregation. Many of the names I knew from my childhood in Birch Hills and connections with the Bible Camp at Christopher Lake, but many of the names were new to me.

I tried to get some picture of the former ministry profile of the congregation. I went through all the files I could find from previous ministries. What had happened in the past? Who was responsible for what areas of work? What programs had been operating, and what were some of the dynamics of Messiah's congregational life?

The cross in the corner of my old office at LCBI came back to my mind. Here too were human lives, which in God's eyes had great value. Each person was a holy life worth dying for so they could live. How far would we go in order to care for these people? What a diverse group of people in this congregation! How diverse would be their needs? And what a diverse community in which we lived! How would one "go" into this community, and what would we encounter in ministry? This was a new adventure.

Over the years I have come to believe that there is nothing that is totally coincidental. I believe our lives are shaped through many things. Some people have been deeply wounded and live in reaction to those wounds. And sometimes one has to accept the limits of what one can do. The circumstances might not always work out well. There was still a need to do what could be done, and even in failure, to take care of the people in the midst of the struggles and sometimes there are wonderful surprises and gifts that come our way.

On the twenty-first day of that first month of work I met a lady in the hospital. She reminded me that we often have no idea what wounds people carry. The first day I visited this lady she was depressed, and almost weary of suffering. This was not misery just because of her health. This was misery that went to the core of her being. My first visit was short.

As I continued to visit this lady I began to learn more of her story. I also got to meet her son who faithfully came to visit and took wonderful care of his mother. With time, her story began to give explanation to her bitterness. There also began to be a sparkle in her eye. She had a great need for someone who would listen to her struggles. She was bed ridden. She was widowed early and had lived in a wheel chair for over twenty years. Life had been very difficult.

After a long stay in the hospital she was moved into the seniors' care home attached to the hospital. This was another difficult time because she realized she might not move back home.

On one visit she was extremely unhappy with the nurses. They had insisted that she go to the dining room for supper, but she was not feeling well and not ready to go for supper. She was ripped.

I suggested that she try to be kind to the nurses because nurses have a difficult job taking care of everyone's needs. She was quite clear in communicating that the nurses did not deserve any kindness.

I suggested that "grace" was "undeserved kindness" so deserved or not, why not share some grace with the nurses. Well, that was a different thought. She informed me that she had never heard it explained that way.

When the nurse returned there was a holy moment. The nurse was afraid. She came in ever so carefully and placed the food on the table.

My friend, squirmed, gave a glancing look at the nurse and then rather strained, but ever so clearly she said, "Thank you very much."

The nurse was startled. My friend was quiet and I must admit I had a delightful inner chuckle. She was venturing onto new ground. It was a little difficult because it was "upstream". I think she kind of liked it.

I have visited this wonderful lady almost every week now for over eight years. We talk about life and faith and pray together. When I walk into the room she beams. Sometimes when I sneak up behind her with some surprise comment; she loves it. She will grasp my hand and hang on. She still has days when the misery comes back, but almost always when I visit she has a smile that would melt ice. She has been a gift to our lives.

She listens to the **Lutheran Hour Broadcast** every Sunday morning on a local radio station. With time she joined, with several other people, in the home for worship and shares in the Lord's Supper with them. It is fun to watch her faith and life blossom even in the midst of all her difficulties. A number of people in the congregation have got to know this lady as well and they stop to see her quite regularly. She has found new fellowship that has been life giving and she is life giving to them as well.

Many people don't believe in miracles today. This woman living in Herb Bassett Home and her growing life is a wonderful miracle of God's grace.

Over the years I have seen many miracles. I have come to believe that one of the signs of our lack of faith is that we have trouble to believe that God (who we confess in the first article of the Apostle's Creed to be the creator of all life), should have trouble to rearrange some body chemistry or bring something new to the human spirit.

I believe another expression of our lack of faith in God's love for his people is that we sometimes feel we have to find the proper methodologies or frame of mind, or the proper words before we think that God can do anything:

> *If you, then, though you are evil, know how to give good gifts to your children, how much more will your Father in heaven give good gifts to those who ask him!* (Matthew 7:11)

The wind blows where it wills. We are not those who are in control. I have had many funerals in the same time. Even the miracle of physical healing is merely an adjustment of the time line that leads to death. The great miracles are in changed lives and the promise of the resurrection. Paul said:

> *If only for this life we have hope in Christ, we are to be pitied more than all men.* (1 Corinthians 15:19)

There is another perspective we seem to have lost. We forget that the Gospel brings new life to the inner person. It has the power to deal with that inner spirit that struggles in its lost and forlorn condition when it is abandoned to itself.

Over the years I have seen so many changes in human lives. I have often seen a new and quiet spirit that moves people to celebrate the gracious gift of life. And when they do, their own life and the lives of others become holy gifts again. This joy and celebration seems to be preceded or followed by a new fellowship with God that finds visible expression in worship and prayer. Over time I have seen the growing fruit of the spirit (Galatians 5:22-23) of love, and joy and peace, and patience, and kindness, and goodness, and faithfulness, gentleness and self-control growing in life. With this so many other things begin to change.

The further blessing of life is that these fruits of God's spirit are lived out in homes, and places of employment, and community life. Isn't this that quiet power that changes our world? These are the fruits that come from living as followers of Jesus . . . upstream living in a downstream world. In the process it has the power to change communities.

Since arriving in Prince Albert I have had opportunity to share many new friendships. The population of Prince Albert was made up of many different backgrounds so there was opportunity to get to know people whose lives and traditions were varied.

I remember one occasion when a corrections worker called and asked if I could meet with a family he knew who were convinced that their home was haunted by strange spirits. I got in touch with the family, although I had never met them before or even heard of their name. They told me their stories of apparitions, sounds, and strange occurrences on their rural property which put their lives in deep fear and uncertainty.

Here was a new adventure. The apostle Paul talks about the reality of evil with which we contend. I never was a great fan on literature about exorcisms and I must confess the evening I entered this home I was not sure about anything. What kind of people were they? Was this stuff real? What could this misplaced farmer who had no great claims of spiritual power or wisdom have to offer this young couple in this circumstance?

The couple were in fact quite delightful. Their experiences were still very real. I listened to their stories and then I introduced them to the One who continually said to his disciples, "Do not be afraid." C.S. Lewis once commented that fear is Satan's tool. Ever since the crucifixion and resurrection of Jesus, Satan, he said, is like a toothless lion. He has no power, so he uses fear to chase people where he wants them to go. Jesus did the opposite. He reminded His followers that the one who was in us is greater than the one who is against us.

In the end we had a simple prayer calling on Jesus, the Lord of life to be with them in their home. In the prayer we reflected on the life lived in each room of their home and asked Jesus the Lord of life to be with them in all their life together and to remove from them all fear.

I remember going home wondering if I had been faithful to the Lord of Life and to this young couple. Yet quietly in the centre of my being I felt quite at peace and expected that likely things would be different in the days ahead. I feel a bit guilty. I never met this couple again, but some months later I got word from one of this family's co-workers that they never had another one of those strange incidents in their home. They were quite amazed.

We often forget the reality of the "living Lord" of life. It is because of that reality that we have faith. It is not the power in us, but the power of the One in whom we put our trust. Would this incident be the beginning of new things for this couple? I hoped and prayed it would. I wondered from what other quarters of God's people there might come more nurture and support for their journey.

Significant to the city of Prince Albert are First Nations people who make up over 30 percent of the population. Early in my time at Messiah I had opportunity to serve a number of First Nations families.

I had a number of weddings of people whose lives were rooted on the Sturgeon Lake Reserve. These were wonderful experiences through which I not only got to know and enjoy the friendship of this larger family, but I also got to meet some very fascinating people.

I always enjoyed attending the receptions after the weddings. One thing I found out early was they had no need for the pastor to pray table grace at the reception because many of the elders and family members could handle this very well. I visited with as many people as possible at all these events. A common thread came out of the conversations: there was a deep desire for integration among the people. This is not as common in those who are politically inclined. The people I met wanted to live in community as people together with everyone else. The gospel was something they seemed to understand and the desire for fellowship was no different than for people everywhere.

I don't know why this would shock us. When European immigrant people came to this country they remained isolated in their ethnic backgrounds for a time, but as they got to know everyone around them they enjoyed each other's friendship and fellowship and integrated into the community.

One of our members who had a First Nations background served for some time on our church council. There was an invitation from the Synod to have two carloads of people from Messiah congregation attend a Native Ministry workshop in Regina. The Synod offered to pay the costs for people to attend.

After the chair of the Church Council read the letter he passed it around to council members and asked for their comments. The letter finally came to our First Nation's member. Having read the letter he flicked it into the centre of the table. Our chair, which did not miss much, continued to ask people around the table what they wanted to do. Finally he asked our First Nations member what he thought.

His comment was striking, "I think this is discrimination. Do we have a ministry to the Dutch, to Germans, to the English . . . I thought we had a ministry to people." There seemed no more need for conversation. The chair moved on to the next item on the agenda. There was no further action on the invitation.

This man has since served a number of years as the chair of our Church Council and a key member in the men's ministry of Messiah congregation and a faithful Sunday school teacher. He has been a very special gift in the centre of the life of our church. He's a good friend on the golf course as well.

We have had up to thirty new members who in the last years emigrated from South Africa and worshiped with us at Messiah. Most of these new members came as refugees from Liberia. I remember visiting with one of these new members one day. They had been with us over a year. He made a comment that I found delightful. He said, "You know, you Canadians are just like us."

These comments made me rethink a lot of the reflex thoughts we have about people of different cultures. Indeed there are different traditions and practices and often a differing socialization process that has happened over the years. Some traditions are strange to us, and we are equally strange to them, but in the midst of all these realities there is a common thread we often forget. We are all 100 percent human beings who on the inside have so much in common. Created in the image of God, every life is holy by definition. In this fallen world we are all "by nature sinful" holy lives profaned by our own sins and the sins of others. And when we view the cross of Jesus, he died for us all:

> *There is neither Jew nor Greek, slave nor free, male nor female, for you are all one in Christ Jesus.* (Galatians 3:28)

One day I was driving a friend I found on the streets of our city to the reserve where his two daughters and grandchildren lived. He talked about how similar we are. This snuck up on him by surprise too. He said that all his life he had been taught that he was so different from all those who were later immigrant people. He had finally associated enough with people of different backgrounds that he too came to realize that we had so much in common. He was also keenly aware of how destructive his lifestyle had been and how destructive the environment in which he had been raised.

As we drove that day he said, "Pastor, you can send us food by the truckload, and you can send us all the money you like, but until we change here (he thumped on his chest), we will destroy everything we receive."

The results are no different for him than for any other human being. As life changed he started looking for new ways to care for his daughters and his grandchildren. He was in his sixties before life turned around. He realized how broad a change was needed in the environment of the community in which he lived. He also realized that change comes one step at a time and he also discovered how easy it was to go back to the downstream flow.

A former Grand Chief of the Federation of Saskatchewan Indian Nations (FSIN) with whom I became acquainted called me by telephone before a major press conference, after a particularly tragic situation for some of his people. He talked about many things but the one overwhelming concern was the deep social problems of his people. He was looking for help to find some means to begin to deal with all that was happening and he asked for prayer.

It strikes me that we have not offered much to help anyone deal with the social environment in which we live. These days we seem to focus on socio-economic issues and the physical environmental issues. We try to interpret social life based on economics. We seek change through an agenda focused on justice which mostly turns on who is to blame and who should pay as a result and produces an adversarial environment where conversation and communication are destroyed. Most relationships end up being brokered by lawyers and the courts.

This does not produce reconciliation. For the most part it institutionalizes the alienation and institutionalized alienation largely fails to bring change since it is itself a part of the destructive lifestyles, which participate in the destruction of that which it seeks to attain in the process.

We live in a progressively growing culture of social anarchy. On the other hand, we have become much less *laissez-faire* when it comes to the physical environment. We seem to believe that the human creature (at least if they are over 18) is infinitely adaptable to anything and everything two (or more) consenting adults can do together. On the other hand, in the physical environment we are convinced there is cause and effect and that we can master many aspects of the physical environment at least to the extent that we can prevent (or at least not accelerate) its destruction.

In the Old Testament book of Hosea, there is an interesting sociological analysis of Israel's life:

> *There is no faithfulness, no love, no acknowledgment of God in the land. There is only cursing, lying and murder, stealing and adultery; they break all bounds, and bloodshed follows bloodshed. Because of this the land mourns, and all who live in it waste away.* (Hosea 4:1b-3a)

Hosea seemed to believe that when there is no knowledge of God in the land, the natural human reflexes of the human spirit degenerate and there are huge social consequences through which human life loses its value and the abuse of life causes huge grief. In fact every aspect of life: social, domestic politics, international politics and religion were affected to their demise. Where there is no knowledge of God, life flows downstream.

And that current catches many adults and also many young people. I remember so many circumstances where both adults and young people got caught in the chaotic and self-indulgent practices, which our culture has rationalized. The promiscuity and self-indulgence of our culture is a runaway. It continues to produce so much confusion and heartache and human degradation of life and relationships. For young people, the dating years are awash without survivable standards for decisions on conduct and care. The consequences are complex but ever so real.

We have much in common with the prophet's observations in his time. When I listened to the Grand Chief and the friends I met on the streets, and think about the day-to-day life of people in community, I began to realize more each day that we have so much in common with the early settlers in Canada as well. In the later immigrant cultures we still have the veneers of prosperity to mask the social chaos of our communities, but the veneers are breaking. We likely have a solid basis to work together.

I had breakfast one morning with another First Nations man I have come to know who owns several businesses and is a business consultant. He had just come back from visiting forty men for whom he had found gainful employment in Alberta and Saskatchewan. These were men who had never worked before in their life and he was pleased how they were all doing. He visited them to encourage them and support them in any way he could but he also realized the limitations of what he was doing.

From his perspective, the economic issues were the easiest issues to deal with; but where he really felt they needed help was spiritually. Until there was a change in the inner life, the outside issues were not sustainable. He said their church on his reserve was abandoned and shot full of holes. For this businessman, the abandoned church was the symbol of their problem.

Here was a huge opportunity for the church to offer that which we have seen and heard. The power of the gospel changes life from the inside. This brings fundamental changes to the way we function in community. Until this change comes one can expect that even the basic provisions of food clothing and shelter for physical life will not be sustainable because of our lifestyles that will destroy it. We might find the gospel to be a greater gift than we imagine. Discovering this to be real has been a part of the adventure. Is that part of the reality of our calling that we have somewhere lost?

In recent years I have spent quite an amount of time in our correctional institutions, both in the provincial jail system and in the federal penitentiary. I have been asked to assist in going through the Fifth Step for the Alcoholic Anonymous program for a number of inmates. Their stories are confidential, but over the years it was striking how similar the stories were. As life was degraded, there was greater ease in doing more that was destructive and in the misery the search for pleasure and escape accelerated the downstream life. The AA program for many was the beginning of exploring new directions. When one has known nothing but destructive living, this is a particularly difficult venture into a new unknown but new life begins on the inside and forgiveness was the only freedom that allowed them to look forward.

The years at Messiah were filled mostly with routine work. I kept my regular office hours and every week there was the routine preparations for Sunday bible study and worship. Every Sunday, worship was the highlight of the week and the reward was to hear more people express their surprise that they looked forward to worship and felt bad when they could not come.

Parish life had many other tasks that were sometimes time consuming, and sometimes just hard work with Ministerial meetings, conference cluster meetings, committee meetings and council meetings and serving on other boards and committees of the church at large and within the community. One can often get caught up in a business that becomes "busyness" and sometimes it is the source of great fatigue. It is always a challenge to be stewards of those extra commitments, which need to be weighed against the more important business of caring for the people, but these were all normal issues that have to be dealt with wherever we are.

During the years at Messiah I was stranded in the mysteries of our church leadership on the larger scale. The view of life at the front lines can be quite different than for those who take positions of leadership in the institutionalized structures of the church. Those different views began to clash in my ministry. The major issue in the early years was abortion. When the leadership got the decision they wanted there, they moved on to the issue of same-sex blessing and finally also ordination of same-sex candidates for ministry. The issues were hugely divisive.

But almost more significant than the issues, was the growing abuse of power and authority used by church leaders to drive their agendas. The strategies to force the last issue through conventions were strikingly manipulative. Only papers in support of the issue were allowed to be published (for discussion) before the convention. The National Church Council had sought out selected people to write papers in support of same-sex blessing. In one of the spring publications of the national church magazine congregations were directed not to argue with the papers, but to consider the wisdom contained in them. There seemed no desire to have informed debate and discussion.

When the vote was taken in 2005 at our National Convention (which by constitution is the highest legislative authority of our church) the recommendation of NCC failed to be passed. It was immediately announced that the Convention had not made a decision.

The issue was returned by NCC as a motion brought before the next National Convention of 2007. Again the convention voted down the recommendation. The relentless pursuit of the national leadership waited out one more convention before they brought the motion again to the convention of 2011 when finally the strategists achieved their goal.

The price of this journey seems to have had its greatest impact on the fellowship of the church. Among clergy there was a growing animosity in the debates. Many people were afraid to speak and opted for silence. This was enhanced by a "Sexual Abuse and Harassment Policy" put out by NCC, a document, which every clergy had to agree to and sign if they were going to continue to be pastors in the ELCIC. That document made it an offence to speak against the issue and indeed any person offended, or third person on their behalf could press charges on anyone who spoke. Conversation was suppressed.

The breach of fellowship could be seen in almost every statistic of the church. Church membership declined, a number of congregations began the process of withdrawing from the ELCIC and financial giving was redirected from supporting the ELCIC. A graph of enrolments at our seminary in Saskatoon produced a forty-five degree trajectory on a descending scale.

It was hard to watch this destruction of the fellowship of the church to which one had committed their life. How does one care? How do you seek to live out that faithfulness to God and to the institution that had embodied so much of what you believed in?

It did not take long to find that if you questioned what was happening you were quickly labelled and from that point on there was little that one could say. The leadership did not seek to enter into discussion with concerns raised. One had the feeling that the tracks were laid, and no one was accepted if they had any question about where we were going.

When leadership loses the hearts of their people it is tempting to demand allegiance by writing policies and rules that force submission to meet the needs of the leaders. The result was the institutionalization of alienation and the growing pile of papers outlining "policy" that seemed to herd the church more than it was designed to lead the church.

During much of my time at Messiah Lutheran I had been involved in the struggle to sort out and try to understand what was happening in our ELCIC. In that struggle I had made a point not to take the issues into the pulpit, but to communicate directly with leadership people as a means to seek to understand what was happening and in more recent years to express my deep concerns that our leadership was systematically tearing this church apart.

The new Sexual Abuse and Harassment Policy implemented by NCC was an obstacle one could not avoid. It is interesting to note that in 1991 a policy had been drafted by the Division of Theological Education at the request of the National Convention. That document was evaluated by the convention and was sent back for some revision, though I believe it was to be used in the interim. (Because of the demise of the working Divisions of the National Church the revisions did not come back to the convention.) This new policy was unrelated to the old, and was never brought to the convention for approval. Based on polity and practice, this seemed like a breach of our constitution.

I contacted my Bishop to inform her that I could not honestly sign my agreement to this policy. I did not believe that this policy was legitimate policy, binding on the church since it had not been submitted to the convention for approval. Second, I was convinced it was a poorly written policy and it exposed people in the church to more problems. I also realized, according to this policy, that if I did not sign that I agreed with the policy and would abide by it, I would not be allowed to continue as a pastor in the ELCIC. Apparently many other pastors could not sign this document either. I asked what I was to do since I could not honestly sign this document: I was simpy informed that I had to sign.

I later wrote my Bishop and informed her officially that I could not sign the policy; however, I would submit to the policy and accept the consequences. She would have to do her job as Bishop. Out of this we finally had a meeting in Saskatoon. At one point in the discussion my Bishop suggested it was as if I was daring her to remove me as a pastor in the ELCIC.

I reminded her that the document suggested that she had no choice. Apparently she was reluctant to carry it out. Indeed I wanted her to see, that though she had signed the document stating her agreement and willingness to abide by the policy, she also was not prepared to abide by it. If she also could not live with the document, it seemed advisable that we set in process some action to make the document one by which she could also abide.

In response my Bishop said she chose to act pastorally, and would not remove me as pastor. I asked for this assurance in writing and received it.

The last I heard, over half of the pastors in our Synod refused to sign the document and this caused tensions. It is too bad. With discussion before these documents were implemented, many of these issues could have been clarified and likely improved. Presented to the convention of the Church for approval, this improved document would also be screened for acceptance by the Church. This did and does not happen.

This growing exercise of power by leadership was disturbing at best. The refusal to be involved in discussion or to hear appeal was even more disturbing. The whole environment of our church was laced with an adversarial spirit. It has certainly been an example of downstream living.

There are a host of stories in the life of our church that have been discouraging to watch and difficult for those involved. Those caught in the web seem to have nowhere to turn.

I was never so aware of the depths of the problem created for ministry until the spring of 2007 when we had set a membership Sunday for the reception of new members. I knew a number of people I would normally have visited to talk over the possibility that they might wish to consider formal membership at Messiah. I did not visit anyone.

I wrestled with the question. Why could I not ask people to consider joining? I spent many sleepless hours thinking about this. It seemed our leadership was determined to go its own course and in the process sought to force submission of pastors and congregations to whatever they decide to do. If nothing changed, I could not believe it would do anything but tear the church apart. Congregations could not isolate themselves from what was happening. Could I invite people into the debacle that seemed to lie ahead if there was no change in direction?

When church bodies and congregations are divided there is not only the carnage it brings to relationships, but also a testimony, as followers of Jesus that is so destructive to life and faith. It was not uncommon for me to lay awake two or three hours a night, trying to understand the destructive spirit that pervaded our church.

The well-being of the church at large in the long run is of huge importance to the care of the congregation. If church structures do not allow for interchange of thought and evaluation of direction, and worse, if it structurally sets out to silence the voice of the people they are called to serve; how does one live out the commission of Jesus and also care for the larger church and the leadership in a way that does not further deteriorate that part of the whole body of Christ we represent as Lutheran Christians?

I had shared how I felt with the Messiah Church Council. I felt I was not doing the job I should be doing to serve our congregation, and they deserved so much better. This led to thoughts of early retirement or to seek a call where I might find a new beginning in a different environment.

I opted to seek a change in environment. In the spring of 2007 I submitted my mobility form (the old form since revisions came later). I suggested I was open to a call. By fall the mobility form had not left the Saskatchewan Synod office.

In conversation with my Bishop I asked why she would not forward my form. She suggested that I might want to reconsider whether I wanted it sent or not. I assured her I wanted it sent.

By this time the new mobility form had been prepared in which one had to agree to the new sexual abuse and harassment policy. The Bishop wanted me to fill out the new mobility form before it was submitted. I suggested the form I filed at the time was likely adequate. She knew I could not sign the new form with its new requirements. I would formally disqualify myself from requesting a call. The original mobility form was finally forwarded to Synod offices.

After a year and a half I called my Bishop to see if my mobility form was indeed active since I had heard nothing and had not been nominated anywhere for call. In that conversation she informed me that because of my age and attitude to the church I just had to accept that I would never get another call.

I was surprised by this admission. I told her I could not do anything about my age. As to my attitude, I had never heard her express any concerns about my ministry and at least to my knowledge I had never been put on trial.

Given the circumstances I had two choices, to fight or to submit. In the end I informed my Bishop that I was not there to fight, so I would choose to submit to her decision, but I did not understand what had happened to the spirit of our ELCIC. I also informed her that she was my Bishop and I would continue to support her. (Asking questions about those issues of concern I hoped was also support).

Since then I have heard of several other pastors who have been similarly told in other parts of the church that they also would not receive another call. How does one understand these things?

One of the unfortunate results is a growing distrust of leadership. Distrust has its own problems. In the absence of information "distrust" speculates the worst. This further poisons the relationships and further deteriorates the environment of our relationships within the church. The fragile gift of relationship is "trust". The replacement of trust from the side of leadership can become the writing of more rules and policies. Without conversation there is little possibility of reconciliation.

The loss of trust and the experience of the abuse of power had a powerful effect on relationships with congregations. Without voice or influence the only means left for communication was for the grassroots to cut off finances and finally many voted with their feet. It is all they had left in the absence of real communication. Some chose to withdraw from the church itself. Some people simply gave up on the church as a whole. In our Evangelical Lutheran Church in Canada, we have lost almost half of our membership since the merger in 1986.

In the spring of 2008 I wrote an open letter to the Bishops of our church. This letter did not pretend to be a comprehensive view of our church but simply to express one perspective on what has been happening in our church since the merger of 1986. I raised some of these issues of concern. I expressed my conviction that it would not be the grass roots people who would tear our church apart, but it would be the leadership. I also suggested that if the leadership did not change direction there was no future for our church except major division.

One Bishop responded and suggested I had accurately described a part of the life of our church. The national Bishop also responded. The Bishop acknowledged my concern for the church but assured me the bishops had the same concern and all we really had was a difference of opinion. I thanked the Bishop for the response. I also assured the Bishop that I would appreciate a response to the issues I had raised and I would wait for a reply.

The national Bishop informed me that she had too many important things to do for her to respond to individual concerns. I offered to meet with her, even to drive to Winnipeg on my own time and at my own expense if she would sit down and provide one hour to talk with me. To this request she did not respond.

Later I wrote the Bishop with the assurance that I would not trouble her further, but that did not mean that the issues would go away and one way or another the church leadership would still have to deal with the problems with which our church suffers.

Will this church survive the prevailing circumstances that divide our fellowship? I see no human reason to believe that it will survive. Having said that, I continue to believe that the Lord of the church is still Lord. Miracles have happened many times in this world; therefore, I will not predict where this will end.

If we ever do come out of it, we will live much more humbly with each other and that means we will be much more ready to be a servant people again. We need "grace" not only in the Pauline greeting but as a central part of our human hearts. And as servant people the Great Commission may again speak to us and give us new direction, not as a philosophical proposition but as the Word of Jesus given to his followers.

This is a commission, not a chosen mission statement. It calls followers of Jesus to share again what we have received from the Lord of life. And through it I believe we will see the miracle of new life, not only for the institution we treasure in our church, but for the people we serve. In so doing I am confident that the church will recover its freedom and its confidence in the documents we claim to have authority in matters of life and faith, because we will learn from them and we will see again the reality of its power to bring new life. This is an upstream journey, but by God's grace it might still come.

If this day comes, we will likely not speak with the same voice as our culture, but we will be ever so real about the business of our calling. Isaiah 55:8 will be relived many times as we come to understand that God's thoughts and ours are quite different. In the journey we will find that it is God who equips us to live and serve in the middle of a very confused world. He has been around a long time. He just might be a little more knowledgeable and equip us to bring something renewing to our troubled world and maybe also to our troubled church.

So, where does one go in these circumstances? It was apparent that I would not receive another call. Almost three years of silence suggested that this was more than theory. I was not sure I could provide a healthy ministry to the Messiah congregation as long as this burden for our larger church constrained me.

Should I retire and just be Grandpa? I had some farmland and could buy more and finish my years as a steward of the land and child of God. I could find other ways to live the Great Commission as the misplaced farmer, returned to the land, a part of the priesthood of all believers.

God only knows and so the journey continued. Upstream living was discouraging, as our church seemed to be moving with a downstream world. I continue to pray for our church and for its leaders.

And in my concern for the church as in every aspect of ministry over the years, I pray that God will protect people from me; for I remain aware, that as much I care, I can care so wrong. Many times I am sure I have handled those concerns badly. Having said that, one thing I am sure of is that the time when we should become most concerned is if we no longer care.

I notified the Bishop that I would resign as pastor at Messiah. If I was not suitable to be a pastor anywhere in our church, I likely had no business to stay in active ministry where I was. I informed her that we would sell our house and prepare to resign and look for a place to retire.

We sold our house and found a small house on an acreage near the city of Prince Albert. The house needed a major renovation. We moved in late fall (of 2010) and I planned to resign the next summer.

All good plans can have problems. In the spring of 2011 we were nominated for a call in Saskatoon. I had no explanation of what had changed. The call was finally offered to us after interviews. The congregation was one we had always said would be wonderful to serve. It was hard to get my mind around continued ministry when I had finally been convinced that we should accept retirement.

There were other circumstances that interfered with our consideration of this call, which I choose to leave behind. We were also in the middle of renovations only partially completed. It could have been a wonderful congregation to serve. The time just did not seem right. We turned down the call, and continued the course to resign as pastor at Messiah. What happened for me to get this call? I can only speculate, so we leave it that way.

We had a wonderful eight years at Messiah in Prince Albert. It was difficult to say our farewells. We planned to continue as members at Messiah and maybe now we could both sing in the choir. It was good to sit in the pew with the people of the pew and feel so at home. What a wonderful experience.

Unemployment meant more time to work on our home. We renovated every square inch. We installed gyproc through the whole house, new oak floors through the whole main floor, a new heating system, finished the basement, and then eleven hundred square feet of new additions. We added a large attached garage, which doubled as a workshop, and the new basement under the dining room addition became a wood working shop. Bev and I loved the new location.

But what would we do? That is a question still being asked and day-by-day we will find its answer. In the meantime, this child of God will enjoy playing hockey so long as the body agrees. There will be time for our children and grandchildren and there will be those continuing encounters of adventure with this sinful world that God deeply loves. Each encounter will be an opportunity to share in the Great Commission and to live out that daily instruction for life, to teach the same, and to love God and to love the people we meet. Each encounter will have that challenge to continue to be a part of the body of Christ that has so many members, such a variety of gifts, and such a holy calling.

The church, like all of us as human beings does not live its whole life at the top of a mountain. There will also be valley days. Our church is there. How can one be faithful also in care for the Church, and in care for all those people of the pews who make up such a large part of the whole body of Christ? Searching for answers to that question, the journey continues.

If it was all about me, I would have abandoned ship a long time ago. But it is not. The work of that body of Christ is what this is really about. When one looks in a mirror, one is so thankful that it is not about us. We are disposable in this world . . . and still not threatened, for our lives in Christ are eternal and holy. It is all about the One who calls us to live as God's people, and in that life to have the freedom to forget about ourselves as we enter into the struggling currents of this world where God still deeply loves people and calls us to "go" and let the world know the gift He brings.

XII POSTLUDE:
Time for Contemplation (2010-retired) with Thanksgiving for the Letter of Call.

There are so many things I continue to think about. I treasure the whole Christian Church and that small part identified as Lutheran. Oh that God would call more people young and old into the holy calling of ministry. That is God's business of course. Those called can turn their back on the call. That is part our struggle.

To encourage more people to consider ministry and to encourage more people to celebrate our life in the "priesthood of all believers" we may need to evaluate what has been happening in our churches over the years.

Does leadership have some responsibility to be involved is such evaluation also? Can pastors in congregations do anything to help the larger church be informed by its history as it seeks to support the front lines where ministry happens? How important is it that leadership people get to know and remember the people of the pews?

When should one speak up and express those concerns? If raising concerns brings silence or abuse, does one become silent? Do you retreat into the congregation you serve and take comfort in that small world pretending that what happens in the larger church will have no effect on the people you serve?

These and many other questions have prevailed in my heart and mind in recent years. Sometimes it was easy to wish one could walk away from these concerns. Like the call to ministry, these concerns have been circumstances one would much prefer to avoid.

In the end I cannot help but believe that the greatest danger is not to care. The on-going challenge is to seek ways to care that are not unnecessarily destructive. So the struggles continue. In the midst of those struggles, how can we encourage more pastors to talk about what is happening in ministry? And where there is a negative view of ministry, how do we bring some healing and new life?

The pastoral role of our Bishops and church leaders play an essential role in this matter. One of the snares for Bishops and church leaders is the illusion of elevation that sometimes can creep in and take over their perspective. Authority combined with this sense of elevation sometimes leaves few people who can assist leaders to find help in sorting out issues in the life of the church.

I used to remind students that whenever we view other people with a descending view (looking down) there is one thing we can know one hundred percent of the time: we are wrong. The Apostle Paul reminded the Philippian Christians of this,

> *Do nothing out of selfish ambition or vain conceit. Rather, in humility value others above yourselves, not looking to your own interests but each of you to the interests of the others. In your relationships with one another, have the same mindset as Christ Jesus: Who, being in very nature God, did not consider equality with God something to be used to his own advantage; rather, he made himself*

nothing by taking the very nature of a servant, being made in human likeness. And being found in appearance as a man, he humbled himself by becoming obedient to death—even death on a cross!

When the ground is level, we find so many more people who can walk with us and yes, even Bishops and church leaders can learn so much more that equips them in their call to service. Of course this instruction is important for pastors and the whole priesthood of believers as we are called to be followers of Jesus.

Bishops and church leaders need to know the clergy who are in ministry. In the adversarial environment of our ELCIC people are more known by which "camps" they are assigned by others on some of the political issues of the day than by their faithfulness (or lack of faithfulness) to their call. Identifying people with labels is usually a shortcut that does not have any understanding of what is really happening in the life of the church or the people we do not get to know because we eliminate conversation. Labels make that conversation unnecessary and in a culture where most everything is defined in simplistic dualisms the equations do not allow for much breadth of thought or movement of thought.

Clergy, as a fellowship of people, together with the Bishops and church leaders would benefit from a rich exchange in discussion and debate that might help us get to know each other on a basis beyond labels.

Some years ago I suggested to one of our Bishops that it would be good if we could get to know each other.

The Bishop replied, "We know you Dan."

The tone of the statement caught me by surprise, but was of great interest. I informed this person that we had not had twenty minutes of conversation with each other in our combined lives. I could not presume to know this Bishop, nor would this person know me to this point in our lives. I also expressed my hope that we could build the kind of relationship that would allow us to get to know each other in the years ahead.

I do not raise this as a criticism as much as a caution for all people and especially pastors. We work with our people, and sometimes know them by the second hand information we might receive from others (with the risk that some could be gossip) and sometimes we just label people without getting close enough to see more. It takes time to get past the veneers to really know our people.

We share this caution with Bishops and church leaders. It also takes time for Bishops and church leaders and pastors to get to know each other. It takes encounter and conversation. In order to support our people we need to spend time getting to know them.

In the last years I have found a growing fellowship with my Bishop through the conversations we have had, even if some of those conversations have been difficult.

We all bring political baggage and personal characteristics and character traits that might be flawed in the eyes of others. When one studies the scriptures, the disciples were a motley crew. But they offered their lives to the calling to which they were called and had to work out their differences. The first century church had many issues to work through and the church in our time has to do the same.

The call to ministry is further refined and identified by our Church in the Letter of Call. (Other denominations will likely have some similar document outlining the responsibilities of the pastoral office.)

I think it is important that people become familiar with the Letter of Call in order to consider the call to pastoral ministry. The Letter of Call can focus some of the clutter that gets in the way of such consideration. It can help church leaders also as they evaluate pastors.

And for the pastor, the Letter of Call is a good template for evaluation to hold against the backdrop of what we are doing in order to see where we are going in ministry.

The Letter of Call is also likely an important document for those who train candidates for ministry. How important for seminaries in conversation with the church to use this document to help shape the curriculum, and how important for the seminaries as a part of the church to be involved in crafting and reshaping this document when it is needed.

While serving on the Board of Governors of our Lutheran Theological Seminary in Saskatoon, I have felt that responsibility and wrestled with the role of a board as it works with the faculty and staff to carry out this holy task.

It has struck me that Jesus spent three years training twelve disciples for the calling to which He had called them. Was that training shaped in part by the road that Jesus knew lay ahead for those he had called?

Our seminary has had three years of classroom instruction and a year where students serve internships to prepare them for ministry. Seminaries need to encounter life on the front lines of ministry in order to understand the training needed for pastoral ministry. The parish may not be a bad place for some sabbatical experience for professors.

It is important that the seminary experience be a healthy experience. In my own journey the early stages of the programmed "crushing" of some parts of our Lutheran heritage within our seminary and in the general life of our church, has had huge consequences. Those labelled "pietists" have been scorned and indeed there was an era in our seminary in Saskatoon when the crushing of "pietists" was a designed part of the program. I believe that this "crushing" is a form of abuse. It has produced problems in the fellowship of our church and has caused deep wounds that continue to influence our life together. Many of our clergy have had to work to disassociate themselves from "pietism" in order to be accepted. Of course it also causes much condescension in our relationships which strains our fellowship.

I believe this is an important issue to evaluate, not to stand in judgment of the past, but to be able to bring something healing to the life of the church so we can get back to our business as a church.

Perhaps we will find that some of our clergy who have experienced this abuse have lived with the wounds of abuse and themselves become abusers. This happens in family life, and I believe is seen in our church as well.

A psychologist stood in the 2005 National Convention of our church held in Winnipeg and said that our ELCIC had all the symptoms of a dysfunctional family. He was discredited because of the nature of the topic of the day, but his observation may still have been more accurate than contrived.

Often the processes experienced in seminary can influence the way ministry is carried out in congregations. Ministry can take on qualities similar to those experienced. The model of life in our seminaries will become a part of the life of our congregations. How important to think this through with great care in those places where our clergy find training.

Pastors have to evaluate their ministry from time to time. The church would do well to do the same, not to defend its integrity, but to seek to test where we have been going and evaluate if there are times when we need to shift our course and find new direction.

The church must often move in different directions to our society. The church is not the adversary of our society any more than salt is adversarial to porridge or that light is adversarial to life when it confronts darkness. Of course it can cause some to feel challenged.

This reminds me of a night in about 1975 when our confirmation students were at Nelson Lake Bible Camp for an intensive weekend of confirmation instruction. Late Saturday night, some of the teachers were having coffee after the young people were in bed. A car could be heard coming toward the camp: we were getting late night company.

Pat (one of our teachers) and I decided to wait for the company to arrive. We walked out on the prairie by the road leading to the camp. There was a chained gateway. Car lights arrived, went out, and six young men evacuated the car and came in the dark toward the girls' cabin. We stood in the dark and let them pass. Then we followed behind at a comfortable distance. They went straight to the back door of the girls' cabin. We watched from a distance as the girls let them in.

Pat wondered what we should do. I suggested we would wait. If they were not out in a few minutes we would go in. Several minutes later they came out the back door and I turned on the large flashlight in my hand. Startled, some hit the ground, some ran in different directions, and shortly they all disappeared. Light is not adversarial to darkness, but put people in the picture and light can become adversarial to what people are sometimes about.

We got in my car and drove over to the car parked at the gate. The young men were returning via the bush instead of the prairie trail to the car they left behind. I left my lights on to illumine their means of retreat. For some reason they did not come out of the bush. I waited. I called them. Nothing happened.

It seemed we should talk but it was not happening. I secured the situation by opening the hood of their car and disconnected their coil wire. The car would not start. I returned to the girl's cabin for a brief visit to ask them for the names of the guys that had been in their cabin. They were reluctant, but finally shared the names.

I returned to the waiting car, and as my lights shone on it I saw only the fleeing forms of young men heading for the bush. I called again, but this time I called them all by name. No response.

I began to feel a certain response in myself. I must say I was a little impatient. So I opened the hood again, took out the coil wire totally, held it up in the light and suggested that I had waited long enough. I would be under the yard light by the dining hall. They had a choice to walk home (six miles) or come and see me. I could wait.

It was some time before two young men came walking under the yard light to where I was waiting. They asked if they could have their coil wire. I assured them that I appreciated their coming and asked why they ran. I asked them if I had ever kicked their butts to make them afraid.

They hung their heads and then one looked up and said, "You would have run too."

I laughed, "You bet your life I would have." Then I assured them I just wanted them to know that we could talk things out and there would be no problem the next time we see each other.

Some conversations are so important one has to push for them. Light helps us deal with reality. I think that is what life and ministry needs so badly. That might be part of the call. How that knowledge of God is utilized and applied to human need is the challenge to grow in the arena of wisdom.

Maybe this was what shaped Jesus' teaching methodology as he took time to sit down and teach them, but then he also walked his disciples through all kinds of experiences with the people of the day.

People were tangibles on the face of God's world. Sin was not a theory but descriptive of that which had the power to make life sick and even destroy it. Grace was more than theory; it was undeserved kindness. One did not have to make "sin" right in order to care for people. Seeing the reality of the power of sin to destroy, the love for people was not changed, and in that love for people grace sought to bring new life, and new direction. The internship program with some practical experience on the front lines of ministry is an important part of training, and the years that follow in ministry are a constant source of learning.

By the way, the story of those six young men did not end there. After putting the coil wire back in the car I called the rest of the young men to come. They stayed in the bush. Finally, I asked the other two to call them. They came with their heads down.

We talked about the situation and I explained the responsibility I had for the "confirmands" and I asked for their support. I also asked them to give me their word that they would not come on the property again for the duration of the event. I assured them that if they kept their word they would have nothing but my respect. They gave me their word and we stood and visited for some time. We had begun a relationship that with time would make us friends. Ministry finds new dimensions we share when we enter into relationships with people.

How do we live grace and still deal with issues that need to be dealt with for the well-being of all? We can talk the talk, but how do we live it in the many circumstances of life? It can be delightfully challenging. It can also be incredibly rewarding. These young men became people of the pew. They came for worship and fellowship. They had more to deal with. They had begun the journey. Thirty years later we still cross paths and those relationships are part of what makes life so rich.

Daniel A. Haugen

As I have been looking back on ministry I have come to treasure the Letter of Call. It has given wonderful focus to ministry over the years, whether as pastor in congregations, teacher and director of public relations for our church school at LCBI, and as president and business manager of the same institution. All these tasks came with a Letter of Call. Each call was a reminder that we are servants of the living God, called to love God and love people. In each call we are directed to forget about ourselves and trust the one who walks with us.

The Letter of Call, to this point has survived the current culture of our church and is well worth evaluating. It provides some "outside" thought that I believe is salutary for those considering a call to ministry and for church leaders who are called to oversee and support the overall life of God's people in and through the church.

In our ELCIC, pastoral ministry is defined in the Letter of Call issued to pastors. We are called to preach the Word, administer the sacraments and conduct public worship in harmony with the faith and the practices of the church. What a wonderful challenge for the pastor to bring the scriptures into the lives of the priesthood of all believers.

I remember a parishioner who suggested that it must be difficult to take a text and build a sermon off that text and to do this every Sunday. He talked of the text as a springboard for thought. I suggested that to use the text as a springboard was likely a dangerous way to preach since one can jump almost any direction off a springboard. Instead I suggested that the text sets the limits of what we can say. When one studies the scriptures our minds often run, and just when we think we are on track, another scripture brings us to a stop.

The scriptures themselves limit the distance we can run with our thought and the directions we might sometimes jump. The thoughts of scripture, which are not our thoughts and the ways that are not our ways wrestle with us and we with them. We walk what we learn into life and it is there we grow in our insight. And having said that, one is reminded that it is still the Holy Spirit who will convince us of the truth that in turn frees us.

This also brings the freedom to preach. Whenever I drive through communities I picture beside every church a large tailings pile (like one finds at many mine sites in British Columbia or the potash tailings piles in Saskatchewan). The picture is a bit humbling. It reminds me that the priesthood of all believers often have to process a lot of stuff to find the treasure in our preaching. It is the Holy Spirit that helps people find what is of value and what to take into the life they live each day in love for God and people. One tries to refine the message to some extent if we seek to care for the flock and feed it. One tries not to mar the landscape with too large a tailings pile.

If our preaching does not speak to the heart of our day-to-day realities, we likely do not understand what we are doing. Jesus seemed to be able to walk through the communities of his day and always had something to bring to people that related to their real lives both in the external realities and the issues of the deeper parts of the human reality. The radical thoughts of Jesus were not some mindless rebellion against cultural norms to fit everything into his own way of doing things (do your own thing of the 1960s) but it called people to obedience to the will of God which itself is a venture in discovery.

Preaching does not take us into a mystical world of swamp-gas and mist, which we sometimes call "spirituality," but into a radical new life in this very real world of form design and substance created by God. Jesus had a deep awareness that life is lived from the inside in this real world. The human spirit was real and by nature twisted:

Daniel A. Haugen

For out of the heart come evil thoughts, murder, adultery, sexual immorality, theft, false testimony, slander. (Matthew 15:19)

It is from what we hold on the inside that we live out our lives in relationship and community. Redemption did not come from a forced submission to the proper external aspects of life, but from a changed human life in the centre.

The Pharisees seemed to write new policies and laws to control the externals of life. It is worth asking whether our theological education has to challenge the thousands of pages of policies we have produced in recent years within our ELCIC. When we lose common values and the heart of our people, by reflex we seek to control externals. Policies no longer guide the human heart but are written to control external relationships and activities . . . and of course they can be used to dispose of those who do not fit the externals we demand.

Preaching and teaching takes us into a much deeper dimension of life. Oh, there is still some need for policies to help us in our disciplines. Indeed civil law is needed to control external relationships in a fallen world so that community can function at all, but Jesus came to deal with the human heart from which a deeper redemptive power is lived out in community that becomes like salt which seasons, and light that shines in the darkness.

In our Lutheran tradition, proclamation of the Gospel and the teaching of Christ has been a central part of worship. As we bow our lives before God, God speaks to us and through his spirit nurtures the life of His people.

Preaching understood as proclamation is also done in the teaching ministries of the church. Christian education is a continual challenge to the cultural voices of the day as those voices are more and more independent of the influence of the Christian church that had a significant role in the development of the world in which many of us have lived.

The teaching of the church is not authoritarian in nature. Jesus' pedagogy was not, "I said it, you better believe it, and that settles it." Rather it was a call to continue in His teaching as his disciples and the truth would be confirmed in the reality of the journey:

> *To the Jews who had believed him, Jesus said, "If you hold to my teaching, you are really my disciples. Then you will know the truth, and the truth will set you free."* (John 8:31-32)

The claims of Jesus teaching are claims, which turn the lights on to see a reality we would never otherwise see.

We also proclaim by the way we live. This is a call for all God's people to walk Jesus' teaching into their daily living. This is the call for the pastor. We have heard the adage, "Practice what you preach." It has also been said, "Proclaim the gospel and if necessary use words."

I expect we will find both are necessary. Jesus seemed to model that. The proclamation task of the pastoral call is a dynamic task that walks one into many adventures in the sanctuary of the church and in the great cathedral of the world where we meet people every day.

I remember entering my favourite coffee shop in my first parish. Four men I called my favourite community delinquents (all over 60 years old) called me to their booth. One was a huge man. You didn't shake his hand. His hand enveloped yours and from that moment the presence of your hand was of small consequence.

Just a few years previous, this man told me of how on one occasion he had been indulging. He found a friend's truck on Main Street with the keys in the ignition. He decided to take it on a ride to a neighbouring community. When the vehicle could not be found by its owner, the police were called, and when they found the truck, they found this man, sitting on the steps of the bar with a bottle of whiskey under each arm.

"Rather pathetic," he had concluded as a coffee shop confession.

One could proclaim God's forgiveness, because of God's Word, not ours. He thought it rather sad that he lived so many years before he came to his senses. I agreed but suggested that his sixty plus years was still insignificant compared to eternity. He agreed.

On this occasion, this man sat with three of his friends. One friend had been in the military and had a high opinion of his ability to have made significant changes in his life without the help of anyone else. He was likely the only man of the group who attended worship in the community with some regularity. Once his own pastor had commented that this man had been raised to respect the clergy, but it just hurt him to try to respect his pastor.

These were not the men one thought of as community theologians but over the years they ventured into the exploration of theology and the deeper things in life. We were good friends and drank many gallons of coffee together. They shared what they had been talking about, and wanted to know what I thought.

I was the ripe age of twenty-seven. I responded to their conversation with usual abandon, but touched a nerve in my military man.

As I completed my response, he clutched the table in the booth with both hands, and declared with great dignity, "I am 72 years old and I have been through the two great wars. I have seen life from the gutter and I have seen it from on top, and I am still not so pretentious to think that I know how to live, and anyone who does is purely audacious."

Of course his eyes were fixed on that young sprout preacher and my response likely was audacious and should have received rebuke through his ever-present cane.

To this man I said, "Anyone who thinks on their own that they know how to live is purely audacious. But God has been around a little longer than even a seventy-two year old and he just might be a little wiser and a little more knowledgeable. And I won't apologize for sharing what he has said, because it wasn't my idea in the first place."

My military man promptly squeezed his portly presence from the booth and with great indignation commented, "It's not much point lingering here" and he walked out. The rest continued in conversation.

Every day I left the office around ten o'clock to get the mail and then I would stop at the coffee shop. Every day I met this man. Every day I greeted him, "Good morning . . ." And every day for six weeks he did not acknowledge my greeting but rather with cane in hand and face set firmly forward continued on his mission to get his mail without a word spoken.

Mondays, no one came to the coffee shop, but on this particular Monday I stopped and had coffee with another man who was struggling to take care of his family. He was a most gracious man, but in many ways a wounded man. As the two of us sat in the empty coffee shop, my back was to the door. I heard the door open, and I heard a thump, thump as someone entered. It had to be my military friend cane in hand.

I turned and sure enough he came, aimed directly at the booth where we sat. The determination on his face told me this was D-Day.

He came to our booth and informed my friend he had to leave. He wedged his body into the booth with the comment, "Plain to see these booths were not designed for real men." Once settled he looked me in the eye and said, "Pastor, how is it that my wife can accept things as a matter of faith and I have to always ask questions? Is it wrong?" That last word ended with a sort of ring to it.

To this military man I replied, "I think people generally do not ask enough questions. But maybe, it is like searching for something by poking your cane in a haystack. If you keep hitting something, there does come a time to finally accept that there must be something there." So began a wonderful visit of almost three hours and a wonderful restored relationship that we enjoyed over many more cups of coffee in the days ahead.

Yes, proclamation happens in the place of worship, and in the great cathedral of our world. We proclaim thoughts that are not our thoughts and ways that are not our ways. Such is the radical nature of proclamation. Though we might have some understanding of what we proclaim, we will discover repeatedly that we have so much more to learn and so much more to share.

This was at once humbling, sometimes confusing, but the adventure to test it out, was always invigorating. It took me into life with a whole new experience of adventure and made me walk paths I would never have taken through choice. On those paths I learned many things. This journey provided an historical reconnect with the scriptures and brought many new insights I shared in preaching.

We speak to a world that has taken on thoughts that are not God's thoughts and ways that are often our ways. There is a tendency in our time to believe that in the evolutionary process, the contemporary mind has evolved to a higher understanding of life than has ever been found in the past (by definition less developed). In contrast to this, experience might suggest that this needs re-evaluation.

T.S. Elliot penned these words in his poem The Rock written in 1934.

> The endless cycle of idea and action,
> Endless invention, endless experiment,
> Brings knowledge of motion, but not of stillness;
> Knowledge of speech, but not of silence;
> Knowledge of words, and ignorance of the Word.
> All our knowledge brings us nearer to our ignorance,
> All our ignorance brings us nearer to death,
> But nearness to death no nearer to GOD.
> Where is the Life we have lost in living?
> Where is the wisdom we have lost in knowledge?
> Where is the knowledge we have lost in information?
> The cycles of Heaven in twenty centuries
> Bring us farther from GOD and nearer to the Dust

The age we live in still moves farther from God. We live in a world quite overwhelmed with its knowledge.

The trouble seems to be that knowledge does not comprehend either the holiness of life, nor the depths of human sinfulness. We look for explanations of the human spirit based on environment, or biological inheritance or chemical imbalance. We have tried to define humanity as a sophisticated mechanism whose origin was chance and whose evolving makeup is that of a sophisticated mechanism. We are playing the great humanistic experiment to explain God as the creation of humanity to meet our own needs. God is ruled out of the practical and real aspects of life and in this great experiment I believe we can see the early stages of the consequences that are inescapable when everyone does what is right in their own eyes. Life is losing its value and though skilled in technology our lives are confused.

Daniel A. Haugen

One should not be surprised. The philosophy of the culture is in some ways embodied in these words of William Ernest Henley (1849-1903).

Invictus

Out of the night that covers me,
Black as the Pit from pole to pole,
I thank whatever gods may be
For my unconquerable soul.

In the fell clutch of circumstance
I have not winced nor cried aloud.
Under the bludgeonings of chance
My head is bloody, but unbowed.

Beyond this place of wrath and tears
Looms but the Horror of the shade,
And yet the menace of the years
Finds, and shall find, me unafraid.

It matters not how strait the gate,
How charged with punishments the scroll.
I am the master of my fate:
I am the captain of my soul.

There is a note of defiance in this poem, and in many ways it captures the spirit of our age. God is abandoned at least in the functional needs of life and it acknowledges with a stoic attitude of submission that there is a price, but who cares?

The price is very high. Listen to what you hear in our society. The voices of oppression are growing and the voices of the oppressed are growing. Listen to the music of the day. There is little joy. Watch television and the themes are dominated with oppression and violence and abusive human sexuality and in so many ways dysfunctional relationships.

Look at what is happening in the streets. Graffiti is growing on public and private facilities. Is this a sign of a growing loss of respect for others by degrading what belongs to others? In Luther's small catechism he relates this to the instruction, "You shall not steal."

> *We should fear and love God that we may not take our neighbor's money or property, nor get them by false ware or dealing, but help him to improve and protect his property and business.*

There is a growing use of body graffiti and other forms of personal physical abuse. Is this simply fad? I expect in some proportion it is, but I also believe it is a growing expression of something far deeper. There have been studies done which suggest that this can be a form of self-abuse. Is life losing its value? Body graffiti and physical abuse with piercings and other distorting adornments is not new. You can study it in what we used to call primitive cultures. It has been found in many cultures. It is worth evaluating what is happening.

Where this road leads, time will tell. The consequences are growing. We might find down the road the need to look for more life-giving options.

How important is "the call" to bring something life giving into the world in which we live? If life is being degraded and losing its value then one does not simply licence all human activity. One identifies the concern, and brings to the concern that which might bring healing. There is reason to share what might be life renewing. It might call people in new directions and maybe it will bring new health and richer lives with new hope that even death cannot destroy.

In a world where people seem to believe "everything has changed" we lose our focus. Certainly we have seen major changes in technology. But there is a discovery in reading the ancient texts that the inner human life, though surrounded by different technologies really has not changed at all. And that which is revealed in scripture helps us understand what is happening in our world cluttered with technology in a way that nothing else seems able.

I remember a young man who came to my office one day. He informed me "everything has changed". We sat at a round table across from each other. I had an object that I pushed over the edge. It fell to the floor. I picked it up and continued to do this without saying a word until the student thought I had lost my mind. I was determined to do this till he spoke. He finally asked what I was doing.

I pushed it again and said, "Look at that, it did it again."

His response, "So?"

I replied, "So, I bet it did that 2000 years ago as well."

He replied, "So what?"

To this I replied, "Some things have indeed changed. We drive cars today, not chariots. But at the same time some things have not changed (I pushed the object again and it fell again). See it still hasn't changed. Now your life is more complicated. Now you have to sort out the things in history that have changed, and those things that have not changed. Have a good day." He left my office.

I hope he enjoyed the challenge to reconnect with a world where some things have changed, but many things have not. It makes life more complicated, but it helps us keep real and if we cannot deal with reality, we have become dysfunctional. This too is part of the call.

Here is one of the great challenges of proclamation and teaching. Here the gift of God's Word is essential for the journey. Proclaiming God's Word is as relevant in our day as it ever could be. Faithful preaching and teaching is an important need for our time and when we become real, the message is still heard.

In the Letter of Call in our church we are called to perform a number of other pastoral activities. We are called to baptize, confirm, marry and perform funerals.

It is difficult to avoid baptism when one holds "The Great Commission" as a focus of our call. Make disciples, baptize and teach is a primary focus of our commission.

Baptism is that wonderful gift of God freely offered as God's gift for faith. United with Jesus in baptism, we are made children of God, and as children, heirs to all God has promised his children.

When families of faith come with their children we celebrate that grace of God. Sometimes we take it for granted as we do so many rich gifts we receive in life. Some replace Jesus with baptism. This is a problem. Our faith is not in baptism, but in the One with whom we have been united in baptism.

Some build fences around baptism to try to force people to take the gift more seriously and it becomes an issue of power and control. Indeed many people keep their faith like a talisman that they turn to as an apparent formality that has little to do with daily living. There is a reflex to try to force them to be more serious. However, the reflex "to force" we might do well to suppress. How then can one help nurture these lives to treasure this gift?

Sometimes we get upset when asked to do some baptisms. On the other hand, they come. The next chapter in this journey is that people do not come. That is also happening today. Should we not celebrate that families do come and each time, enjoy this as an opportunity for ministry?

How many people came to Jesus for so many different reasons? He did not question them or interrogate them to see if their motives were pure or if they were worthy. Each encounter was an opportunity. He responded to their needs.

Some saw their need, and some did not. He did not licence things that were wrong to make them feel better. He always sought what might be redemptive in their circumstance and sometimes they turned away. Jesus did not send them away.

How do we share with every family the reality of baptism and the gift of fellowship with the living God that it provides? What challenges parents as they are now called to nurture the life and relationship we find "united with Christ" in baptism? Is there not something sobering about the responsibility? We proclaim the reality of this gift for us and for our children (Acts 2:38-39) and in the light of that reality they have to make decisions. Should we let the parents make their decision? Should we then support that decision and continue to seek to nurture life and faith for these families? And if they should turn away . . . Jesus seemed to always understand that this was a possibility.

Confirmation can be another challenge. We have often chosen the "lost years of education" (grades 6-8) as the primary time for confirmation instruction. Sometimes I think this needs re-evaluation. It is good if we can find a way to connect with these hormonally disoriented youth who have trouble to focus on education at the best of times. On the other hand we can tokenize the years and major in mediocrity as a form of despair that simply finds a way to technically fulfill the requirements.

The challenge to connect with our youth can be a fascinating adventure. It also may call us to go beyond the standard protocols to find the ground where we can engage their minds. Engagement is not the sole purpose. To bring them into an encounter with Jesus and with thoughts that are not our thoughts and ways that are not our ways is to lay foundations for the future. Some might say, what better time than this time of confusion when so many issues in life are beginning to be sorted out.

In this time of transition, from childhood to adult life, young people are going to have to make some decisions in life. Parents will have to progressively relinquish that calling and turn it over to their growing adolescents who one day will move into adult life and have to make even more decisions about the life God has given them.

Of course, every pastor is not a teacher and sometimes needs help from the priesthood of all believers. This ability to see ministry as a shared venture with our people brings another dynamic that can stir one into new places one would not have thought to go. We share with a larger priesthood who bring gifts we will never have, to the work of the church. This corporate work in a society that has become so individualistic is itself a challenge. We often have limited skills and disciplines to work as teams. Here is an adventure in itself; to celebrate the gifts each person brings especially where we ourselves are weak. We have to find the disciplines to allow others to be involved in a corporate venture in order to fulfill our calling.

I remember an incident in our first parish. There were far too many students and classes for one pastor to cover and we needed someone to teach confirmation. I liked to get some men involved so I asked a local farmer who was a member if he would be interested. I always encouraged people to feel free to say, "No." I did not want people teaching simply out of duress. That would likely not make for a good teaching environment.

This man thought about the question of teaching and said, "I don't know if I can teach, but I took confirmation and I should have learned something. Tell you what, I will try it. If it does not work I will let you know." He had never taught before. It was an adventure and he became a wonderful teacher for our young people.

It is not a bad thing to help our youth share their gifts and thoughts in worship as a part of that nurture of their life and faith. It is likely more important for youth to be involved in worship than in Church Council (this has often been a frail token that produces very little benefit).

We have had our youth provide a brief meditation on the Psalm for the Sunday, read the scriptures, and assist with communion and ushering and as worship assistants. There are many areas where we can help our young people find productive ways to share in service opportunities that help them live that life and faith as followers of Jesus. Young people can assist as teachers in Sunday school. They can visit elders and get to know their stories of life and faith. They can get involved in areas of service within community. The important thing is not to tokenize our youth, but to allow their involvement to be real and suitable to their gifts. That has to be an essential part of our nurture of life and faith in the lives of our young people.

I once dreaded performing marriage ceremonies. I sometimes thought there was more hope in funerals than there was in some marriages. Again, sometimes we set up protocols and process simply to get through this aspect of ministry. If we live in a society that does not hold marriage in high regard we will find that couples will be deeply influenced by the perspective of the community. When they come to get married (if they come) they are often uncertain about its importance.

I expect over 90 percent of those I have married in recent years have lived common law prior to marriage. In the face of this reality I have tried some upstream adventures that have proven quite delightful and have changed my attitude to marriages.

Upstream Living in a Downstream World

I love meeting with couples who are considering marriage. The real issues are not whether they are contributors to the church or whether they are members or whether everything has been the way it maybe should have been. I do not really care if they come because we have a beautiful sanctuary or because they cannot get a marriage commissioner or judge to go where I might go to marry them. Every time people come there is opportunity to serve in some way.

I love to remind couples that my job is to help them find the rich life God offers in Jesus and to do this we have to get real. I remind them that I am not their judge, and I also inform them that I will not decide if I will marry them, but after we have met they will have to decide if they want me to be the pastor at their wedding. Having thought this through, I will support whatever they decide.

This has given me new freedom as a pastor. It allows me to be as frank as seems necessary to help them face the question, "What is marriage?" Sometimes there is a need for some change in direction. Sometimes they need encouragement for the way they are going. Sometimes the freeing gift of forgiveness and a new beginning called marriage is the beginning of a renewed journey of faith and life.

Sometimes there are questions that need to be raised. What is happening in our promiscuous society? Have we taken the holy gift of life and degraded it? Is marriage a holy relationship ordained by God and to be held in honour by all? And we explore the implications of marriage for the future for them and their children and the communities in which they will live.

In the end, these couples are not on trial. If anything, the pastor is on trial. I give them a model of a wedding service for them to talk over and evaluate. That is their one assignment. I want them to ask each other what those words mean, and if it means something to them. I want them to examine the scriptures, and the thoughts expressed. What is marriage? What will we build our marriage on? What will be the measures we use as we seek to build our life together and our home?

Then they generally call me a week later to let me know if they want me to be their pastor for their wedding and we proceed from there. Seldom do they say no, but some do. Almost always they thank me for helping them sort out what they are doing. This is much more adventurous than simply setting up a screening process and running people through it. Every encounter, under whatever pretence, healthy or not is an opportunity for ministry.

Sometimes they feel that they have messed up. One couple shocked me at a rehearsal. We were there to work through the logistics of the service when the couple took me aside and asked if they could share in the Lord's Supper that night. They felt that their life had been so wrong in the past, and wanted to share in God's forgiveness so that their wedding day would indeed be a new beginning. They asked me to invite the wedding party to join them and asked that I explain to the wedding party why they wanted to do this. This was all their idea.

Wow... we sometimes propose these things as spiritual leaders, but when it comes from the genuine hearts of our people one knows something is happening.

Over the years this happened a number of times. Forgiveness... provided freedom from the past, and the ground for a truly new beginning. The real purpose is to help people who are considering marriage to find something real on which to centre that relationship that we find in fellowship with God and each other.

Are the results always positive? Of course the results are not always what one would hope for. Are there many surprises that are celebrated signs of new life? There are many. The challenge to seek to be faithful in every circumstance never changes.

Upstream Living in a Downstream World

Visitation of the sick, the distressed and burying the dead can be difficult parts of the call for many reasons. I always hated hospitals. In my early ministry I went because it was my job to go. I set it into a disciplined time or I would find excuses to stall and not get there. I still find it rather uphill to keep that appointment every week, but over the years so many wonderful experiences have come out of that uncomfortable environment.

One gets many calls from people distressed by issues of health, family circumstances, addictions, financial crisis and every other form of distress imaginable. These calls can come when one is tired, or busy with other matters, and it is not difficult to feel stretched beyond our elastic limits. At the same time, every one of these calls come from human beings who have value in God's eyes.

No person or pastor is gifted in every area. We can only do what we are able to do. Here too there are often others among the priesthood of all believers who have more to offer than we will as pastors. The needs of our people take us out of our offices and into the real world that God deeply loves. There we are called to bring that redemptive life through the gifts God has given us. We will always feel inadequate if we are honest, but we can still offer that which we have heard, that which we have seen, and that which we have touched with our own hands. I will always remember that lady in the hospital who said that sometimes it was not so much the words we say; just coming sometimes meant the most of all.

And then there are funerals. I dreaded my first funerals. In my first parish after ordination I had three funerals in the first week. I am not at all sure I knew what I was doing, but I tried to take care of the living and that became my focus for funerals. We entrust those who have died into the hands of God. We are not their judge. We can do no more, and we would do no less. Our ministry is to the living.

I have never minded having anyone come whether they have a faith background or not to request that I take a funeral. I find every funeral a chance to proclaim God's Word and care for people.

We always talk about outreach. Some people will go knocking on doors to meet people and I have never understood when they come to our doors that we turn them away.

When we have a funeral we are not breaking a bottle of champagne on the casket to christen the dead into heaven, nor is it our job to declare judgment in a black shroud. Jesus is the judge; we are not qualified.

We are called to minister to the living. What a wonderful freedom, and with open doors we have opportunity to meet and discover human lives we would never otherwise meet. We can share that which we have seen and heard.

Funerals are often a time for people to reconnect with the fellowship of God's people. It can be one of the more honest times in people's lives and at so many funerals you have a chance to proclaim God's Word to hundreds of people you would never otherwise see. That however is the secondary task. If we do not care for the grieving, there is little reason for others to believe we have anything for them also.

I attended a funeral once in another church. I was appalled that the focus of the service was not in care of the people who had lost a loved one. The service was viewed as an opportunity "to get people". The person who died was young and the death very unexpected and it brought a huge crowd. One felt that if the grieving family had left it would not have been noticed. It was a terrible experience. It was an example that held up great caution flags for ministry that I could never forget. How easy to slip by reflex into the abuse of people instead of genuinely caring for them in every circumstance.

In many ways the funeral is just the beginning. I remember an early funeral where the widow had a very difficult time for two years in sorting out the grieving process. I visited her at least once every month over that period of time and together we journeyed through that time of healing and adjustment.

That process of caring found its limitations, especially in one year of ministry when I had over thirty funerals. How do you take care of people? Again I could not help but turn to the great work of the people in the pews who shared in that ministry. How wonderful to see the priesthood of all believers at work.

In an age that seems to almost adore "impiety" the directive in the letter of call "to inculcate piety" is itself an upstream adventure. What is piety? I suppose it can be many things to many people. I believe in part it is what Paul encourages in his letter to early Christians in Rome:

> *Therefore, I urge you, brothers and sisters, in view of God's mercy, to offer your bodies as a living sacrifice, holy and pleasing to God—this is true worship. Do not conform to the pattern of this world, but be transformed by the renewing of your mind. Then you will be able to test and approve what God's will is—his good, pleasing and perfect will.* (Romans 12:1-2)

Piety was in some ways the opposite of living the reflexes of the reality, "by nature sinful". Piety was for the Apostle Paul, to live the new life directed by God's spirit:

> *Those who live according to the sinful nature have their minds set on what that nature desires; but those who live in accordance with the Spirit have their minds set on what the Spirit desires. The mind controlled by the sinful nature is death, but the mind controlled by the Spirit is life and peace. The sinful mind is hostile to God; it does not submit to God's law, nor can it do so. Those controlled by the sinful nature cannot please God.*
>
> *You, however, are not controlled by the sinful nature but are in the Spirit, if indeed the Spirit of God lives in you. And if anyone does not have the Spirit of Christ, they do not belong to Christ. But if Christ is in you, then even though your body is subject to death because of sin, the Spirit gives life because of righteousness. And if the Spirit of him who raised Jesus from the dead is living in you, he who raised Christ from the dead will also give life to your mortal bodies because of his Spirit who lives in you.* (Romans 8:5-11)

So much of Paul's teaching through the letters written to the first century churches are instruction in a piety that is lived out in response to God's calling and purpose. It is not a legalism to be lived "in order" to be acceptable to God, but it is instruction to live in the new ways of the Spirit that honour God and care for life.

This is really an understanding of the original meaning of "torah" in the Old Testament. I remember reading a book by a Jewish author named Peli titled *Torah For Today*. In this book he suggests that God's "torah" takes dysfunctional people and makes them functional again. Functional people can be a blessing to others.

I think the low point in the past years of ministry was the banquet celebrations at our church convention in 2011. The theme for the banquet was the celebration of "profanity" and "toasts". It seemed the antitheses of this part of our call. Life is holy by definition. It is not to be used, abused or denigrated. Profanity is by definition the use and abuse and degradation of life. Profanity is what we nurture when love for God and people is lost. This experience reminded me that, even with good intention we can drift a long way off course when we live in ambiguous times without compass or guide.

It seems quite suitable that in the Letter of Call this task of inculcating piety is tied to the pastoral support of the schools and auxiliary groups of the congregation. Christian education is in part at least, the extension of "torah" as instruction for life and faith. It is a means by which piety is nurtured so that God's people live lives, which honour God and are equipped to share in word and in actions the knowledge of God that brings guidance and instruction that cares deeply for the care and nurture of human life. We have a model in Jesus who was known as "rabbi" which means teacher. The teaching role of the Great Commission extends this calling to the life of the church and the pastor.

The Letter of Call also called the pastor to tasks tied to the institutional church. Pastors had duties of installing members of Church Council who were elected by the congregation. Pastors were to seek out qualified people to prepare for ministry at home and abroad, to encourage members to support the church and to keep congregational records and make reports to the larger church, and commend members to other churches wherever they might move.

Here are some of the descriptive works of ministry tied to the institution that are designed to bring together a corporate expression of the body of Christ for the purpose of ministry. Here we can get deflected into the ministry of having people serve the institution, instead of having the institution as a corporate embodiment of our service to God.

In our Letter of Call, the pastor is only advisory to the Church Council and its committees (based on the model constitution for congregations), but together we work to bring the corporate gifts of the people into the frontlines of ministry where we serve to nurture those who form that body, and where we seek to move that body of people into the broader interface with people among whom they live as instruments of God's grace and witnesses to the life of Christ.

One of the great tasks of the Church Council and pastor is to mobilize the priesthood of all believers in the work of God's kingdom. If there is sometimes a sleeping giant in the church it is this wonderful priesthood of all believers, the people of the pews, who need to be nurtured and encouraged and helped to see the daily opportunity to be God's people wherever they are.

Some of the difficulties in this area may also be increased when the corporate church loses some of its focus. If we have lost focus for ministry we are not sure what design our institutions should take. This can happen at every level of the church as institution.

There will always be a need for prophetic evaluation of our institutions to critique what is happening. We can easily become so rocked in the arms of our culture that we become the culture and move away from "thoughts that are not our thoughts, and ways that are not our ways". Our focus on scriptures gives us the tools for evaluation. We often restructure institutions for survival, but we seldom restructure based on a refocus of our mission.

Upstream Living in a Downstream World

It is easier to cut and walk out of institutional relationships than it is to work for renewal. We easily lose identity, forfeit loyalty and end up with little sense of belonging. Commitment in difficult times is a challenge.

We live in a time when there is a growing confusion and disillusionment with leadership. In this loss of trust, the church as institution often becomes more demanding and assertive to gain control of people. The disillusionment is accelerated. Living in this environment is an upstream journey unless one simply submits and goes with the flow. The results will show up in statistics and in a progressive dysfunction within the church as institution. The work to bring something healing to this time of struggle encounters many head-on currents. God will call people to serve in the middle of these times.

The bottom line; however, is that the Lord of the church is still Lord. The venture into the unknown includes the adventure of seeing how God will still prove to be Lord. In the meantime we will have those human decisions to make about how we will fulfill God's calling and purpose. That is not always as clear.

So, if ministry is first and foremost, "not about us" . . . how does one become involved in ministry? Is this like choosing any other career path? Is this something we do to meet personal needs? Is there anything at all unique about being called to be a pastor?

These and many other questions can arise when one considers entering ministry as a pastor. I have come to believe that we are all provided with different gifts and abilities. If one is tone deaf, one likely should not consider being a choir director. I also believe that every gift and ability is God given.

To go into ministry to "prove a point" is likely destructive. To go into ministry to seek to meet one's own needs is likely not helpful. To go into ministry to seek power or position or prestige .

. . (is likely illusion) but will also be destructive since it serves our need, not the need of those to whom we go.

God calls and we have to sort out what to do with the gifts we have received. On the other hand, when one reads the scriptures, it seems God can do quite as He pleases when he calls people. Indeed the wind blows where it wills. Is there some solid rational process to identify and define a true "calling" of God? I know of none. I am also quite certain it is different for different people.

In the Old Testament we read of a variety of experiences of God's call to a variety of people and a variety of tasks. Though we know little of the particulars, Abraham seemed to take up his call quite freely to be the father of a great nation, though he struggled with many uncertainties in the journey.

God called Moses to be a liberator of his people from Egypt. Moses felt in every way disqualified as a murderer hiding in the wilderness of Sinai and he felt he was slow in speech (though quite agile in speech for excuses). He had a lot of excuses not to listen to his call, but finally submitted. Joshua seemed to take his calling to be a great military leader with full determination from the beginning. Gideon on the other hand debated God's call to military service and demanded signs to convince him. Samuel was a very young man when God called him to be a judge in Israel. Isaiah felt disqualified by his own sinfulness at his call to be a prophet. Jeremiah was a youth who felt disqualified by his age to speak on God's behalf as a prophet, but was informed by God that he had been chosen even before he was born. Hosea the prophet began his call with the strange instruction to marry a prostitute and Amos, the sheepherder from Tekoa was called to be a prophet.

In the New Testament, Jesus called such a variety of people to be His disciples. And that Paul, a persecutor of the followers of Jesus should be chosen by God against Paul's will, to be a great

Apostle and servant to the Great Commission is likely a reminder that indeed, the wind blows where it wills. Paul was not likely an eloquent speaker (as even he recognized Apollus to be):

> *And so it was with me, brothers and sisters. When I came to you, I did not come with eloquence or human wisdom as I proclaimed to you the testimony about God.* (1 Corinthians 2:1)

God does as God chooses and we may never quite understand why.

Paul saw ministry as a great partnership with others. No one was adequate in themselves:

> *What, after all, is Apollos? And what is Paul? Only servants, through whom you came to believe—as the Lord has assigned to each his task. I planted the seed, Apollos watered it, but God has been making it grow. So neither the one who plants nor the one who waters is anything, but only God, who makes things grow. The one who plants and the one who waters have one purpose, and they will each be rewarded according to their own labor. For we are co-workers in God's service; you are God's field, God's building.* (I Corinthians 3:5-9)

God's people react in many different ways to God's calling. In that calling God's people often journey in ambivalence and uncertainty, but even when driven by realities that God's people cannot define or understand, God has the power to convince His people to move on and take the challenges of God's call.

In the journey the doubts might come and go, but in the journey there is the discovery that we are not alone, and the adventures and surprises can finally convince us to trust God and to enjoy the challenge of honouring God as we set out to serve where we have been led to serve. In the journey we come to believe with greater confidence that this is really not about us, but about the One who is with us.

On the other hand, for those who think it is all about them, ministry can be a very trying experience. Many become the oppressors of their people. For some pastors, congregations can never do enough to take care of them. I recall stories of pastors who accepted a call and the terms of the call and once arriving in the parish immediately complained that the terms were not adequate. This is always difficult for congregations to figure out when the terms were accepted in the first place.

Some pastors come with an agenda to straighten out the congregation. They seldom have a good experience. Some pastors never seem to know if they are working or not working. They have no schedules they follow because they like to be adaptable for the other things they might want to do. The congregation often is equally unsure if they are working or not and it often produces conflict and in an age where many are really not sure what our mission is, life can be very confusing for everyone. Sorting out the stewardship of one's working relationships with people is an important process for pastor and people.

As Lutherans we hold that God works through Word and Sacraments and the Holy Spirit convinces people of the truth and they are set free. If faith is the assurance of things hoped for and the conviction of things not seen, it is less a leap into an abyss than the hesitant journey into the future where we finally become convinced of that which the rational mind otherwise might have trouble to comprehend. In doing so we are not less rational, but the rational mind discovers realities it would otherwise not have discovered with which to work. I think this is something I learned from the old saints one encountered in ministry.

The assurance and confidence is not unlike that found in the story of Abraham. God had promised his offspring a land. It seemed hard to believe. God had promised him offspring. His wife was so old. God had promised to protect him, but on his entry into Egypt during the time of drought the first thing Abraham does is pawn his wife off as his sister to gain the favour of Pharaoh. When his betrayal of trust was discovered he was kicked out of Egypt.

Abraham had trouble to believe that he would have a son in his old age, so he worked it out his own way with Hagar. It was as if God had to work harder to convince Him that he would have his own son. Later when there was conflict at a well with Abimelech, Abraham returned to his Egyptian ploy and passed off his wife again as his sister.

If one studies Abraham's early life he often ventured into the unknown, and manipulated his own security when threatened. Each time he was messed up by his own action for self-preservation. Still protected by God, it finally seemed to sink into the centre of his being that God could be trusted. It is not until one encounters Abraham near the end of his life, when going up the mountain to offer the sacrifice of his son, that Abraham faces his son's question: (Genesis 22:7b-8) *Behold the fire and the wood, but where is the lamb for the burnt offering?*

Abraham answered, *God himself will provide the lamb for the burnt offering, my son.* And the two of them went on together.

Near the end of life's journey, Abraham had come to understand with confidence the reality of God's care and provision. It was no longer an academic proposal, and it was not irrational, but a confidence and certainty he could not escape. It was a testimony that has challenged the heart of God's people ever since.

So in the journey of life, God seems to have the ability to convince us of that which we struggle to believe. He convinces us that we can be "called" and that God can continue to work through those whom he calls to do what he chooses to do, and that which we could never do ourselves.

It does not take long to feel inadequate. I would often reflect on:

> *Love is patient, love is kind. It does not envy, it does not boast, it is not proud. It is not rude, it is not self-seeking, it is not easily angered, it keeps no record of wrongs. Love does not delight in evil but rejoices with the truth. It always protects, always trusts, always hopes, always perseveres. Love never fails* (some translations: love never ends). (I Corinthians 13:4-8)

The encounter with human need did not take long to also teach one to pray. I prayed for God to provide what people needed to find for wholeness and life. I also prayed that God would protect people from me, for as much as one cared, one could care so wrong. I think this awareness protects people from us.

When my mother was in her early 80s she told me that as her children grew she always prayed that God would protect them from their parents because "as much as we cared, we could care so wrong."

At the time she shared it, I set out to defend her. In a short time; however, I came to have deep respect for her perspective. I should have understood immediately because for years in parish ministry I prayed the same prayer for my parishioners.

Does one never give up? Is that a realistic perspective for ministry? I remember writing this question in my random thoughts book. "When does one work and not give up? At what point does one let go and leave it in God's hands?" I don't think there is a final answer to this question.

One works as long as there is something more that can be done. One stops when convinced one has done all that you can. One prays that God will have other servants who may step in when we seem to have failed, but one continues to pray. It is still God's business to which we have been called.

I remember a young teacher in British Columbia. He was a wonderful faith-filled teacher who had a deep commitment to his students. On one visit I became concerned that he was pushing himself to the point of breaking and I finally asked him to stand up. He was a bit uncomfortable but stood at my request. I asked him to reach with one hand as high as he could. He did. Then I suggested that God had designed him with this ability to reach so far. Indeed he could pile boxes, climb on them and reach higher, but he could not live that way all the time.

One has to remember that we are not God and we have normal limits. Those limits are by design. Some people can reach higher and go further than we can. We have to accept the givens that we have received and enjoy living in those limits. The rest is still in God's hands and he may take our frail efforts and bring results well beyond our reach, but that is His business.

In the face of both failings and limitations, the cross became a visual reminder of our task and of our freedom. I treasured that cross that stood in the corner of my office. It had come from the offices of the Evangelical Lutheran Church Canada when the offices of the new Evangelical Lutheran Church in Canada were set up in Winnipeg in 1986. I remember days of frustration with some students who struggled with deep life issues. In my concern and frustration I remember looking at that cross.

It reminded me that in the eyes of Jesus sinners were worth dying for so they could live. If God in Christ would go to the point of dying so sinners could live, how far should we as staff go in caring for these students? I am sure the staff got tired of hearing me preach this perspective for the care of our students. And if you are thinking, then you also know, that this preacher often had to look at that cross to remember that the cross was there for me too.

The cross is a reminder that we must also care for church leaders, sinners for whom Jesus died. Yes, they too can stray as we can. They need people to move upstream to seek to bring redemption even as we all do.

The cross is a constant reminder of the love to be lived and the forgiveness to be shared as we too live in the never ending love of God that works patiently in and through those He has called, and gathered for the work of the kingdom. The empty tomb reminds us that the life we have in Christ is eternal. That reality sets a frontier for life and thought that takes us a lifetime to explore.

In 1977 I was given the privilege to speak at the Service of Dedication of newly built facilities for Christ Lutheran Church in Kelowna B.C. This was my parent's home church after their move to British Columbia. The recessional hymn was a great hymn of praise that filled my heart and that of the congregation gathered.

Upstream Living in a Downstream World

This hymn still fills my heart and mind having been given the privilege to serve as an ordained pastor within our Lutheran Church. My prayer is that the call to ministry would continue to bring music to the lives of our people and gratitude to our hearts.

Now Thank we all our God

Now thank we all our God,
With hearts, and hands, and voices
Who wondrous things hath done,
In whom His world rejoices
Who, from our mothers' arms,
Hath blessed us on our way
With countless gifts of love,
And still is ours today.

O may this bounteous God
Through all our life be near us,
With ever-joyful hearts
And blessed peace to cheer us,
And keep us in His grace,
And guide us when perplexed,
And free us from all ills
In this world and the next.

All praise and thanks to God
The Father now to be given,
The Son, and Him who reigns
With Them in highest heaven:
The one eternal God,
Whom earth and heaven adore;
For thus it was, is now,
And shall be evermore

ABOUT THE AUTHOR

Pastor Haugen holds a B.A. with a major in Western European History from the third to the nineteenth century and a minor in Political Philosophy. He also holds an M.Div. degree with a Biblical major and later completed an S.T.M degree in Old Testament studies.

The author has been a Pastor in the Lutheran Church since 1973. His pastoral experience included 18 years of parish ministry and 19 years at a Lutheran High School; 17 of those years as President of this educational institution of the church. In 1997 Pastor Haugen was invited to be a guest lecturer in Bogotá, Colombia on Torah for Today and Youth Ministry and in 1999 was a participant in an International Lutheran Education Conference on the Gold Coast of Australia.

Now living on a forested acreage where two rivers meet near Prince Albert, Saskatchewan, retirement has been a time for reflection on ministry, preaching by invitation (on most Sundays) and the enjoyment of family and grandchildren. In the winter months Pastor Haugen still plays hockey three or four times a week before a couple months of winter escape to Arizona.

Printed in Canada